WITHDRAWN

THE MARKET SYSTEM,
STRUCTURAL CHANGE
AND EFFICIENT ECONOMIES

WITHDRAWN

THE MARKET SYSTEM, STRUCTURAL CHANGE AND EFFICIENT ECONOMIES

The International Trend Towards Indicative Targeting

Edited by
Bodo B. Gemper

Transaction Publishers
New Brunswick (U.S.A.) and London (U.K.)

Reissued in 1990 by Transaction Publishers, New Brunswick, New Jersey 08903
Copyright (c) 1988 by Verlag Weltarchiv GmbH, Hamburg. Originally published as *The International Trend Towards Indicative Targeting.*

All rights reserved under International and Pan-American Copyright Conventions. No part of this book may be reproduced or transmitted in any form or by any means, electronic or mechanical, including photocopy, recording, or any information storage and retrieval system, without prior permission in writing from the publisher. All inquiries should be addressed to Transaction Publishers, Rutgers–The State University, New Brunswick, New Jersey 08903.

Library of Congress Catalog Number: 89-5176
ISBN: 0-88738-805-1
Printed in the United States of America

Library of Congress Cataloging-in-Publication Data

The Market system, structural change, and efficient economies: the
    international trend towards indicative targeting: case studies on
    Canada, Ghana, Great Britain, the People's Republic of China, South
    Africa, the Soviet Union, Taiwan, and West Germany / edited by Bodo
    B. Gemper.
        P. cm.
    ISBN 0-88738-805-1
    1. Economic policy–Case studies. 2. Capitalism–Case studies. 3.
    Mixed economy–Case studies. 4. Marxian economics–Case studies. I.
    Gemper, Bodo B.
    HD82.M367   1989
    338.9-dc20
                                                                89-5176
                                                                CIP

Preface

The aim of this volume "The International Trend towards Indicative Targeting" is to present contributions having a thought-provoking effect on the reader who is interested in an answer to the problem: What kind of an economic policy should – for example – the market economies actively pursue under the pressure of accelerating change? More government or less government? This is the central question. To deny this question would be to deny the solution. Policymaking and conscious shaping of the future presupposes both, intuition and science. Given the magnitude of rapidly increasing change industrialized economies as well as developing countries must fashion policies to enable them to shape the development of the changing structures.

What kind of economic policy and what kind of government might we declare to be the desirable one?

Clarifying today's situation and being prepared for the future is not only a question in advanced market economies. It is also an issue in dual economies like South Africa. Furthermore, we observe the changes which are taking place in reform-orientated Soviet-type economies, too. They see the difficulties involved in implementing new methods and measures, as first started to happen in Mainland China and is now taking place in the Soviet Union: "Gaige" (modernization) and "Kaifang" (policy of the open door) in China and "Perestroika" (restructuring) as well as "Glasnost" (more openness about public affairs in every sphere of live) in the URSS, are the keywords.

The Walberberg System Symposia arranged by The Independent Institute for Jurisprudential, Social and Economic Sciences, Bonn, provide a setting for the debate of crucial issues, which the Federal Republic of Germany and her partners face worldwide.

As editor of this book and as organizer of the 14th Walberberg System Symposium, held at the Dominican Monastery St. Albert, Bonn/ Bornheim-Walberberg, West Germany, on "Meet the Trend: The Path towards Indicative Targeting", I would like to thank all contributors who made the symposium and the presentation of these case studies on Canada, Ghana, Great Britain, the People's Republic of China, South Africa, the Soviet Union, Taiwan and West Germany possible.

I am also very much obliged to the donors who with their financial support made it possible to organize the symposium and to realize this publication.

I am especially indebted to Dr. Otto G. Mayer of the HWWA-Institut für Wirtschaftsforschung, Hamburg, for accepting this volume as part of the Verlag Weltarchiv publications.

The members of the Independent Institute for Jurisprudential, Social and Economic Sciences desire to provide the readers with stimulating views of these challenging socio-economic policy issues. They would welcome comments or suggestions.

Grissenbach, 20th October 1988

Bodo B. Gemper

Address of the editor:
Prof. Dr. Bodo B. Gemper
Grissenbach, Luisenstr. 11
D 5902 Netphen 3
(West Germany)

Contributors

Dr. James C.W. *Ahiakpor*
Professor of Economics, St. Mary's University, Halifax, Canada

Dr. Richard L. *Brinkman*
Professor of Economics, Portland State University, Portland, Oregon, USA

Dr. Rolf *Dittmar*
Ministerialrat, Federal Ministry of Economic Affairs, Bonn, West Germany

Dr. Bodo B. *Gemper*
Professor of Economics, University of Siegen, West Germany

Dr. Charles *Grant*
London School of Economics and Political Science, London, U.K.

Dr. Helmut W. *Jenkis*
Professor of Economics, University of Dortmund and Director of the Association
Niedersächsisch-Bremischer Wohnungsunternehmen e.V., Hannover, West Germany

Dr. Tillo E. *Kuhn*
Professor of Economics, York University, North York, Ontario, Canada

Dr. Dieter *Loesch*
HWWA - Institut für Wirtschaftsforschung, Hamburg, West Germany

Dr. Herbert *Schmidt*
Ministerialrat, German Federal Chancellery, Bonn, West Germany

Dr. N. J. *Schoeman*
Professor of Economics, University of Pretoria, Pretoria, South Africa

J. J. *Swanepoel*
Economist, Industrial Development Corporation, Sandton, South Africa

Dr. Geert L. *de Wet*
Professor of Economics, University of Pretoria, Pretoria, South Africa

Dr. Nicolaas *van der Walt*
Professor of Economics, Rand Afrikaans University, Johannesburg, South Africa

Dr. Rong-*I Wu*
Professor of Economics, National Chung Hsing University, Taipei, Taiwan,
Republic of China

Contents

1. The Market System and Structural Change

2. Technological Change and Development in Dual Economies

8

1.

The Market System and Structural Change

Redefining the Government's Role
in Contemporary National Economies:
Essentials of State Participation in Market Economies

by Bodo B. Gemper

1. The Situation

Choosing this topic is likely to attract the attention – particularly at the present time – of at least two groups. The first group comprises all those who are concerned with the role of the state within the economy, mainly under the aspect of accelerating technical progress and how problems emerging from this may be mastered for the economy and society as a whole. Within this group there are two political schools: the first one represents all who feel upset when they hear the word government because they oppose persistent interference by politicians in everyday life, and they reject the continually expanding involvement of the state in the running of both the economy and society; the second school represents those who believe it would be better to strengthen the government's role because they think this is necessary in order to keep economic and technological progress in balance with the reality of society and in particular with the goals of a socially caring state. However, both schools do not like officialdom at all.

The second group of people to be interested in this topic are those observing the changes which are taking place in reform-orientated Soviet-type economies. They see the difficulties involved in implementing new methods and measures, as first started to happen in Mainland China and is now taking place in the Soviet Union. Here I am referring to both China's budding markets, the strategy of intensive growth begun by Deng Xiaoping in 1978 to improve the economy's efficiency and boost people's living standards, and the economic reforms in the Soviet Union, commonly known as "Perestroika" and "Glasnost", initiated by Mikhail Gorbachev in 1985. However, ten years of "Gaige" (modernization) and "Kaifang" (policy of the open door) in Mainland China, and three years of "Perestroika" (restructuring[1]) as well as "Glasnost" (more openness about public affairs in every sphere of life[2]) are not long enough periods of initiated change to enable a comparison of both reforms, or even to allow comments to be made about them owing to the lack of evidence. There can be no doubt that a large field of research lies ahead of us, to be harvested scientifically in the future – a most tempting challenge.

I believe that most of us belong to one group or the other, and all of us, wherever we are, worry about the omnipresence of the state often enough to be anxious to know whether and how these reforms are succeeding. I shall refrain from discussing both extreme positions – on the one hand that the state, which is accused of being repressive, should be abolished, and on the other that total control over all individuals in a society is necessary to guarantee law and order – because these are issues discussed by only a very small number of people, who believe either that we can do without government authorities completely, or that social welfare is solely the responsibility of the state.

2. Legitimation and Limitation

Often we can observe the uneasiness felt by people when thinking of government decisions about various areas of life. More and more people are questioning the legitimacy of state intervention. They feel almost no commitment to the state in which they live. Special studies, therefore, deal with the question of whether the modern state has reached a critical stage, and we even hear about 'the crisis of the modern state'[3]. In my capacity as an economist, I have also come across this problem whilst doing research in the field of structural industrial policy. I therefore feel entitled, or at least competent, to look at the government's role from the standpoint of an economist.

The Government's Role in the Past

I shall focus my interest on aspects of the government's role in a federal state and discuss this issue against the background of the process of integration in West Europe. I shall also look at the role played by the government in important fields of practice. Past experience has shown that the problem cannot in any way be reduced to a common denominator. One only needs look at the government's role in Canada, the USA or Switzerland as well as in Germany; although these countries are all democracies and states with a federal structure, they differ considerably as does quite clearly the role of the government.

I would like to stress that I believe in the future of federalism as a political answer to the challenge we will have to face. Europeans especially should accept these challenges created by accelerating technical progress, and the member states of the EC should do their best in forming the United States of Europe on the basis of the Single European Act and the domestic European market, envisaged for completion by 1992. I also believe in federalism as a prime mover for fundamental change in dual economies such as South Africa. I think federalism is the master key for opening the door to a future-orientated structure for the state and the economy of South Africa. This concept could at the same time form a basis model for a non-racial constitution in South Africa. Speaking frankly, I should welcome any constructive change – as long as people take the time to listen to each other. We are living in a very remarkable period of transition, and this issue is, in a certain sense, of universal implication for both the way in which to live and in which to govern, and finally it could be applied to the question: "Redefining the government's role in contemporary market and collectivist systems: new trends of convergence, or inevitable pragmatism in East and West?" What type of government might we declare to be a desirable one?

As a rule, governments in the past were dominated by (a few) outstanding politicians. They were authorities in the field of the executive and their counsellor was political wisdom. They understood how to run the civil service in the interest of the public and for the sake of the common good. In a word, they were statesmen. Compared with the size of government which they considered to be best, all governments nowadays are much too big. In those days the scope of the public authorities, in particular the official machinery, was very limited. Statesmen then were content with, as a rule, five ministries, which are now referred to as the "classical" ministries:

1. the Foreign Office, Department of State or Ministry of Foreign Affairs;

2. the Ministry of the Interior or Home Office;

3. the Ministry of Finance, the (Board of the) Exchequer or Treasury Department;

4. the Ministry of Justice or Department of Justice;

5. the Ministry of Defence or Department of Defense.

The Government's Role Today – Two Examples

How many ministries do you think we have in the Federal Republic of Germany. 5, 10 or 15? We have infact 17 ministries and one minister without a special portfolio. And this is only at the federal level! The eleven federal states (Laender [4]) also have their own ministries or departments. Besides the five "classical" ministries mentioned above, we find at the federal level the following additional government departments: 6. Economics, 7. Food, Agriculture and Forestry, 8. Inter-German Relations, 9. Labour and Social Welfare, 10. Youth, Families, Women and Health. 11. Transport, 12. Environment, Nature Protection and Reactor Safety, 13. Post and Telecommunication, 14. Regional Planning and Urban Development, 15. Research and Technology, 16. Education and Science, 17. Economic Co-operation, and, not to be forgotten, the 18th Federal Minister, who takes care of special responsibilities and is also in charge of the Federal Chancellor's Office at the same time.

Whilst we may count 17 full ministries in West Germany, Switzerland has had the good sense not to increase the number of ministries over and above the absolutely necessary number and thus we find only two ministries other than the five "classical" ministries. These are the Federal Department of Economics and the Federal Department of Transport and Energy.

With a little good will West Germany could reduce the number of ministries without difficulty from 17 to 9.

Since the Minister without Portfolio has the final say in decisions concerning inter-German relations, the Ministry for Inter-German Relations could be completely abolished. The Ministries for Food, Agriculture and Forestry, and for Regional Planning and Urban Development could also be abolished. Special tasks which still existed could be transferred to the other remaining departments. The main functions of the Ministry for Youth, Families, Women and Health could be looked after by the Ministry for Labour and Social Welfare. A similar condensing could take place by assigning the central tasks of the Ministry for Research and Technology and the Ministry for Education and Science to one Ministry for Education and Research. Even the responsibilities of the Ministry for Environment, Nature Protection and Reactor Safety could be integrated into this Ministry for Education and Research. Why do we need separate Ministries for Transport and for Post and Telecommunication? One would be sufficient to meet completely the needs of both. Finally, there is no need for a special Ministry for Economic Co-operation, whose central tasks could be dealt with by both the Ministry of Economics and the Ministry of Foreign Affairs.

As a rule, it can be said that a large degree of state intervention in a country deters foreign investors from spending their capital because the higher the level of intervention, the greater is the danger that the market mechanism will be disturbed in this country.

The reason for this reduction in the propensity to invest is that government interference causes unnecessarily high business risks, allocative efficiency drops and as a result the performance of the national economy also suffers.

The survey below reveals that West Germany holds a relatively moderate position at the present time. Moreover, it is one of the few countries where the share of the state in distribution has declined since 1980. Only Great Britain has been better in this respect.

The Role of the State:

The Share of the State in Distribution[1]			
Country	1970	1975	1980	1987[2]
FR Germany	38,6	48,9	48,3	46,5
USA	31,6	34,6	33,7	36,5
Japan	19,4	27,3	32,6	34,0
Great Britain	39,8	47,3	46,0	42,5
France	38,9	43,5	46,4	53,5
Italy	34,2	43,2	46,1	60,0
Switzerland [3]	21,3	28,7	29,3	30,0
Sweden	43,4	48,9	61,6	64,0
Netherlands	43,9	52,8	57,5	57,0
Belgium	36,5	44,5	50,8	51,0
Austria	39,2	46,1	48,9	52,0
Spain	22,2	24,7	32,9	41,5

[1] Total state expenditure as a percent of gross domestic product
[2] Estimates
[3] Current public expenditure only (not including public capital expenditures)

Source: OECD; 1987: IW-Estimation and (German) Council of Experts for Evaluation of the Overall Economic Development, Annual Assessment 1987/88.

It should be mentioned that this comparison is of limited value only to the extent that the figures shown above are of different quality. For example, whilst in the U.K. the downward trend of the state's share in distribution is primarily a result of the forced privatization of public enterprises, the falling quota in West Germany is to a large degree caused by the reduction of producutive expenditure by the public authorities. Moreover, Britain's policy of handing public utilities over to private ownership shows two effects of leverage: firstly, the returns of a sale are to be seen as negative expenditures; secondly, the privatization itself has led to an acceleration in the rate of economic growth.

3. The Market System and the Government's Role in the Economy

It is small wonder, in view of the extent of the tasks regarded by the government as its responsibility that it appears impossible not to regard the political system as being omnipresent. People ask the question: "Is it really necessary?" and the answer is a definite "No!". Everybody knows that the activities undertaken by the public authorities would in most cases be tackled much more quickly, much better and much more cheaply by using private initiative and the forces of the market.

For this reason it is necessary to reduce the public debt considerably in order to reduce the tax burden imposed on taxpayers and thus to bring back the willingness to work and to produce.

The market mechanism of competition is the most powerful mechanism for not only rewarding hard work and risky investments, but also for sanctioning mismanagement and bad investment.

This means that the government of a free society must do its best to establish the legal and social framework such that in the first instance it pathes the way for free competition. This holds true even for the sphere of environmental protection. Technical progress must take the environment into account. But environmental problems can best be solved within the market, not outside it. Since environmental goods such as fresh water and clean air are to be seen as critical items, they are economic goods and must have a price. This, however, does not mean that there are no responsibilities left for the government. A modern industrial state cannot do without standards and the government must lay down laws relating, for example, to the protection of the environment, and the government also has to make clear the high priority to be attached to environmental policy.

Here we can see that the government must assume the role of a guardian, and must stipulate and guarantee general institutional conditions for providing back-up support and preserving social peace. The abuse of freedom, particularly behaviour which is not in line with real market conditions, violations of environmental laws etc. must be prosecuted. We all accept that a main function of the government is to ensure law and order in general: But the government must also make special provisions for guaranteeing economic competition as well as for defending the economy against protectionism, and the national currency must be secured against depreciation. The institutions in West Germany, which are responsible for these matters, are, for example, the Federal Trade Commission (Bundeskartellamt) and the German Central Bank (Deutsche Bundesbank) not to mention the Law Courts.

These federal agencies are a conditio sine qua non in a (free) market economy as the market mechanism tends wo weaken itself. This is because those who emerge from competition as winners try to compete with each other until only one remains. Therefore the functioning of counterbalancing powers must be guaranteed by law in order to strengthen the market mechanism. Here are three examples: the Federal Trade Commission is the safeguard against unfair competition and takes steps against restrictive practices in the market economy. A hard currency is also the result of a consistent, straightforward monetary policy pursued by an independent Central Bank, which cooperates with the Federal Government in order to maintain successfully both the constancy and internal consistency of economic policy. In 1966 the Federal Constitutional Court of West Germany declared the turnover tax to be unconstitutional because as a cascade tax it led to a vertical concentration in the economy and so in turn to a weakening of economic competition. On account of this the tax system had to be changed and this was one reason why West Germany came up with value added taxation. Another reason was its interest in promoting integrative processes in the EC by means of pushing forward the harmonization of indirect taxes. In addition to the harmonization of direct taxes, there was and still is an urgent need for closer alignment of indirect taxes as a part of the efforts by the EC Commission in Brussels towards greater conformity between the economic and social policies pursued by member states.

4. More Government – Less Government?

More government or less government? This is the question. To deny the question would be to deny the solution.

To allow free competition implies a fundamental decision to establish a free market economy. The organization of the division of labour within this market mechanism requires the precondition that all the plans of producers and consumers can be coordinated, not to forget the importance of the free functioning of money and capital markets – both national and international. These fundamental decisions must not be left to the anonymity of the numerous interest groups within a society. They have to be taken by a constituent assembly, which sets the basic law structure and lays the foundations for the form of both the state and the economic order.

The answer to the question "more government or less government?" must be obvious to all who wish to be free citizens and are, therefore, also supporters of the free market economy. Less government within the framework of a state and economy, which guarantees political democracy and economic competition, means reducing the interference of the state in private lives, concentrating government activities on securing the political system and economic stability by setting the economic framework, and ensuring that there is competition. There is no doubt that we also need devices to hold economic power in check.

Between the state, that is, government regulations, and private decision-making processes we find the activities of intermediary agencies. By this I mean, for example, the Technical Inspection Service Corporation. All of us know this institution, since it is entitled to inspect and control the safety of machinery, vehicles and vessels, not only for the benefit of both the owner and driver but also in the interests of the public, that is, all who come into contact with such machines whilst they are in operation. There are quite a number of such quasi-public corporations at the service of all citizens and even the most consequent advocate of the free market accepts these public authorities and intermediary institutions.

Point of Departure: Towards an Innovative Structural Industrial Policy

Due to the fact that information technology and the accessibilty of information are rapidly changing, an innovative economic policy, conducted by a sophisticated industrial state, has not only conceptual but also executive tasks to fulfill [5]).

It should provide help in the form of pre-starting-up assistance, starting-up assistance, adjustment assistance, re-inforcement assistance and breaking-up assistance - and this, in the first instance, to small and medium-sized businesses. What does this mean exactly?

1. Providing pre-starting-up assistance by setting up technology centres as important institutions means improving the local and regional innovation infra-structure, intending in particular to:

- strengthen the consultancy services in the region through concentration and cooperation based on the division of work;

- motivate those interested in establishing new enterprises, developing and strengthening their entrepreneurial abilities;

- and finally, to serve as a forum or catalyst for joint and collective activities with a view to supporting innovation and technology transfers at local and regional levels.

2. Providing starting-up assistance means acting as a promoter. This involves paving the way for entrepreneurial independence. It supplies back-up support by strengthening the market position of entrepreneurs of already established firms, which penetrate the market in an innovative manner.

3. Giving adjustment assistance implies offering technical advice and managerial support to enterprises with a sound entrepreneurial structure, which are - temporarily - unable to cope with the pressures of adjustment.

4. Offering re-inforcement assistance is aimed at strengthening a provincially-managed enterprise's adaptability to the accelerating speed of economic and technical progress, by re-inforcing its ability to regain economic vitality and become competitive once more.

5. Providing breaking-up assistance, in extreme cases winding-up assistance, is aimed at shortening the liquidation process for those firms which are no longer competitive and which, therefore, must be taken out of the market as quickly as possible.

This kind of innovative policy, conducted by the government, requires assistance measures which impose a high degree of responsibility on public authorities and on the private banking system alike.

This policy approach is a very controversial socio-economic policy issue in West Germany. For example, Hans Besters, a leading economist from the University of Bochum, totally denies the short-sightedness of the market mechanism vis-a-vis future-orientated developments in technology. He says: "All those who produce and utilize durable capital goods are bound to take future developments into consideration." [6] A strong argument against Professor Besters' hypothesis is the pursuit of profit at any price, even to the extent of ignoring the fundamental principles of an over-all economic policy, such as the principle of liability. Pertaining to this rule, anyone who benefits from something must also bear the costs of any damage which it may incur. And Walter Eucken said: "Those who are responsible for the plans and actions of firms and households must also be held liable if anything goes wrong." [7] The increasing disregard of this pay-for-your-damage principle is in itself evidence that the far-sightedness of entrepreneurs should not be believed in too much. Most of them suffer from a typical myopia as soon as responsibility proves to be costly. Moreover, an entrepreneur loves fast money rather than social responsibility, as can be seen by looking at the American economy. The neglect in the past of environmental factors in the corporate planning of industrialists and the need to pass extensive environmental laws as a means to sanctioning entrepreneurial behaviour are other examples.

5. Fewer Administrative Authorities – More Political Leadership

What are the consequences of modern private decision-making, both public and private?

The continuing debate about an "active" industrial policy, to name but one field of problems, has its origin in the acceleration of scientific and technical evolution and the concomitant impact of this upon the socio-economic systems of advanced industrialized countries, and it leads to the question of whether there is a need for redefining the government's role, even in free enterprise economies or socially tempered market economies. Entire branches of trade and industry are old and dying, established economic regions are undergoing substantial changes in structure. Completely new industries are emerging, modern production methods as well as the service sector are expanding. These problems of structural adjustment are no longer being settled in a perfectly competitive manner by the market.

The point is whether market forces are able and fit enough to solve the problems of economic change in due time and in a socially responsible way. The question arises, does the "invisible hand" need assistance? And from whom?

For dynamic, forward-looking economies much will depend on the answer to these questions. It is as important to give society direction and confidence in the future as it is to maintain law and order. Therefore a government has at least two sets of new functions to carry out: *orientating functions* and *initiating functions.* These orientating functions are:

1. The task of providing information and additional transparency to private sector activities. This means public authorities and/or intermediary agencies should increase the level of information in three directions:

   – for the private sector;

   – for the policy makers themselves in the Federal Government as well as at the level of the Laender, and

   – for the public.

2. The task of publicizing very new developments in order to prepare people for future decisions and to inspire "frontier" thinking.

3. The task of making people aware and open to that which is in the making.

The initiating functions of the government are as follows:

1. The signal function. This means the setting of goals which form a point of orientation, encouraging people to practice aim-orientated behaviour.

2. The function of inducing personal initiative.

3. The function of promoting innovation creating.

4. The function of revitalizing economic activity.

5. The function of strengthening efficiency-orientated attitudes.

These are just some examples to explain what is meant by initiating functions. These orientating and initiating functions of the government constitute *indicative targeting* for the sake of individuals, the economy and society as a whole.

6. Political Leadership and Private Leadership - Hand in Hand

Indicative targeting makes it possible to discover systematically signals, which could become points of reference (landmarks) for the way into the future, and indicative targeting enables us to trace out future trends by extrapolating current data onto new territory. Desirable trends and ideas should be encouraged, unwelcome and risky developments or trends should be suppressed. The government's role in meeting the future must be based on *intermediary consultancy* processes between private industry and commerce, private banks, the Central Bank and the Government, and also to a certain extent on applied research since it is responsible for the correct use of a set of policy measures. This system of an intermediary consultancy should correspond to a federal state structure and a free market economy. The need for redefining the government's role in contemporary market economies should have high priority because of the huge and still growing number of problems as yet unsolved, which have been caused by the accelerating rate of technological change. Neither the market mechanism nor discretionary government measures have been able to meet these challenges in Europe.

The precise point of departure must, therefore, be found by carefully analysing the extent to which the framework of *the vital functions of socio-economic development dynamics* have themselves changed in their structure as a result of accelerating technological change and by evaluating the impact on the economy and society.

The result will enable us to open up new vistas for bringing economic policies uptodate and will give us a clear answer as to what the ideal relationship between decision-making units of the private sector and the state should look like. Redefining the government's role means clarifying today's situation and being prepared for the future.

Notes

1. Cf. Mikhail Gorbachev: Perestroika. New Thinking for Our Country and the World, London 1987, p.17

2. Op.cit., p.75

3. Cf. Bernd and Ingeborg Guggenberger: Die Legitimitaetskrise des modernen Staates – Ist die Massengesellschaft noch freiheitlich regierbar? (The Legitimacy Crisis in the Modern State – is it still possible to govern a Mass Society in a liberal manner?) in: Material zum Problem der Legitimitaet im modernen Staat (Evidence on the Problem of Legitimacy in the Modern State), Politische Akademie Eichholz, Bonn 1975, p. 28–47.

4. Baden-Wuerttemberg, Bayern (Bavaria), Bremen, Hamburg, Hessen (Hesse), Niedersachsen (Lower Saxony), Nordrhein-Westfalen (North Rhine Westphalia), Rheinland-Pfalz (Rhineland Palatinate), Saarland, Schleswig-Holstein, Berlin (West).

5. Cf. my article "Industrial Policy in a Free Market Economy: A Matter of Conviction or Desperation?" in: Bodo B. Gemper (Ed.) Industrial Policy – Structural Dynamics, Hamburg 1985, p.18, and New Brunswick (USA) and Oxford (U.K.) 1987, p.18

6. Hans Besters: Neue Industriepolitik oder Rueckkehr zur Ordnungspolitik? (Towards a New Industrial Policy or a Return to Ordnungspolitik?) in: Joachim Klaus und Paul Klemmer (Ed.): Wirtschaftliche Strukturprobleme und soziale Fragen. Analyse und Gestaltungsaufgaben. J. Heinz Mueller zum 70. Geburtstag. (Problems of the Economic Structure and Social Questions. Analysis and Creative Responsibilities. Commemorating the 70th Birthday of J. Heinz Mueller), Berlin 1988, p.58.

7. Walter Eucken: Grundsaetze der Wirtschaftspolitik (Principles of Economic Policy), 4th ed., Tuebingen and Zurich 1968, p.281.

Social Market Systems: International Perspectives

by Tillo E. Kuhn

1.   Definition and Meanings of 'Markets'

The terms "markets" and "market systems" are in widespread use. They are an integral part of everyday commercial language. There is no economics. management and business text, nor indeed any serious newspaper, without reference to markets. Politicians love to pepper their pronouncements with observations on the real or imagined attributes of various market forms. Statesmen in the Eastern nations nowadays naively place great faith in the invigorating powers of market forms. And in the West we are awed by the enigmatic messages issueing from "fickle", "depressed", "panicky", "buoyant", "uninspiring" etc. markets, revered by many avid followers, in their high-technology manifestations, almost like electronic Delphic oracles.

Basic Definition

What is at the core of all this verbiage? Here is a definition of our own which might capture the essential elements of contemporary market systems:

> "A market is an area, or a network, or a set of arrangements, within which buyers and sellers accomplish exchanges of tangible and intangible goods and services, assets and liabilities, for use now and in future, with or without deploying money as the medium of exchange. The varying degrees of market power and knowledge possessed by the different market participants will materially influence the eventual outcome of their transactions."

Note the wide technical scope of market transactions envisaged by the definition, as well as the important role assigned to "power" and "knowledge", given that these are to some extent substitutes for each other.

Three Levels of Meaning

In current debates about markets, at least three levels of meaning can be iden-tified:

(a)   At the *theoretical level*, there are the rigorously specified market prototypes in orthodox economic analyses. It is worth recalling that these range:

–   from pure or perfect competition ("many" individually powerless sellers and buyers; costless market entry and egress; homogeneous commodity; total resource mobility: perfect knowledge of all participants);

–   through oligopoly and other market imperfections;

–   to monopoly (single seller) and monosopsony (single buyer).

We observe with great regret that the theoretical economist's perfectly competitive market theorems, while pedagogically elegant and politically seductive ("powerless economic agents toiling for the common good"), have hardly any practical significance. Each semester my graduate students and I try diligently to come up with real world applications; each time we fail. Monopoly examples abound, on the other hand. And the rather stilted market imperfection models in economic theory simply do not justice to the big, messy middle range, where so much activity takes place in modern economies.

(b)   At the *empirical level,* much creative scientific work can be done, given imaginative terms of reference and interdisciplinary approaches, to answer questions such as these: what are objective performance indicators to judge the effectiveness of different market forms? To what extent do history, social attitudes and political beliefs determine the most suitable market form for particular cultures? Should the innate characteristics of the object marketed determine the market system configuration, or vice versa?

In the real world, we find an impressive diversity of markets which seem to function very well. An imaginary stroll around the downtown core of the City of Toronto will provide vivid illustrations. To start, the St. Lawrence Market represents the highly successful fresh produce markets for fruits, vegetables, meat, fish and dairy products found in such vibrant profusion from München (Viktualienmarkt) to Montevideo and even Moscow. Success ingredients: direct transactions between producer and consumer; no fussy advertising; flexible pricing; good municipal infrastructure; and sensible regulations.

In Toronto we next reach the Eaton Centre, an impressive array of stores, restaurants and other establishments, all under one roof and directly linked to the subway – really a North American version of the Great Bazaar in Istanbul. Native Torontonians call it The Great Vacuum Cleaner for its ability to extract real or plastic money from the users' pockets as they walk through.

We conclude our little stroll in Toronto's financial district, where huge masses of money, shares and commodities are traded worldwide, in geographic space and in time at electronic speed.

To reflect, within a radius of one kilometer, we observe an astonishing range of markets: apples and beans purveyed under municipal auspices; an ultramodern amalgam of private, public and joint shopping facilities; and a global trading offspring of the information revolution.

Each one of the three types represents a valid and fully functioning market system in the real world. Each one fits our basic definition quite well. To none would one apply orthodox economic market concepts without all sorts of disclaimers and qualifications, if at all. Why is there this obvious gap between concepts and reality, between theory and practice?

Right there, there is scope for a productive research agenda: honest descriptive work on extant market systems: development of taxonomies and empirical generalizations; these would eventually lead to formulation of fruitful hypotheses, empirical testing and thus rejections or conditional acceptances of various market theories.

(c)   A *third level* of meaning of markets has unfortunately emerged in recent political and ideological debates. It has arisen out of the inconsistencies and contradictions between rather sterile economic textbook theorizing about markets, on the one hand, and the puzzling and complex manifestations of real markets in the modern world, on the other hand.

At this third level, the term "market" has become a *metaphor,* a loose set of symbolical references and allegorical allusions, with implied resemblances to empirically observable market phenomena and/or rigorously constructed economic models.

The market metaphor is a powerful tool of political rhetoric. If combined with the other potent metaphor'"freedom" and served up to the voting public as the "free market system", it rivals motherhood as something intrinsically good and obviously desirable.

The western world has gone through an ideologically conservative phase, associated with such heads of government as Kohl, Thatcher, Reagan and Mulroney in Canada. Simultaneously, the emergence of television as the key political communications medium, coupled with the short attention span of the viewers, has fostered the punchy political message, the theatrical side of politics and emphasis on the personality of leaders. Such slogans as "free enterprise", "private initiative", "curbing of government meddling and interference in the market place", come across the screen very smoothly into millions of living rooms. Of course, five minutes later the viewers do not remember what was said, leave alone what it all really means. Instant responses, imagery and leadership cults are enemies of careful thought.

The Canadian communications sage, Professor McLuhan, summed up our age beautifully: "The medium is the message". To illustrate, many millions of dollars later, Torontonians wonder whether the recent Economic Summit of the heads of the seven richest industrial democracies here went beyond a gigantic international media circus. Does anybody remember, or even care, what transpired? How does one reconcile the free market rhetoric of those seven leaders with farm subsidization policies in the EEC, Japanese protectionism and the prime role of the defence establishment in the U.S. economy?

To sum up, as scholars of the subject, we are obliged to treat the obviously vital concept of the market with great care and respect. In particular, we must sharpen and upgrade our theoretical tools, in order to more effectively address the bewildering varieties and complexities of real market systems in the modern world. In scientific parlance, we must simultaneously deploy both inductive and deductive reasoning and research methodologies, with the aim of reconciling and integrating the two approaches.

This in itself would reduce the scope for deceptive market metaphors, loose political rhetoric and extravagant claims made for the capabilities of particular market systems configurations nowadays.

2.   Paradigm Change: Policy Analysis applied to Market Systems

How can we reconcile these different visions of markets? Is it possible to integrate the theoretical and empirical manifestations of markets? And if so, will this enhance our understanding of the true nature of the political rhetoric surrounding the subject?

If we succeed in answering these questions, we are better equipped to tackle the more complex notion of *social* market systems,the core topic of this paper.

The Concept of a Paradigm

At this point it is fruitful to draw on the powerful notion of a scientific paradigm, developed by my distinguished namesake Thomas S. Kuhn, in his work *The Structure of Scientific Revolutions*[1]:

"In its established usage, a paradigm is an accepted model or pattern ... Paradigms gain their status because they are more successful than their competitors in solving a few problems that the group of practitioners has come to recognize as acute." (p. 23)

"One of the things a scientific community acquires with a paradigm is a criterion for choosing problems that, while the paradigm is taken for granted, can be assumed to have solutions. To a great extent these are the only problems that the community will admit as scientific or encourage its members to undertake. Other problems, including many that had previously been standard, are rejected as metaphysical, as the concern of another discipline, or sometimes as just too problematic to be worth the time." (p. 37)

Thomas S. Kuhn, after examining the nature and necessity of scientific revolutions, then states: "scientific revolutions are here taken to be those non-cumulative developmental episodes in which an older paradigm is replaced in whole or in part by an incompatible new one." (p. 92) And he concludes significantly: "In learning a paradigm the scientist acquires theory, methods, and standards together, usually in an inextricable mixture. Therefore, when paradigms change, there are usually significant shifts in the criteria determining the legitimacy both of problems and of proposed solutions." (p. 109)

Desirable Market Paradigm Changes

There can be little doubt that economic theories purporting to explain markets qualify as genuine paradigms, in the way Thomas S. Kuhn sees them: market theorems are accepted models or patterns; they are applied by practitioners (such as advisors, consultants, forecasters) to problems in the real world which are assumed to have solutions; they are part of the "community's paradigms. revealed in its textbooks, lectures, and laboratory exercises." (1, p. 43)

Economists get into serious difficulties, though, when they move certain models from the cognitive, or descriptive, mode to the normative one. Let us examine the perfectly competitive market paradigm, which fills a lot of pages in Western microeconomic textbooks and learned journals and, willy-nilly, still seems to impress some of our political leaders. If desired we can thoroughly track, with the aid of Joseph A. Schumpeter's monumental work *History of Economic Analysis* [2], the root idea from "free" competition (in 'classical' economic writings), through the 'perfect' version (Boisguillebert, Cournot) to 'pure' competition (Jevons, Walras, Pareto, Marshall and many others) in its contemporary disguise.

There is nothing wrong in using the perfectly competitive market model as a pedagogical device in the classroom, as a benchmark case and as a starting point for seriously working one's way from this one extreme end of the market spectrum over to private and public monopolies, at the other extreme.

One might legitimately go even a step further and devote some study to the concept of "equilibrium", including the static or stationary state (which Schumpeter calls a "simplifying device" and "nothing but a methodological fiction"), dynamic versions and even the highly contrived general equilibrium theorems.

But it is quite another matter to elevate these theoretical, "what is" or even "what might be" artifacts, into "what ought to be", i.e. into normative prescriptions for policy makers.

Once economic scholars and practitioners have slipped from the theoretical, cognitive mode into the normative, prescriptive mode, which asserts that perfectly competitive markets maximize welfare, then massive economic policy interventions suggest themselves: enforcement of competition; anti-combines legislation; privatization; deregulation; minimization of the role of the state.

It is my firm contention, shared by many, that economics cannot be value free and ethically neutral. As a social science it is obviously deeply embedded in human nature, human knowledge, human behaviour and human concerns about the future. Economic policy analysis, which provides the linkage between "what is" and "what ought to be", *must* be driven by clearly articulated value judgements of the society it is supposed to serve.

In this light, the perfectly competitive market apparatus, seen as a normative policy prescription device, must be regarded as an obsolete paradigm. I leave it to others to judge whether, following Thomas S. Kuhn, it should be "rejected as metaphysical, as the concern of another discipline, or ... just too problematic to be worth the time." It is up to its proponents to demonstrate conclusively and consistently, with empirical evidence, that it has advanced measurably human welfare across societies with different value systems. Any takers?

This does not diminish its usefulness as a teaching tool and, going further, as a "means to an end", as one of several possible instrumentalities which one might deploy to achieve goals derived from the particular society's value system. By all means, let perfect competition compete with other policy delivery approaches in the real world, all of them to be judged on the basis of objective performance indicators derived, of course, from society's goal structure. How this might be done in practice will be examined now.

Fundamental Logic of Policy Analysis

A thorough exposition of this weighty topic is obviously not possible here. But with the aid of the numbered modules in Figure 1, key features can be explained briefly, specifically with the aid of Canadian examples (The author has been fortunate enough to test and perfect these policy formulation processes in a number of national settings, especially in developing countries.):

Module 0:

Identification of the "client" (decision maker, executive body, policy implementer) is probably the single most important decision any analyst has to face. Sometimes there are several clients with conflicting goal structures, e.g. the Inter-American Development Bank plus the Republic of Paraguay in field work the author carried out with a Canadian engineering-consulting team.[3] Here we assume simply Canada as the relevant geographic, legal etc. domain and the Canadian Federal Government as the power base (Module 6).

Module 2:

Scenarios, a well-developed analytical device, reflect exogenous factors (givens, assumptions, anything outside the client's domain and power reach), such as demographics, climate and international factors.

Figure 1

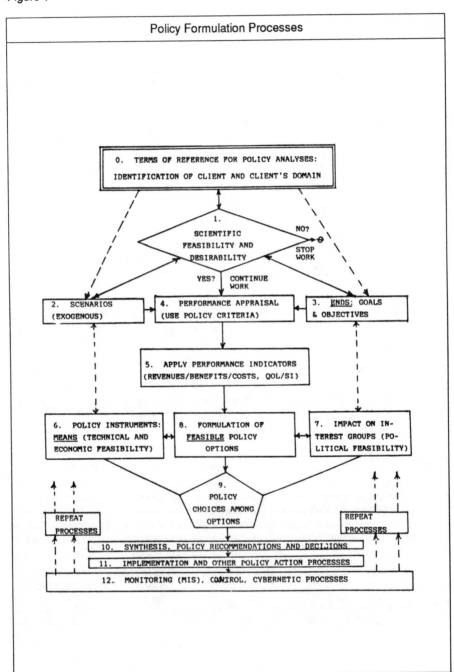

Policy Formulation Processes

Module 3

Ends: goals and objectives (strategic and tactical achievements sought by the client, are naturally derived from Module 0. But they are also influenced by various interest groups and political pressures (Module 7), especially in democratic systems, as well as by Glasnost innovations in the USSR, it seems. And, rather subtly, Modules 6 ("means") and 3 ("ends") are functionally linked. The Canadian goal structure is remarkably stable[4], rather free of political ideology, beyond the parties' natural desire to get elected into power. Pragmatism prevails and Canadian decision makers will ask policy analysts: tell me what is possible (Module 6) and I will adjust my goal structure (Module 3) accordingly. Methodologically this can be done by running several policy option iterations (Module 8, via 4 and 5, plus the others), giving the client the final choice among several crisply presented alternative policy packages (Module 9).

Clearly, then, market systems belong into Module 6 (policy instrumentalities) and their particular merits must be objectively appraised with the aid of performance indicators (Module 4), which in turn are derived from the given society's value system, in this case Canada's goal structure (Module 3), in the light of threats and opportunities arising from changes in the external environment (Module 2). To illustrate, Canada recently overhauled its national transportation policies (a massive undertaking for the country, the second largest in the world after the USSR) along the lines sketched here.

3.   Synthesis with Social Market Systems

A synthesis between the principles and applications of policy analysis, just outlined, and the concept of social market systems should now be attempted.

The author, although German (Bavarian, more specifically) by birth, did all his studies and academic work in England, the USA and Canada, apart from visiting professorships and advisory assignments in other parts of the world. He has therefore had regrettably little exposure to the Concept of the (German) Social Market Economy,[5] also known as The 'Freiburg School'. Apart from the creative stimuli received through the proceedings of the Fourteenth Walberberg System Symposium, April 1987, he found the writings by Bodo B. Gemper[6], Richard L. Brinkman[7], Horst Friedrich Wünsche[8], Helmut W. Jenkis[9], particularly helpful, while acknowledging that there are several other important contributors in this field.

With this disclaimer as background, a perusal of this extremely stimulating literature indeed reveals convergence between the approaches originating from the opposite sides of the Atlantic Ocean. Jenkis, for instance, cites Alfred Müller-Armack, the intellectual father of the concept of the social market economy (Soziale Marktwirtschaft):

"While it is necessary to understand and secure the interconnected wholeness of the market economy, it is equally necessary to be aware of the technical and specific character of the market economy. The latter is merely a purposeful mechanism but nothing more: and it would be a disastrous error to expect that the self-regulating mechanism of the market could fulfil the task of creating an acceptable and valid social order and could pay attention to the needs of public and cultural life."[10]

This represents a forceful distinction between ends and means, basic to policy analysis. Gemper[11] likewise stresses the need for "a goal-oriented conceptual framework", where "The objective of political policy is, in the final analysis, the concern for a dignified life and for the development of man's potentials." In the same spirit, Brinkman[7] states: "In theory and in practice, an unregulated market system is anachronistic to the needs of a modern industrial society. ... The process of economic evolution, as measured in advances in economic production and higher levels of energy control, serves as a necessary but not sufficient condition for human progress. The numeraire or basic unit of account in assessing progress, to our view, should not simply be economic production but rather should focus on Homo sapiens, as humankind." And Wünsche, in an interesting essay on Ludwig Erhard's conception, concludes: "An economist must regard the demand for a desirable social product as the primary goal. The economy must not be allowed to become an end in itself."

This small sampling of social market systems scholars shows persuasively that their concepts, in a way, furnish the basic intellectual components for policy analysis, which then provides the necessary processes, or logic flows, for the evaluation of alternative policy packages.

In conclusion, there is a synthesis: the two approaches are symbiotically related. There is much room for learning and innovation here.

4. Some Canadian Applications

Following a brief exposé of the Canadian setting, some cases illustrating the pragmatic interplay between public policy and productive enterprises in our country will be of interest.

The Canadian Setting

Canada, as the second largest country in the world, obviously had to rely heavily on government as the logic source of capital and power to establish and maintain the massive infrastructure required for the linking and physical survival of the far-flung portions of its domain. This factor, coupled with strong British, French and other European traditions and attitudes, has made Canadians far more receptive to government leadership and intervention in the economy than is the case in the USA, the giant entity roughly ten times the population and economic size to the south.

These two nations, while deceptively similar at a superficial level, are really quite different in fundamental ways. Rightly or wrongly, Canadians pride themselves on their superior social and health services (by international standards, these do not put heavy tax burdens on Canadians), their moderate foreign policy stance and defence commitments. As a nice compliment, Peter Ustinov once described Toronto as "New York run by the Swiss". Fear of being politically and culturally absorbed by the United States via an impending free-trade pact, is causing bitter debates in Canada right now.

Important for the theme of this paper is the seemingly non-ideological nature of our political life. Canada is a federation of ten provinces, a total of eleven governments, plus two (in future three) territories in the north approaching self-governing status. Within this political quiltwork, it is hard to tell who is on the right and who is on the left. Parties probably tend to get elected on grounds of their perceived team quality and management ability. Canadians like to cover their political bets: right now, following a pattern, the conservatives hold federal power in Ottawa, but the liberals govern in Ontario and Québec, the two most important provinces.

While there are sharp regional differences, Canadians enjoy considerable economic prosperity. According to comparisons among OECD nations[12], Canada scored as follows in 1984 or 1985:

- US $8484 per capita private consumption (2nd after the USA)

- a low population density of just 3 inhabitants per sq. km

- 421 passenger cars per 1000 inhabitants (3rd)

- impressive economic and social indicator performance in general, as revealed also by a survey in *The Economist*[13].

And Ontario, bigger than Spain and France combined, has the thirdhighest disposable incomes in the world and its economy is growing twice as fast as that of Japan.

Finally, there are many indications that Canada has already moved well into the third economic-industrial revolution: towards the information and communications society.

Pragmatism in Defining Public and Private Roles

Given its small population size (25 million in 1985), Canada must constantly reconcile the quest for economies of scale, which would favour monopolies, with the desire for efficiency, easiest achieved through competition in the right settings. The following contemporary cases demonstrate the pragmatic accommodations that have taken place recently:

(a)   Petro-Canada is one of the many Canadian Crown Corporations, which can be defined as "government-controlled enterprises producing goods and services, typically for sale, while ultimate formal authority is retained by the state". Petro-Canada was established in July 1975, grew rapidly both in size and scope of operations, partly by acquisitions, and by 1985 was the largest fuel retailer in the country.

The Conservatives, who came to power in 1984, had vowed to privatize Petro-Canada. They desisted after opinion polls revealed solid public support for the Crown Corporation. Canadians like a public presence among the multinationals.

(b)   Air Canada, another Crown Corporation formed as long ago as 1937, has served the country and its customers well. After doing nothing for four years, the Conservatives recently announced that the national airline would be "privatized", to the possible extent of 50 per cent of shares.

However, there is no ideology involved. Air Canada has to raise capital to purchase 34 Airbus A320s for C$ 1.8 billion, in order to replace its ageing fleet of 33 fuel-guzzling Boeing 727s. Raising money from private sources (including employees) is sensible, since the Federal Government is already burdened with big deficits and a massive national debt.

(c)   Bell Canada is an interesting hybrid which functions exceptionally well in the sophisticated telecommunications field: while owned by many small investors, Bell's key policy decision variables (rates, investments, etc.) are controlled in the public interest by the Canadian Radio-Television and Telecommunications Commission. By international standards, Bell's service quality was always exceptionally high and rates are also very low. Recently, CRTC effected further substantial long-distance rate reductions and off-peak discount features. Well-researched consumer advocacy group interventions are an important part of the regulatory process.

An international telecommunications survey put out by *The Economist* in 1985[14], revealed gross inefficiencies and high rates of the Bundespost's telecommunications system, by contrast. And a June 1988 guest at a hotel in Bonn had to surrender 80 marks (= C$60) for a three-minute call to North America in prime time. The Bell rate in the opposite direction is a mere C$2.72 for the initial minute and $1.81 for each additional minute at the regular rate, with big savings during off-peak periods. If you are German, it is best to let Canada call you!

It would be interesting to determine the reasons for the big differences in service quality and costs between the Canadian and German systems: Is it the regulatory regime in Canada? The vertical integration of Bell, the operator, and Northern Telecommunications, the technically advanced and internationally aggressive Canadian supplier? The outstanding research done by Bell-Northern Research, a jointly-owned company? What is the role of the Bonn Government and Siemens in all this? And what inferences can we make regarding social market systems capable of sustaining the information and communications revolution which is upon us?

(d)   Magna International Inc., Canada's largest manufacturer of automobile parts, finally, illustrates an innovative combination of impressive private entrepreneurship in the ferociously competitive North American motor vehicle market, with a unique, socially balanced corporate culture, described as "fair enterprise".

Briefly, this culture recognizes that it takes three ingredients to be successful in business, namely: management, employees, and capital. Each of these in-gredients has a right, enshrined in Magna's Corporate Constitution, to share in the profits that it helps to generate. The company is a leader in productivity improvements through new technology, while emphasizing human capital through the upgrading of wages, environment, safety in the workplace, fairness and equal opportunity for advancement. In 1985, manufacturing and office employees owned more than $30 million of Magna stock, as did members of management. Consequently, all participants have an interest in protecting the value of their investments and in sustaining the continuing healthy growth of this company.

Other critical components of the corporate culture include a commitment to keep all Magna plants small with a maximum of 100 employees each, emphasis on research and development, profitsharing and a range of social benefits from day care for employee's children to a company-owned conservation and recreation area.

The professional economist notes that Magna reaps economies of scale within the huge US-Canada free trade market in autos and auto parts, by centralized planning, market intelligence, financing, R & D., and other functions. At the same time, it avoids the diseconomies of scale by small autonomous operating units (cell-splitting them, when they get too big), which often compete with each other. And, one might say, the unique corporate structure and employee profit-sharing arrangements, are further potent decentralizing devices. Interestingly, unions have not taken hold in Magna; maybe they are not necessary.

The history of Magna is really the entrepreneurial life story of Frank Stronach, an immigrant to Canada from Austria, who founded, the company in 1957. In the last 15 years

Magna grew continually in sales and profits at an annual rate of 30 per cent or more and by 1985 was opening one new factory every six to eight weeks to keep pace with demands. This big enterprise has been very successful financially and, under its constitution, it allocates from profit before tax 7 per cent for research and technology development, plus 2 per cent for charitable, cultural, educational and political institutions "to support the basic fabric of society".

Frank Stronach, while continuing as Chairman of the Board, recently withdrew as Chief Executive Officer of Magna, to enter the next Canadian Federal Election as the Liberal Party candidate in a Toronto riding. Depending on the political fortunes, his unique vision of the innovative and socially balanced competitive enterprise may be projected onto the national scene.

The Private-Public Enterprise Spectrum in Canada

In the following tabulation, our Canadian benchmark cases are placed in appropriate spots within the total private-public enterprise spectrum:

Ownership/Control	Examples	Public Interest	Performance
Private Corporations	Numerous	Minimal	Mixed
"Fair Enterprise"	Magna Inc.	Safeguarded by innovative balancing of interests	Very good
Crown Corporation	Air Canada	As for other (private) airlines	Competes successfully
Crown Corporation	Petro-Canada	Provides a Canadian presence in a foreign-dominated oligopoly market	Competes successfully
Publicly Regulated and Privately Owned Utility	Bell Canada	A natural monopoly, in many ways	Excellent technical, cost and rate performance
Traditional Government Ministries	Many	Presumed to be predominant	Mixed; hard to assess objectively

The Canadian pragmatism is evident in the middle range, where there are numerous public-private and hybrid arrangements, with or without regulatory or other government interventions. Ends to be achieved have largely dictated the means, as it should be.

5. Concluding Observations

The following conclusions and observations on this important topic are offered:

(a)   Past economic-political ideologies (Marxism, Capitalism) have erroneously focussed on *instrumentalities* (ownership of means of production, particular market systems configurations), rather than on ultimate ends which should be pursued for the advancement of humankind.

(b)   These ideologies also attributed unsubstantiated motivations and behaviourial patterns to the "actors", or dramatis personae, in the schema of the economic process, such as capitalists (greed vs. efficiency), bureaucrat and central planner (benign servant of the collective will vs. corrupt bungler), landowners, labourers, and so on. Such presumptions would not receive passing grades nowadays in an organizational behaviour and industrial relations course.

(c)   In the contemporary setting, any systematic study of ultimate goals held by different societies (such as internal and external peace and stability; creative opportunities for the population; a decent life style; a sustainable man-nature balance: equity and social justice; law and order; tolerance; and so on) would probably reveal far greater similarities than differences. Furthermore, if the Canadian example serves as a guide, these societal value structures are probably quite stable over time.

(d)   It follows that different societies should be free to search for their own, unique means – fashioned by culture, customs and history – to achieve roughly the same goals. May the best goal delivery systems win in a peaceful and cooperative world setting.

(e)   The social market system perfected in Germany is attractive for other societies, such as Canada, since there can hardly be any disagreement on the explicitly stated social goals.

(f)   However, the environmental dimensions – which are coming to the fore very rapidly – must be addressed vigorously. After all, it is rather presumptuous to treat humans as the focal point of the universe. "Respect for life in all its manifestations" might be a better paradigm. Humans, uniquely equipped with powers of reason, might ideally be seen as custodians of the manifold marvels of nature and life. This would also safeguard our own social survival.

I would like to end with the magnificent address by Chief Seattle in 1854 (the city was named after the Dwamish Indian leader), to an assembly of tribes, which were preparing to sign a treaty with the white man:

> "How can you buy or sell the sky, the warmth of the land? The idea is strange to us. If we do not own the freshness of the air and the sparkle of the water, how can you buy them? Every part of this Earth is sacred to my people. Every shining pine needle, every sandy shore, every mist in the dark woods, every clearing and humnimg insect is holy in the memory of my people. The sap which courses through the trees carries the memories of the red man."

> "The white man treats his mother, the Earth, and his brother, the sky, as things to be bought, plundered, sold like sheep or bright beads. His appetite will devour the Earth and leave behind only a desert."

> "Where is the thicket? Gone. Where is the eagle? Gone."

> "Whatever befalls the Earth befalls the sons of the Earth. Man did not weave the web of life; he is merely a strand in it. Whatever he does to the web, he does to himself."

> "The whites too shall pass, perhaps sooner than all other tribes. Continue to contaminate your bed, and you will one night suffocate in your own waste."[15]

Notes

1   Thomas S. Kuhn, *The Structure of Scientific Revolutions,* 2nd edition, enlarged, International Encyclopedia of Unified Science, The University of Chicago Press, 1970, vol. II, no. 2.

2   Joseph A. Schumpeter, *History of Economic Analysis,* Oxford University Press, New York, 1955.

3   *Feasibility Study for the Trans Chaco Highway,* report prepared for the Ministry of Public Works, Republic of Paraguay, and the Inter-American Development Bank, Washington, D.C., by Delcan International, Asuncion, 1969.

4   Tillo E. Kuhn, *Canada's National Goals and Objectives,* Strategic Planning Branch, Transport Canada, Ottawa, 1979.

5   Helmut W. Jenkis, *The Concept of the (German) Social Market Economy,* Summary, Hannover, 1987.

6   Bodo B. Gemper (Ed.), *Industrial Policy - Structural Dynamics,* Verlag Weltarchiv GmbH, Hamburg, 1985.

7   Richard L. Brinkman, "Democratic Planning in a Free Economy and Social Values," in Gemper (Ed.), (6), pp. 21–36.

8   Horst Friedrich Wünsche, "Does Industrial Policy Comply with Ludwig Erhard's Conception of the Social Market Economy?" in Gemper (Ed.), (6), pp. 37–43.

9   Helmut W. Jenkis, "Stabilisation of the Social Structure versus Change of the industrial Structure – The Case of the Ruhr District," in Gemper (Ed.), pp. 57–88.

10   Alfred Müller-Armack, *Wirtschaftslenkung und Marktwirtschaft,* Hamburg, 1947.

11   Bodo B. Gemper, "Industrial Policy in a Free Market Economy: A Matter of Conviction or Desperation?," in Gemper (Ed.), (6), pp. 11–20.

12   OECD, *Economic Surveys 1986/1987: Canada,* Paris, 1987.

13   The Economist, "Nirvana by Numbers", December 24, 1985.

14   *The Economist,* "The World on the Line: Telecommunications – A Survey," Nov. 23, 1985.

15   Extracts. The speech was recorded and translated by a Dr. Smith. It is printed in its entirety in vol. 42, no. 11 of *Fellowship,* from the Fellowship of Reconciliation, 523 N. Broadway, Nyack, N.Y., USA, 10960.

The Social Impact of Small Business

by Herbert G. Schmidt

I. Economic Policies for Small and Medium-sized Businesses

Current questions of interest

Structural problems of small and medium-sized businesses are not limited to the national level. Lobbies, associations, institutions and government agencies dealing with the problems of small and medium–sized businesses exist in virtually all countries. At present, the Federal Republic of Germany is being faced with more and more problems of adjustment posed by the introduction of new technology, in particular electronics, and by the demands of international competition in industry. The integration of the European Economic Community (a domestic European market is to be realized by 1992) has not only created access for national products to new markets, but has also made demands on the vitality and competitiveness of businesses, a problem which must be seen both in the national and international context. At the moment, small and medium–sized businesses are gaining in importance as a means of combating unemployment and of stimulating the economy.

My remarks here serve to characterize the features of German national policies for small and medium–sized businesses within the framework of a social market economy. Due to its economic and social significance, intercompany co–operation is to be seen as an instrument of government policies for small business to help the economy help itself, with a particular view to maintaining the viability of independent businesses and at the same time ensuring jobs for the employees. Co–operation can, however, also be of importance in setting up businesses, especially for those not in a position to do so on their own.

Structural data on small and medium-sized businesses in the Federal Republic of Germany.

The category of small and medium-sized businesses comprises owners of independent companies who have invested in a financial venture, are taking the risks involved, are managing their companies and usually work in them. A small businessman is commonly defined as someone who is in danger of going broke and losing his money.

(a)   Classification according to size of the business

There are no uniform criteria as to what constitutes a small, medium-sized or large business. There is no homogeneity in the structure of business size. Business sizes sometimes vary substantially within a particular branch of industry. In order to set up an exact classification of small and medium-sized businesses, one would have to define the many qualitative traits, which comprise organizational, legal, social, sociological and economic aspects.

For the implementation of government policies for small and medium-sized businesses the size of a business is defined by the *number of employees* and the *annual turnover*.

On the whole, small and medium-sized businesses comprise economic units of less than

500 employees and
DM 100,000,000 annual turnover.

The following sub-classification has proven useful:

Business size	No. of employees	Annual turnover in DM
very small businesses	1 – 2	up to 100,000
small businesses	3 – 49	100,000 to 5,000,000
medium-sized businesses	50 – 499	5,000,000 to 100,000,000
large businesses	over 500	over 100,000,000

In accordance with this classification, the structure of business sizes in the Federal Republic of Germany for commercial businesses (excluding agriculture) and for liberal professions is as follows:

Employees	% of businesses	% of employees
1 – 2	52.0	6.8
3 – 49	45.7	31.2
50 – 499	2.1	24.2
over 500	0.2	37.8
	100.0	100.0

(b)   The social contribution of small and medium–sized businesses

The significance of small and medium-sized businesses in a social market economy can be characterized by the following features which also serve to underline the economic importance of the various business sizes:

–   Over half of the gross value added (excluding accomodation rental and government) was attained in small and medium-sized businesses,

–   over two-fifths of private fixed asset investment (excluding housing construction) was in small and medium–sized businesses,

–   about two-thirds of all employees in private industry were active in small and medium-sized businesses,

–   over four-fifths of trainees received their vocational training in small and medium-sized businesses and in centres of study for the liberal professions,

–   about 70 percent of all corporate taxes and 62.2 percent of all social security contributions derive from small and medium-sized businesses,

–   about four-fifths of inventions for which patents have been applied come from small and medium-sized businesses.

(c) The proportion of self-employed persons as a basic criterion:

A basic criterion to appreciate the significance of small and medium-sized businesses is the proportion of self-employed persons. This is the proportion of such persons in the total labour force which in the Federal Republic of Germany is now 9.5 percent. This figure varies, however, from industry to industry. The proportions of self-employed persons in 1985 were as follows:

—	in agriculture	36.2 %
—	in trade and transportation	13.8 %
—	in the service sector	8.2 %
—	in manufacturing	5.2 %
—	in craft industries	12.9 %
—	for self-employed persons in commerce and the liberal professions (excluding agriculture and forestry)	8.0 %

In order to increase the prospects of self–employment in industry, the Government of the Federal Republic of Germany is endeavouring to keep the threshold for self-employment as low as possible for anyone possessing the qualities and motivation for such an entrepreneurial venture.

The freedom to choose one's profession and place of work guaranteed in the constitution would not be a reality without small and medium-sized businesses. A strong entrepreneurial sector will therefore continue to be the best guarantee for the maintenance of a free economic order in our country and is thus viewed as one of the fundamentals of a free and democratic society.

Policies for small and medium–sized businesses in a social market economy

The basis of the vitality and competitiveness of small and medium-sized businesses lies in their ability and constant willingness to adjust to structural change in industry.

In our dynamic economy it is often difficult for the owners of small and medium-sized businesses to deal with such problems of adjustment, to recognize them in good time and to take appropriate action. Industry and business associations in all industrialized countries have therefore always been demanding active government policies to support small and medium-sized businesses. Today as in the past, many representatives of independent small and medium-sized businesses, influenced by traditional class thinking, still regard this as the "protection of small and medium-sized businesses" or indeed as the maintenance of the number or proportion of small and medium-sized businesses. Such ideas amounted to a restriction of the right freely to choose one's trade guaranteed in a social market economy. Those responsible for the elaboration of government economic and social policies in the Federal Republic of Germany have felt obliged to adhere to these principles inherent in a social system of government. A prime element of policy for small and medium-sized businesses has therefore been to adjust such business to changing market requirements.

The edging out of the market of small and medium-sized businesses in a social market economy has not been interpreted as proof of the Marxist postulate that in the final analysis only big industry will survive the process of industrial growth. On the contrary, the process of industrial and economic growth has shown that variety in the crafts and trade sectors and in a number of other service industries has increased as a result of the growing diversification of production structures. Nor can we ignore the fact that the trend towards bigger companies also exists in small and medium-sized businesses, i.e. one cannot talk about a general transfer of functions, in craft industries, for instance, to big industry, though the number of companies is decreasing.

Joseph Schumpeter followed Karl Marx in regarding the concentration of power in the hands of big business as the price society had to pay for prosperity. Technical progress in Schumpeter's view could only derive from the research centres of big business. However the advantages generally attributed to big business must be differentiated. The optimal size of a company varies from branch to branch. One may assume for craft industries, for instance, that the more individual a product or service is, the greater the advantage of small or medium-sized businesses over big companies which manufacture more cost-effectively in uniform mass production. The rise in living standards in the Federal Republic of Germany, for example, has created lasting stimuli especially in the field of individually manufactured products, those in limited series and other high-quality services.

The traditional German term „Mittelstand" or Middle Class is now quite foreign to a German society which has become more functional and oriented to concrete tasks. Government support measures are therefore devoted to the maintenance of those private businessmen in small and medium-sized businesses whose goods and services, in an economy based on the division of labour serve concrete needs, are produced cost-effectively and are in demand on the market. They must fulfil their functions in their own economic sectors.

Particular attention will be paid below to the multifaceted social significance of small and medium-sized businesses. One postulate may, nevertheless, be put forward here: the gradual elimination of cultural lag is serving to close the gap between the developing and the industrialized countries. The resulting change of mentality in the field of economic activity arises primarily from healthy small and medium-sized businesses. Great importance must be attached to them in development policy. In countries willing and able to develop, our government development policies, in their initial phase in particular, should be directed towards the creation of viable structures for small and medium-sized businesses. No decisive and lasting progress can be made in national industry and development without economic policies devoted to the particular problems of small and medium-sized businesses.

The lasting viability of small and medium-sized businesses and their ability to expand has been tested and proven over and over in the industrialized countries. The "classic" Socialist countries are increasingly accepting the existence of small and medium-sized business structures. Such family and part-time business activities have become a major stabilizing factor in providing the population in the Eastern bloc with goods and services. Large State-run companies are not in a position to show such flexibility and efficiency.

These points serve to stress why the Government of the Federal Republic of Germany, in its development policies, attaches such great importance to the promotion of small and medium-sized businesses in developing countries.

II. Development Prospects for Small and Medium-sized Businesses

Hypotheses on the disadvantages of small and medium-sized business structures

Small and medium-sized businesses are often lumped together and classed as being inferior to big business because of their size. The following arguments are usually given as proof of negative aspects:

- In the long run, only big companies can survive in production and market activities; a concentration of industry is inevitable;

- new technologies are proving so complex that they can only be applied within the production and organizational structures of big companies;

- innovation processes require a high level of capital investment in their development and realization phases; small businesses which only manufacture one or two products and are usually lacking in capital are not in a position to distribute risks effectively;

- changes in global economic structures and the international increase in the division of labour are, in terms of comparative cost, confronting small and medium-sized businesses with unsolvable problems; the opening up of new markets as a result of European economic integration or the global market only offer opportunities for big companies.

It is also the disadvantages posed by the size of small and medium-sized businesses which are usually referred to in calling for independent government policies for small and medium-sized businesses to be pursued by business associations. This has also been true for a number of years now of preparations which the Commission of the European Community has been making to create a supranational policy for small and medium-sized businesses. The first informal council of small and medium-sized businesses in the European Community met in the Federal Republic of Germany in May 1988 during the current German Presidency of the Council under the chairmanship of the German Minister of Economics. In June 1988 concrete decisions concerning a European policy on small and medium-sized businesses are to be made by the Internal Market Council. These will comprise three social aspects in particular:

- creation and consolidation of dynamic, independent businesses,

- creation and consolidation of jobs, utilization of opportunities to reduce high unemployment,

- creation of a framework for an improved qualification of employees, in particular of young people who have not yet had any career opportunities.

Special opportunities for the development of small and medium-sized businesses

Small can be beautiful. The above-mentioned hypotheses on the alleged inevitable advantage in productivity and competitiveness of big business are one-sided and wrong. As opposed to major technological innovations of the past, new technologies can be utilized more easily by small and medium-sized businesses. Microelectronics, for instance, offers completely new approaches. It increases the flexibility of production. New solutions to technical functions suitable for small-scale businesses enable the latter to add value more quickly becaue they are simpler to operate. New creative developments and inventions are improving the viability of businesses and their optimal capacity. Impediments to innovation increase with the size of the business.

The strength of smaller and medium-sized businesses lies in their ability to close gaps in the market quickly. This market orientation in turn promotes the lasting success of modern technological innovations. In the Federal Republic of Germany, four-fifths of all innovations derive from the recognition of a new market and only one-fifth from a technological discovery. It is nevertheless essential to support independent businessmen in their wealth of ideas. About four-fifths of inventions for which patents have been applied in the Federal Repulic of Germany are from small and medium-sized businesses.

Proof of the efficiency and productivity of small and medium-sized businesses can be seen in the willingness of more and more major corporations to make use of them as subcontractors. Whereas the flexibility of major corporations decreases the more the production level increases, smaller companies can raise their optimal output with increasing technological progress and become just as viable and competitive as the big companies. The IFO Institute of the German Economy in Munich noted in a special study of applications for inclusion in the 1979/80 suppliers catalogue for craft industries, which serves to promote the division of labour between businesses by means of co-operation, that the proportion of subcontractors was

90 – 100 %   for 45 % of businesses, and
25 – 90 %   for 25 % of businesses.

Nor have any one-sided dependencies arisen as a result of the increasing shift of functions from big corporations to small and medium-sized businesses. With the additional flexibility brought about by new technologies, it is becoming easier to respond to the various supply and demand specifications and to attain a diversification reducing risks. Over 50 percent of small businesses have 10–40 customers. Only 4 percent of businesses work for 1 to 3 customers. Modern technology is thus improving the viability and competitiveness of small and medium-sized businesses.

The Federal Republic of Germany and the other highly industrialized EC Member States recorded a slow-down of economic growth. The location advantages of the trading partners in the EC and in the world economy will become increasingly evident in international competition. It is assumed in the Federal Republic of Germany that opportunities for development exist in particular in those branches of the economy relying on highly developed technologies (electronics, chemical industry, mechanical engineering) in which new and improved versions of products replace older ones (automotive industry, precision engineering and optics).

In other branches, the location advantages of NICs, the Newly Industrializing Countries, or so-called threshold countries will make their influence felt. These are the countries which have surpassed the level of the developing countries and are beginning to compete with the industrialized countries. Additional influence will be felt from the OPEC countries which, together with the NICs, form the "upper-tier countries".

III.   The Social and Regulatory Significance of Small and Medium-sized   Businesses

Differentiation and decentralization of economic activity

Small and medium-sized businesses have a social and political significance of their own. The large number of businessmen who are independent, achievement-oriented and willing to take risks constitutes a stabilizing factor for the development of an economy. A balanced regional distribution strengthens the supply function and impedes distribution bottlenecks. This is particularly true in rural areas. Many developing countries could deal with their grave problems of urbanization, i.e. the migration of large sections of the rural population to the big cities, with the help of regional economic and structural policies in support of small and medium-sized businesses. The decentralization of decision-making is a basic element in a market economy. It counteracts regional imbalances and ensures the ability to react quickly and adapt to changing market conditions. Uniformity in production is thus replaced by heterogeneous productivity which is a guarantee not only of pluralist development, but also of stability and continuity because of the self-reliance of businessmen and their ability to calculate risks. The freedom and scope within which this guarantee is maintained constitute in turn the pillars of a well-functioning competitive system.

At this juncture, I should like to refer in particular to small and medium-sized businesses in the field of agriculture. Large production units are not favoured in the Federal Republic of Germany and in most parliamentary democracies which safeguard private property, as opposed to the agricultural kolkhoses and sovkhoses in the Socialist countries. The family farm and the farmer as a self-employed person predominate despite the increasing use of technology in this sector in recent years. The social significance of this sector of the small and medium-sized business community is similar to that of the business community in crafts, trade and commerce, industry and in the service sector.

Small and medium-sized farms are also faced with additional tasks as a result of increasing ecological awareness. They are eminently suited to dealing with nature and animal protection. Agriculture is gaining a new social dimension which is arising with the increasingly urgent need for harmonization between economy and ecology. It can act as a catalyst between the negative effects of a highly industrialized society and ecological interests which conform to the needs of environmental protection. Among the latter are nature protection, water and air quality, stimulation of natural regeneration, creation of other forces to preserve the ecological balance. Many of these goals have traditionally (and unintentionally) been cherished by the farming community in their daily work and in their production methods. With an increasing awareness for problems, specific preventive and corrective measures are, however, required. Who could better carry out such activities than well-functioning farms within a balanced regional agrarian structure?

The plurality of small and medium-sized businesses which are to be found in all economic sectors, branches and regions ensures a lasting ability to take advantage of economic creativity and achievement. A large number of independent and hard–working entrepreneurs is also an important factor in combatting unemployment. Heterogeneity in the structure of a country's work force is an expression of the variety of business activity and of the resulting job and career situation. Let me repeat that about 99 percent of businesses with 62.2 percent of employees in the Federal Republic of Germany are small and medium-sized businesses with up to 500 employees. 37.8 percent of all employees work in large businesses.

Small and medium-sized businesses in the human assets and creation of jobs.

Small and medium-sized businesses play an important role in the development and utilization of human resources in the economy. The right to choose one's career and job and the right to education are pillars of a social market economy. Four-fifths of young people in the Federal Republic of Germany received their training in small and medium-sized businesses. The proportion of trainees in companies with up to 49 employees is 9.2 percent. In companies with over 5000 employees, it is only 3.9 percent. The majority of all men employed in industry have completed company vocational training, but less than half of them received such training in industry itself. Most vocational training takes place in small and medium-sized businesses, in particular in craft industries. A substantial proportion of human resources in major corporations was "educated" in smaller-scale enterprises. Even with an increasing awareness of the role of human assets in business, the function and reality of education in small and medium-sized businesses will not decline in importance.

It is no coincidence that the Government of the Federal Republic of Germany pins its hopes on smaller-scale companies in particular in its appeals to create more training for unemployed young people. Over the past few years, for instance, despite economic difficulties, the number of training contracts has been rising constantly, mostly in craft industries. About DM 28 billion are now being spent in the Federal Republic of Germany for vocational training, five times more than what was spent 15 years ago. This shows the high level of flexibility and the extent of social responsibility felt in small and medium-sized businesses.

In small and medium-sized businesses there is a high level of security for existing jobs and more and more new jobs are being created. In a social market economy, great importance is attached not only to the viability of small and medium-sized businesses, but also to ensuring jobs. In view of the high rate of unemployment in the Member States of the European Community, the EC Commission is increasingly viewing small-scale companies as the target of its employment and structural policies.

During the Social Democratic-Liberal coalition (1969–1982), government employment programmes were introduced on several occasions, especially in the 1970s. They, however, proved unable in the long run to create new jobs and lower unemployment. Government programmes to stimulate employment would seem inappropriate therefore. Centralist programmes to combat unemployment are ineffective because there is no clear-cut definition of what a dynamic businessman constitutes. Experience gained in the Federal Republic of Germany would seem to argue rather for the maintenance of good overall conditions for business activity, including those for small and medium-sized businesses within the framework of a well-functioning competitive social market economy.

Job satisfaction and conflict management in small and medium-sized businesses

Social harmony in the country, job satisfaction among the employees as individuals, and companies with harmonious labour relations are goals pursued by everyone. Here we can see the advantages of small-scale companies. Small and medium-sized businesses, because they constitute smaller production units, would seem predestined to ensure a humane employment structure. Opportunities for individual development are furthered by a recognition of production processes and, at the same time, individual achievement. The individual capabilities and knowledge of the employees and their problems can be recognized more quickly and easily and dealt with by the personnel management in such companies. Anonymity and monotony on the job decrease the smaller the company is.

The potential for conflict in labour relations is likely to grow over the next few years in view of the coming structural changes in the economy which will arise for technical and organizational reasons. The German parliament is now (1988) endeavouring to give e nployees more say and more rights in the introduction of new technology in companies. The Works Constitution Act is to be updated.

It can already be said, however, that small and medium-sized businesses have particular advantages when it comes to dealing with problems resulting from technical innovations. The small scale permits conflicts to be solved in a friendly and balanced manner. Problems in companies of between 100 and 500 employees and above make institutionalized forms of democracy and the setting up of works councils in such companies indispensable in finding equitable so-lutions to conflicts between employees and management. Any company with at least 5 employees would seem to need a works council. This does not, however, mean that all companies of this size in the Federal Republic of Germany indeed have works councils. Only about half of those employed in industry are represented by works councils. All big corporations have established works councils; this form of employee representation is also increasingly to be found in medium-sized businesses. It is estimated that about one-tenth of German employees are employed in companies which are not big enough to have their own works councils and one-fifth in companies which, though big enough, do not have shop councils. These three—tenths of employees are to be found primarily in small and very small businesses.

IV. Strengthening Industry's Will to Help Itself

Promoting viable small and medium-sized businesses

For the various reasons referred to above, it is essential to follow economic policies which account for the legitimate interests of small and medium-sized businessmen and their ability to function in our society. The tone set by national economic policies for small and medium-sized businesses is determined by regional, economic and social needs. Conditions of location, deposits of natural resources, transportation, the social infrastructure (education, social institutions), the extent and quality of labour and the presence of capital and technical skills play a role. The significance of an open-minded progressive attitude in the country and its shaping in the interests of economic and social change must be underlined here.

Dynamic small and medium-sized businesses develop their own force which bears its mark on employer and employee alike and radiated into society at large. Aggressive behaviour on the part of all those involved in the creation of value in industry can be supplemented by an achievement-oriented class of independent entrepreneurs. The idea of co-operatives and co-operation between business partners, in addition to individual initiative, is to be stressed.

As opposed to that of less developed countries, the policy for small and medium-sized businesses pursued in the Federal Republic of Germany shows a different emphasis. It is designed to preserve the standard of achievement attained and the social position thereof. In a social market economy, policy for small and medium-sized businesses in the past few years has developed into an economic policy caring for the needs of small and medium-sized businesses, a policy which, to a great extent, has to be structurally oriented to business sizes. Such a policy is not limited to the fields which small and medium-sized businesses traditionally make up: craft industries, shops, restaurants and bars. Indeed it has been technological advances which have caused the rise of many small and medium-sized businesses in the field of industry and transportation, many of which now compete on the market with larger companies in a highly successful manner.

A modern structural policy oriented to business sizes lays emphasis on the promotion of the will of small and medium-sized businesses from all branches of industry to help themselves and on their readiness to adjust to change. In line with the basic principles of a social market economy, those responsible for government economic policies and policies for small and medium-sized businesses have adapted their activities to support initiative in industry and help co-ordinate the organization of viable self-help associations designed to help increase productivity and improve structures.

Intercompany co-operation as an instrument to promote small and medium-sized businesses

Since the second half of the 1960s, great importance has been attached in the Federal Republic of Germany, and increasingly so in the European Economic Community, to the endeavour of many businesses to deal with difficulties of adjustment and transformation by uniting in a larger association or by intercompany co-operation. This is a form of economic co-operation surpassing the idea of co-operatives in its effects. This form of co-operation is to be understood as that between two or several businesses jointly exercising several functions to attain greater profit by means of rationalization or division of labour while maintaining their independence. As opposed to concentration in the form of merger, in which at least two businesses lose their economic and legal independence to form one business unit, co-operation, though involving restrictions in the economic freedom to make business decisions, means the co-ordination or integration of business operations in one or more fields such as advertizing, acquisition, financing, order handling, administration and marketing. Such co-operation can take the form of giving up or transfer of functions, specialization, diversification or the concentration of functions. One can differentiate between horizontal, complementary and vertical co-operation with either the same business levels, complementary ones or different levels.

The promotion of such co-operation between businesses is an instrument of structural policy oriented to specific sectors and business sizes. Such activities to increase the output and competitiveness of businesses also form part of regional policy. Government measures to promote co-operation have received special emphasis in the Federal Republic of Germany since it is such activities in particular which help strengthen the will of industry to help itself. Market mechanisms are not infringed upon by this type of co-operation. On the contrary, their ability to function is stabilized and strengthened by such adjustment activities based on the free will of businessmen. We are talking about the concept of "group industry competition", i.e. co-operating businesses in competition with other individual businesses on the market and with other co-operation businesses, so-called co-operation families.

The fact that co-operation promotion as an instrument of policy was instigated and propagated under the administration of Ludwig Erhard, leading proponent of a Social market economy is proof that intercompany co-operation conforms to the system and the market, of course within certain limits which do not impede competition. This is especially true of small and medium-sized businesses and suppliers etc. During a speech he made in Munich on 8 June 1966 at the annual meeting of the Federation of German Industries (BDI), Ludwig Erhard, then Chancellor, stated, "We particularly welcome the fact that we have found a form of co-operation in the wide field of small and medium-sized businesses which can no doubt be improved even further. It helps on the whole to maintain the principle of competition and not to destroy its highly beneficial effects."

Co-operation between businesses is usually seen in its most problematic aspect, that of anti-trust laws, i.e. price-fixing agreements to control the market which are unlawful in the Federal Republic of Germany. The law against restrictions on competition which entered into force in 1958 resulted in a number of legal ambiguities, which caused adjustment difficulties especially for small and medium-sized businesses. In 1963, in order to improve mobility of production factors and facilitate business adjustment oriented to company size, the Federal Minister of Economics publicly outlined the possibilities of legal co-operation by publishing a co-operation handbook. Forms of co-operation which did not hinder competition were propagated and declared irrelevant to anti-trust legislation.

Co-operation in the exchange of experience, information and opinions is thus not subject to authorization or anti-trust legislation. Specialized forms of co-operation in a company's areas of activities such as production procurement sales, research and development, marketing, administration, turned out to be particularly effective once they were authorized by legislation. The distribution of possible risks in opening up new markets and in introducing new products and processes had a lasting effect on increasing productivity and at the same time ensured the viability of businesses and jobs. Equal opportunities on the market for small and medium-sized businesses are furthered by political measures to encourage competition.

Social aspects of co-operation

Concentration and co-operation processes in industry always have a social component. Intercompany agreements sought for economic or technical reasons encourage rationalization which in general has repercussions for labour, personnel and society. This means:

– redundancy (rehiring in some areas),

– change of activities,

– change in the structure of employment, jobs and organization,

– change in economic conditions etc.

It is important from the very start to include these aspects in plans for business mergers. In this manner, social problems and transformational difficulties within the company in question can be reduced and "maintenance of company independence", the goal of co-operation, can be linked to "saving jobs". Public information and close co-operation between employers and employees during such adjustment processes have substantially reduced impediments to adjustment at this scale in the Federal Republic of Germany.

Aside from the above-mentioned co-operation problems, labour, personnel and social aspects can themselves be the subject of co-operation agreements, either on their own or in the form of supplementary agreements between two or more businesses. Fields of such co-operation can be personnel planning, training activities, manpower pools, job rotation between companies etc. Joint facilities such as lunch-rooms, medical services, training centres, kindergartens, jointly-run trading and craft facilities (joint usage of commercial facilities) are examples of other forms of co-operation. Although usually restricted to specific functions, the results of these activities in all fields have been positive from the very start and have been internationally recognized because of the significance of export co-operation.

Policy for small and medium–sized businesses in the European Community

Both the Commission of the European Community and the European Parliament deal with the problems of small and medium-sized businesses in the Community. Endeavours are based on the principle that "a healthy and strongly developed small and medium-sized business community is a prerequisite for the proper functioning of a modern economy". In the European Community about 30,000,000 people are employed in labour-intensive small and medium-sized businesses. Flexibility and quick reaction to structural change are considered just as important as the free development of the personality of employees and the opportunities for self-employed businessmen to develop their own talents.

International trade and supplies, and participation in public contracts in the European Economic Community have received strong and lasting impetus by transborder business co-operation. For instance, an office for business co-operation was set up at the Commission of the European Communities to promote international co-operation in industry and to support international co-operation agreements and mergers of companies from the various Member States (Commission directive of 21 June 1973). The field of activities of the co-operation office of the EC Commission was later extended to facilitate industrial co-operation between Community businesses and those of third countries (supplementary directive of 20 July 1977). This step helped improve the economic and labour structures of countries willing to join and now promotes increased integration on the road to the 1992 European domestic market. Studies carried out by the EC Commission have shown that countries with a large percentage of small and medium-sized businesses, often with outdated production methods and insufficient capital resources, are encountering particular difficulties in the integration of the European Economic Community.

This situation in Germany and Europe is exemplary for similar initiatives to strengthen the limited capacity of small and medium-sized businesses in the developing countries. International division of labour is promotede by the active participation of national economies. Impetus for growth can be made use of and learning processes can be carried out. The prerequisite is, however, a willingness to adhere to the principle of free trade, i.e. to do away with protectionist interference in international trade. One element of this is the elimination of administrative impediments at the national level as unfortunately exist in many developing countries as a result of misinterpreted government activity.

The role of government in economic policies designed for small and medium-sized businesses

In conclusion, we can note the following with respect to policies designed for small and medium-sized businesses:

Government is devoting special attention to:

- improving basic conditions for economic activity, e.g. right of competition, relieving the tax burden on small and medium-sized businesses and giving the self-employed access to old-age pensions;

- promoting an increase in productivity by financial support for rationalization, innovation, research and development;

- strengthening the financial power of companies in investments particularly important to structural policy, promoting the setting up of businesses, exemplary co-operation projects and the establishment of vocational training facilities (supporting the qualification campaign of German industry, in particular for small and medium-sized businesses).

Private financial and credit institutes play an important role in financial promotion activities. Banks grant loans to small and medium-sized businesses at favourable interest rates. Credits are government-guaranteed and publicly funded. The principle behind all these activities is subsidiarity, supplementing and encouraging independent business activities. Responsibility for active co-operation policies must also remain in the hands of private industry, even when businessmen show no particular will to help themselves. Government activities should be purely ancillary. Nevertheless, government has particularly great responsibility when there is a danger that its action or lack of action is a decisive factor in the failure of a business on the market which is not the fault of its owner, e.g. lack of clarity in overall regulatory conditions or infringements on competition by imbalanced subsidies. An important role must also be attached to studying the international constraints which might have unfavourable repercussions at the national level, in particular for employment and the loss of jobs.

The ideas presented here on administrative policy, on the social and economic significance of small and medium-sized businesses and on the activities carried out for them are all indications of the will of small and medium-sized businesses to survive and adapt to a socially just and functioning market economy. In the Federal Republic of Germany, the independent owners of small and medium-sized businesses have maintained their strength, as have the regulatory plans and instruments of policy in their interest within the framework of a social market economy. Owners of small and medium-sized businesses are the pillars of our social State based on competition and a liberal market economy. Citizens, businessmen, trade unions and government administrations are all bound to act in a socially responsible manner in accordance with our constitution. In industry, it is this economic and social countervailing power which of course serves small and medium-sized businesses by helping safeguard their ability to thrive and compete on the market and to remain an important part of our society.

Policies for Employment Creation

by Charles Grant

The employment problem in Europe

Several years on from the worst phases of the stagflationary experience, the (developed Western) world economy appears to have recovered remarkably smoothly. Inflation is still with us, but the concern is now to keep it below five instead of ten percent per annum, and there has been a steady, if unspectacular, expansion of activity which is now quite long by historical standards. True, the U.S. government deficit and the related problems of developing-country debt and proliferating trade barriers are major threats on the horizon, but so far the world economy has managed to avoid disaster.

However, the one area in which performance has been poor is with respect to unemployment, particularly in European countries. A good example of this is the case of Britain today, where real growth this year is forecast to exceed that of any of its trading partners (perhaps for the first time in living memory), but "official" unemployment remains above eleven percent of the labour force. Excluding changes in the official definitions and youth-training schemes, it is claimed that the true rate might be something nearer to seventeen percent (Bean et al (1986)), in which case we are approaching the situation characteristic of the early 1930's. The problem is certainly immediately apparent to anyone travelling through parts of the older, Northern industrial regions of the country, and has become noticeable in other parts of Continental Europe as well.

Potentially, persistent unemployment could be a greater problem than any of the more immediate pitfalls facing the world economy. The loss of potential output is an obvious cost, but the deeper changes in social attitudes towards work and welfare, perhaps even towards property entitlements in general, have yet to ermege. Who, for example, would have thought that the archetypically stable British society would in this decade hit the headlines with riots in London and Liverpool?

From the late 1970's on, Western governments aimed to solve this problem through monetarist rectitude. Excessive money growth – often thought to be the result of excessive government spending – had led to spiralling inflation and a consequent distortion of economic activity. If M-whatever could be controlled, inflation would abate and the underlying market forces of supply-and-demand would eventually restore "full" employment. Thus, the previously-held Keynesian beliefs in the possibility of deficient demand (e.g. because of insensitivity of spending to interest rates, or the stickiness of these speculatively-determined rates) were almost totally rejected.

However, there was still some debate about the speed with which the labour market would clear. The Rational Expectationists had by this time appeared on the scene to assert that the process of adjustment to full equilibrium should be virtually instantaneous, whereas the view of their more orthodox 'Friedmanite' colleagues was that the historical record showed the inevitability of a more protracted and painful adjustment. Nonetheless, according even to the latter group it should not have taken as long as it has to reduce unemployment to more normal or "acceptable" levels, and we certainly should not have seen such a sharp *rise* in unemployment as we have done. By any New Classical reckoning, despite the initial setback of a sharply-rising pound, the election of a committed and credible Thatcher government in Britain in 1979 should by now have yielded more positive results.

The logical conclusion which many economists have now reached is that labour markets are malfunctioning, with wages being rigid and employment fluctuating rather than vice versa (for a discussion of this problem see McDonald and Solow (1981)). In a sense this is a return to the simplest of the Keynesian explanations of unemployment, at least in so far as it refers to *nominal* wage rigidity. In fact, the U.S. experience can be taken as a good example of this phenomenon, with expansionary fiscal (and lately, monetary) policy putting sufficient upward pressure on prices to offset money wage gains. The result: an economy that has managed to sustain itself near to full employment, despite a rapid increase in its labour force, through effective *real*-wage flexibility (i.e. virtually no rise in real wages for a decade-and-a-half).

In Europe, however, the situation may be different in that we are facing rigidity in real wages. For example, in terms of the usual Mundell-Fleming analysis, the U.S. economic expansion should have had a greater impact on European employment through the relative depreciation of European currencies and consequent improvement in competitiveness. However, the currency depreciation translated itself immediately into higher domestic prices and thus triggered compensating money wage rises. If this is the case, then Europe has a problem: no increase in demand, whether government-, consumption-, investment-, or export-led, can succeed in reducing unemployment but will merely fuel faster wage rises for those who stay in work.

This problem is illustrated quite simply in *Figure 1*, where at wage w there is initial unemployment of amount N − L (N being the short-run measured labour force). Unless the government can cause productivity improvements, there is no way that it can shift the aggregate labour productivity (demand) schedule. All it can do is to shift this schedule in nominal terms, but with w defined in real terms this merely implies an equal shift of the supply schedule. Socially and politically this situation might be very bad, but it is arguable whether there is any *economically* measurable loss, since the perfectly-elastic labour supply schedule indicates that the opportunity cost of not working is equal to the utility deriving from employment. That is indeed precisely what some economists have argued, as a criticism of the overly-generous unemployment benefits which European states provide in contrast to the less generous American system. Cutting these benefits would presumably shift the supply schedule down to w and thus restore full employment.

A related line of thinking, which many Europeans at least would consider more civilized, is to cut the "wedge" between employers' and workers' payments and receipts. For instance, a cut in employers' social security contributions would shift the demand curve upwards in real terms, while a reduction in the employees' taxes would result in a downward shift of the supply schedule (Bean et al (1986)).

Both of these solutions assume that the reservation-wage of the unemployed exerts pressure on overall wage levels, as with any other market mechanism. However, there appears to be a growing body of opinion that the labour market does not function this way. Instead, there are "inside" workers and "outside" workers, with the latter having

only a small impact on wage bargains in regard to the former group (a distinction emphasized by Layard (1986)). If so, then there may no restraint on wage increases apart from "moral suasion"; e.g. the wage could be pushed up to w' even 'though the willing

Figure 1

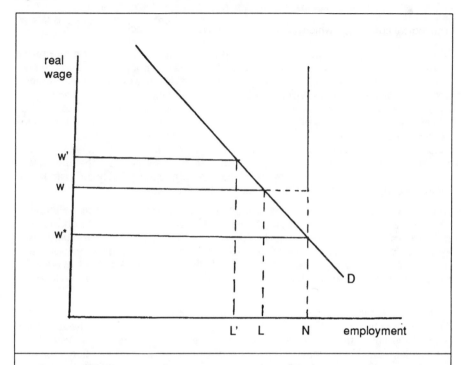

"Insiders" may push wage up to w' despite elastic supply of "outsiders" at initial w. Problem is to halt this separation, and to reduce labour costs to w*.

ness of outsiders to work remained elastic at w (the reduction in employment being effected through non-replacement of leavers such as retirements, etc.)

In Britain at least there seems to be considerable evidence of this phenomenon, with real wage increases being maintained at high levels despite massive unemployment. This has given renewed importance to the idea of taxes on wage increases, which although originally conceived as counter-inflationary, could in principle apply equally well to increases in real terms. An interesting variant on this theme has been proposed in the form of a linkage between previous wage increases and unemployment benefits, so that the latter would be reduced progressively as the former were higher (Brown and Levin (1987)).

However, apart from the well-known distorting effects that pay policies (in whatever guise) have had on labour markets, this approach is primarily designed to hold the line on the rate at which wages can increase, rather than being focused on the more basic problem of reducing the overall *level* of real wages. Of course, exponents of wage-increase taxation (WIT) could reply that eventually their policy would have this result, but if so, it is important to note that the tax schedules would have to be so severe as to keep net nominal wage increases *below* the rate of price increases. This seems most unlikely to be politically acceptable, and again suggests that such taxes would be most useful in merely keeping the rate of wage increases at or not much above the rate of price increases: i.e. as a counter-inflationary device.

Thus, the problem can be essentially reduced to how best to exert effective downward pressure on the current level of real wages. The answers to this depend on the perceived differences between inside and outside workers. In one view, the chief difference is that the outsiders tend to become less productive the longer they are unemployed. That is, they lose skills as well as work discipline and cease to be "employable" regardless of their willingness to work for lower wages. This is clearly the thinking behind retraining schemes, which in Britain have taken large numbers of generally younger people off the unemployment registers. An alternative strategy would be to shift the onus of training on to the potential future employers themselves (as in the apprenticeship system found in Germany), by providing a large enough subsidy for them to assume the direct re-training and implicit future job responsibility.

The other view of this problem tends to emphasize the role of unionization in European labour markets, and therefore to see the solution in terms of reducing their power and influence. However, it has been shown often enough that employers are frequently willing to bargain with workers collectively, and if so, even cosier arrangements between firms and their employees could result. In fact, in the U.K. the driving force of wage increases seems to be emanating from largely non-unionized sectors (e.g. the financial sector).

Possibly, a combination of these various measures will serve to bring down unemployment. On the other hand, the *ad hoc* nature of many of the proposed remedies has not been encouraging and has led some economists to look for more radical solutions to the problem. By far the most prominent of these is the idea of profit-sharing (see Weitzman (1983)). This accepts the fact of collective, or even collaborative relations between employers and employees, and indeed encourages this mutual interest. At the same time, the wage bargain itself is radically altered in such a way as to maintain a given level of the net wage while simultaneously creating an incentive for employers to hire additional labour. This thinking has already influenced recent U.K. tax policy, and shows every indication of spreading to other countries. A strong argument in its favour is that profit sharing is almost identical to a bonus system related to profitability, a practice associated with successful Japanese firms.

The claims for profit-sharing are almost too good to be true, and include not only the co-existence of high take-home wages with increased employment, but also an automatic stabilizing property such that labour costs decline in response to adverse demand shocks. In the next section I will demonstrate that although these claims are partly valid, profit sharing has an incidence on the economy similar to that of profit taxation, and therefore causes both a short-run and long-run loss of efficiency. Furthermore, its stabilizing properties depend on an initial situation of excess demand; if the labour market is initially clearing, then it is no better than a pure wage system (and may be worse). In the following section I will then go on to demonstrate that a system of wage subsidization financed by profit taxation is economically superior.

Profit sharing in a general equilibrium context

The analysis of profit sharing in the partial equilibrium context of a single firm or sector should be familiar to most readers. Instead of facing perfectly-elastic labour supply at some going wage, competitive firms become mini-monopsonists whose workers are paid a basic wage (w_b) in addition to a share (h) of gross, or accounting profit per head. Thus, total unit labour compensation (w) is simply: $w = w_b + h (F - w_bL)$ where F = total revenue and L = labour input. Maximization of net, or economic profit with respect to labour input yields the result: $dF/dL = w_b$ i.e., the profit-sharing firm will operate at the point where marginal revenue product is equal to the *basic* wage rate, effectively ignoring the profit-related component.

Figure 2

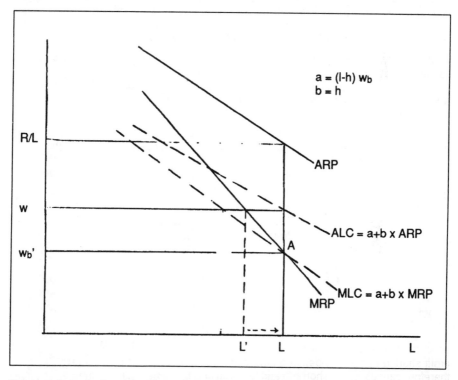

This result is depicted in *Figure 2,* where in addition to the average and marginal revenue product schedules (ARP and MRP), the average and marginal labour cost schedules (ALC and MLC) are also shown. It is a simple matter to show that under profit sharing, the ALC curve – in effect, the negotiated labour supply curve – is a linear transform of the ARP schedule: *viz.*, $w = (1-h)w_b + h(R/L)$ and that: $d(wL)/dL = (1-h)w_b + h(dR/dL)$. Hence, the intersection of MRP with MLC, indicating the formal profit-maximizing level of input, must occur at w_b.

The way in which the diagram is drawn makes the benefits of profit sharing obvious. If the original competitive wage rate had been w, then employment in this firm would have been only L'. However, the profit-sharing agreement has replaced the perfectly-elastic supply schedule with the negotiated ALC schedule. Hence, the firm will seek to increase employment to L where the associated MLC schedule intersects the (unchanged) MRP schedule. However, at this increased level of employment, total unit labour compensation is precisely the same as under the pure-wage system. This is a clear illustration of the fact that the firm's owners are in effect subsidizing workers' incomes, by the amount $(w-w_b)L$ in this example.

Of course, this negotiated subsidy element must have a further impact on the firm's decisions. In order to see what this is, set out the firm's cost condition: $C = w_bL + rK + h(R - w_bL)$ where C = total cost, K = capital input, r = rental rate on capital (given).

This shows the interesting feature that the firm's costs are not independent of its revenues (although we have already used the reduced form to establish the profit-maximizing labour input decision). However, if we assume competitive product markets, then $R = C$ and this reduces to: $C = w_bL + rK + (h/1-h)K = w_bL + (r/1-h)K$.

That is, at the same time as the cost of labour has been reduced (to w_b), the cost of capital has effectively been raised (to $r/1-h$). This implies a reduction in the desired level of the firm's capital stock simultaneously with the increased demand for labour, with the cost-minimizing condition for tangency between any given isoquant and constraint line (not shown) now becoming: $MRS = MPL/MPK = w_b(1-h)/r$.

Of course, in a general equilibrium model intersectoral adjustments will occur to re-establish full employment of both capital and labour, the latter consistent with higher take-home pay than would occur in a pure wage system. Thus, the main purpose in this section is to investigate what the likely effects of profit sharing might be in this broader con-

Table 1

Comparative equilibria			
	(1)	(2)	(3)
n	1.0000	.9190	1.0000
w	.7364	.8000	.8000
wl	.7364	.7352	.8000
w_b			.7299
PRP/w			.0876
h_1			.4166
h_2			.1582
r	.2636	.2648	.1598
r_1			.2740
r_2			.1899
v	1.0000	.9398	.9844
(1)	pure-wage full-employment		
(2)	fixed wage (unemployment)		
(3)	profit sharing		

text. This requires us to actually solve for general equilibrium values under pure-wage and profit-sharing regimes, and as is well-known, even for simple two-sector models this typically requires numerical solution.

Table 2

Comparative dynamic incidence		
(1)	(2)	(3)
t_r 0	.2595	.2413
k 1.0000	.6871	.7084
y 1.0000	.8448	.8558
w/y .7365	.7923	.7881
r .0289	.0283	.0284
r' .0289	.0346	.0341
v 1.0000	.9870	.9891

(1)   pure-wage equilibrium
(2)   profit-sharing
(3)   wage subsidy

Our basic results are set out in columns 1–3 of table 1 for such an economy in which goods in both sectors (1,2) are produced according to CES-type functions. Identical individual utilities (v) are likewise of the same general form: $v = (aX_1^P + (1-a)X_2^P)^{1/P}$ where X_1 = current consumption of good i (i = 1,2).

In defining the utility function, the parameter 'p' was set equal to 1/6, implying an elasticity of substitution of 1.20, and 'a' – roughly, a "share" parameter – equal to 0.60. As it happens, however, our results are not very sensitive to these choices. In production, for good 1, the value of a (= a_1) was set at 0.8, and for good 2 (a = a_2), at 0.6, with p_1 (=p) = 1/6 (as for utility). The elasticity of substitution between labour and capital in the second sector was taken to be 0.90, implying p_2 (=p) = −1/9. These values conform reasonably to empirically determined magnitudes, with elasticities of substitution not too far from unity (i.e. the Cobb-Douglas case), and as can be seen from column 1, the share of wages in total income is 73.64 per cent. The capital-labour ratio in this stationary economy was fixed at unity for convenience, as was total nominal income per unit of labour. Since this is our *numeraire* condition, it is thus necessary to measure the effects of profit-sharing and other variations in terms of the utility of the representative individual, which in any case is the ultimate criterion for analysis of this kind.

The numeraire condition, together with the demand equation for either good derived from the utility function, the two production functions, the full-employment condition and the competitive input-price conditions serves to determine equilibrium. Our first variation is to drop the full-employment condition and to fix the wage rate at w = 0.80, which is above the market-clearing level of w = 0.7364. This causes the employment ratio(n) to drop from one to 0.9190, an unemployment rate of just over eight per cent. Given that this unemployment is wholly due to an excessive (real) wage, adding so-called "frictional" elements would give us an overall unemployment rate not too dissimilar to those found in European countries today. As is also apparent, the share of total income going to labour has actually fallen very slightly, and the utility measure has declined by about six per cent..

Now we introduce profit-sharing. Formally, this introduces four new variables: w_{b1}, the basic wage in each sector, and h_1, the share of (gross) profits in each sector. However, we also re-introduce the full-employment condition, together with the following conditions: $w_{b1}, = w_{b2}$ $w_{b1}+(h_1/1-h_1)rK_1 = w_{b2}+(h_2/1-h_2)rK_2$ and $w_{b1}+(h_1/1-h_1)rK_1 = 0.80$ where K_i = capital input in sector i (i = 1,2).

These require merely that the basic, or "guaranteed" wage (w_b) be the same in each sector; that the overall wage, or total unit labour compensation (w) also be equal between sectors; and that this overall wage should be equal to that prevailing in the initial (unemployment) instance. The results are shown in column 3 of *Table 1*. The initially-excessive labour compensation is now consistent with full employment. The basic wage rate is equal to 0.7299 (so that profit-related pay is just under nine per cent of total remuneration), and workers get a 41.66 per cent share of profits in sector 1, and a 15.82 per cent share in sector 2. The first of these may seem rather high, but even if both sectors were equally capital intensive, the required share of profits would be nearly 26 per cent just to provide the same level of implicit subsidy. Higher "replacement rates" – in the U.K. 15 per cent has been often suggested as a "significant" proportion of profit-related pay (PRP) – would therefore seem to imply very high profit shares. The *net* rental rate on capital, or equivalently in this model the rate of profit, interest, or return is now only about 16 per cent as compared to above 26 per cent in the two preceding cases. However, the gross rates of return are 27.4 and about 19 per cent in sectors 1 and 2 respectively.

This differential alerts us to the possibility shown in the last entry: that individual utility is lower than in the first, full-employment case by just over 1 1/2 per cent. The reason for this is that profit-sharing acts exactly like an interest-income or profit tax – albeit voluntarily negotiated levied at differential rates between sectors. Thus, even though factor incomes are in this stationary context pure rents, as has been well-established in the literature of public finance, differential taxation generates an excess burden which we are able to measure in terms of utility loss. Note that this differential exists in order to ensure that total unit labour compensation (w) is equalized between sectors, given that basic wage rates are also equal. It would therefore be possible to construct a model in which the shares – and equivalently, the implicit profit tax rates – were equal but in which these basic wage levels differed. This would seem to be an odd type of labour supply function however, since workers in the lower-guaranteed-income sector would also be facing greater risk from fluctuations in profits.

In the long run, the results of analyzing profit taxation are again applicable. In particular, the lower net and higher gross rates of return imply reduced savings and capital formation. In order to investigate this dynamic incidence of profit sharing it is convenient to adopt a one-sector model, in which the price of the single (consumption/capital) good is fixed at unity. This means that output as well as utility can now vary, although as before it is the latter measure which is of ultimate significance (all individuals being identical). Numerical simulations were again based upon assumed values for CES-type functions, with the utility function now being defined in terms of consumptions in each of two periods: work and retirement. The value of the coefficient 'a' was set at 0.70, with the elasticity of substitution between consumption in the two periods given a fairly high value of thirty (p = 0.9667). Much of the work on lifetime utility functions assumes additivity, implying an infinite elasticity of substitution, and although for practical purposes this was infeasible, our choice reflects this tendency. However, it must also be admitted that dynamic incidence effects are highly sensitive to this parameter; in particular, low elasticities of intertemporal substitution may give rise to *increased* saving and capital formation. In production, the elasticity of substitution between labour and capital inputs was set at 1.03, and the value of the "share" parameter ('a') was taken as the weighted average of the two-sector share coefficients (a = 0.7236), weights being equal to the proportions of total value of output. These parameter values were consistent with an initial equilibrium labour share of 0.7364. Hence, we start with a one-sector dynamic model in which the initial conditions are the same as in the foregoing static two-sector model.

Now introduce a profit tax – identical to a profit-sharing scheme – at the rate of 25.95 per cent. This is the percentage of total profits taken as wage shares in the static model, although it will be seen that the overall wage is slightly less than 0.80 due to other effects. However, the approximation is sufficient for our present purposes. From table 2 (column 2) we find that the equilibrium capital-labour ratio falls by over thirty per cent. This reflects the high degree of intertemporal substitutability. Output per unit of labour(y) likewise declines by over fifteen per cent, but utility of the representative individual only decreases by about 1 1/3 per cent,.again a reflection of the dominance of the shift in consumption pattern. As mentioned, models of dynamic incidence tend to be sensitive to parameter values, but at least for the values which we have selected it is clear that there will be both short and long run efficiency losses.

Of course, this comparison is misleading if we are taking the unemployment case as our benchmark. That situation gave rise to a permanent 6 per cent loss of welfare in our example, and so a profit-sharing solution is clearly preferable. On the other hand, there may be alternatives which are better still, and we shall examine one such in the next section. First, however, it is of interest to examine an additional claim regarding the *stabilization* properties of profit-sharing systems: i.e. that a deflationary shock will cause profits to fall, hence total unit labour compensation to fall, hence employment to be cushioned. From our earlier analysis it should be apparent that this is simply not true, since it is the basic wage rate that determines employment, and indeed in *Table 3* (column 1) we show the effects of a demand shock in our static two-sector model (which of course is the appropriate context for this type of analysis).

Specifically, the utility parameter 'a' is assumed to change from its initial value of 0.60 to 0.33, while all other parameters remain unchanged. This causes the (full-employment) equilibrium wage rate, and consequently the share of wages in total output, to fall from 0.7364 to 0.6714, a drop of nearly nine per cent. In contrast, if we start from the assumed situation of unemployment, with the wage rate fixed above its market-clearing level at 0.80, then as shown in table 3 (next Page) (col.4) the unemployment rate rises to almost 16 per cent, and the utility measure is now 11 per cent below its general equilibrium value.

However, the profit-sharing regime also produces unemployment. If the basic wage rate remains fixed at $w_b = 0.7299$, and the respective shares remain fixed at $h_1 = .4166$ and $h_2 = .1582$ then the unemployment rate rises from zero to 7 1/2 per cent – nearly as much as the increase occurring under the fixed-wage situation – and in consequence, the utility measure is now 5 1/2 per cent below its full-employment equilibrium value, a fall of another 4 per cent. The second column of table 3 shows that if full employment
Table 3

Table 3

Effects of a change in demand parameter ('a')			
	(1)	(2)	(3)	(4)
n	.9248	1.0000	1.0000	.8408
w		.8000	.6714	.0800
w_1	.7936			
w_2	.8036			
wl	.7397	.8000	.6714	.6726
w_b	.7299	.6978		
PRP/w		.1022		
PRP/w_1	.8027			
PRP/w_2	.0917			
h_1	.4166	.8037		
h_2	.1582	.2371		
r	.2603	.1660	.3286	.3274
r_1	.4460	.8458		
r_2	.3091	.2371		
v	.9458	.9553	1.0000	.8900

(1)	fixed basic wage and profit shares
(2)	flexible basic wage and profit shares
(3)	flexible pure-wage equilibrium
(4)	fixed-wage system

is to be maintained consistently at w = 0.80 then the basic wage must fall to 0.6978 (nearly 4 1/2 per cent), and the shares of wages in profits must rise to 80.37 per cent in the first sector (from 41.66 per cent, or nearly double in proportional terms), and to 23.71 per cent in the second sector (from 15.82 per cent, or roughly half again as much). In addition, although we have not calculated the long-run effects, with these substantial rises in what amount to effective profit tax rates there is likely to be further diminution of the capital stock, output, and welfare (given our selected parameter values).

A superior alternative: employment subsidies

The fallacy underlying the belief in the automatic stabilizing properties of profit sharing schemes is that firms respond to the overall unit cost of labour, when in fact economic analysis shows clearly that it is the guaranteed, or basic wage rate, relative to the overall cost of *capital* that is of key importance in firms' input decisions. Thus, in the preceding example in which the basic wage and profit shares had been initially fixed, the result of the demand shock was to automatically reduce labour's total compensation, not by means of the per unit compensation of those remaining employed, but by inducing unemployment. The effect was like that of a fixed-wage system, and full employment was only restored through negotiated changes in both basic wage rates and share ar-

Figure 3

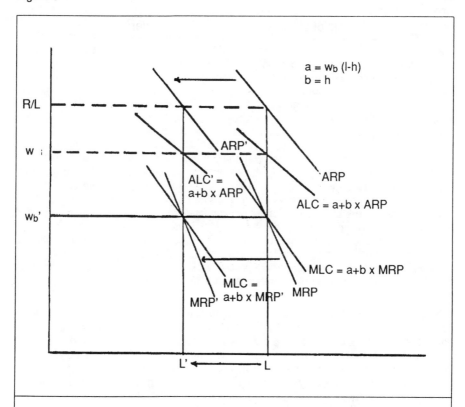

A shift in (derived) labour demand curve (MRP → MRP') also shifts MLC to MLC', hence L falls to l' (w$_b$, h uncanged) w and R/L remain the same!

rangements (which, it could be argued, is no different from what is required in the pure-wage system, with the latter having the advantage that only the wage rate needs to be re-negotiated, and if this leads to the restoration of full employment there is no excess burden in either the short or long run). In terms of partial equilibrium analysis, *Figure 3* shows that a demand shock is perceived by the firm as a leftward/downward shift in its ARP and MRP schedules. However, under profit sharing it must be the case that both the ALC and MLC schedules shift in exactly the same proportion, so that the entire impact is on employment with both the basic wage as well as total unit compensation unaffected ('though in the results of table 3 general equilibrium effects do serve to affect w slightly).

However, these observations also suggest that a system in which the relevant – i.e. basic – wage rate could fluctuate automatically would be able to achieve the desired stability of employment. Consider then the obvious device of a direct wage subsidy financed by a universal profit tax. Going back to our original example, workers could receive a wage equal to 0.80 while the effective cost to firms was only 0.7364 if there were a subsidy of 0.0636 (just under 8 per cent of the gross wage). This could be raised by a uniform tax of 24.13 per cent on gross profits. An immediate conclusion we can draw is that in the short run context there would be no excess burden effects. With capital and labour (implicitly) in fixed supply, taxes and subsidies applied at the same rate in all sectors would have no distortionary effects on resource allocation. On the other hand, there would still be long-run dynamic efficiency effects, but these would be no greater than those arising under profit sharing. In fact, the method of financing wage subsidization by profit taxation is merely convenient for comparisons with profit sharing. Income taxation, expenditure (consumption) taxation, or any other revenue base could be used for this purpose, although the efficiency effects would need to be investigated further. We know that income taxation is effectively equivalent to taxation of both capital and labour income, so that to the extent that workers pass on higher taxes in higher wage demands we arrive at something nearer to pure profit (interest-income) taxation. However, if labour supply is not uniquely defined in terms of real wages – i.e. there is some degree of "illusion", or if it is insensitive to real-wage variations anyway – then the burden on capital is lessened and with it, the long-run effect on capital formation. Alternatively, although again higher consumption-good prices may be reflected in real wage demands, the exemption of savings from an expenditure tax base would additionally tend to compensate for any decrease in the rate of capital formation, and on the face of it this seems to be the most promising means of financing wage subsidies.

The point is that profit sharing represents a severely-constrained and relatively distortionary way to reduce the cost of labour to firms while maintaining higher take-home pay. Of course, its advocates would assert yet another virtue of profit sharing, in that it encourages harmony of interest between management (presumably representing capital owners' interests) and employees. It is possible to argue that this is likely to occur, but it could lead to even cosier arrangements to obtain high wages at the expense of employment. There is nothing in profit sharing to say that the basic wage and/or profit shares have to be consistent with full employment, whereas employment subsidies can be controlled by the government to reflect the state of the labour market. Moreover, if the real aim is to encourage mutuality of interest, these subsidies could easily be awarded contingent upon agreements such as employee share-option (that is, stock-option) schemes or even some forms of worker participation in managerial decision-making.

Finally, it might be objected that although wage subsidies are fine in theory, their actual implementation would lead to a disastrous wage inflation. This would be possible if there were no check on the rate at which firms were awarding pay increases; however, as we mentioned earlier, proposals for exactly this type of monitoring system – conceived of as a penalty rather than as a subsidy system – have been around for some time. For example, having decided on some aggregate level of subsidization, the government could administer these on the basis of changes in a firm's revenues per (full-time) employee – that is, average-revenue product – in relation to total compensation per employee. Subsidies could then be given to firms whose ARP had fallen, indicating contracting demand and/or lower output per employee (due to additional employment), conditional upon unit labour costs not rising above a certain rate, which could be linked to the change in ARP. Again, the purpose in this present paper is not to set out a definitive subsidy program, but merely to offer the view that wage subsidization is perhaps a feasible and attractive alternative to profit sharing as a means to restore and maintain full employment in a sticky labour market.

Do employment-creating measures inhibit progress?

Looked at from a purely formal point of view, if by "progress" we mean the rate of increase in per capita consumption (and therefore, in our preceding utility measure), then any measures that take the economy towards its golden-rule state are an improvement, and vice versa. Typically, we assume that the market-determined rate of profit or interest exceeds the rate of population or labour force growth. Therefore, it is implied that the *laissez faire* situation is one of capital deficiency, in which increased saving and capital formation would yield even greater output benefits.

If so, then to the extent that employment-creating policies *reduce* savings and capital formation, they perforce must inhibit "progress" as defined. As we have seen (table 2) this is indeed the outcome of either profit-sharing or wage-subsidization schemes, although it must be stressed again that under alternative parameter assumptions it is possible to generate equilibria with *increased* saving and capital formation. Furthermore, if the capital stock embodies new technology, this diminished rate of accumulation will also reduce the rate at which technical progress – defined as an exogenous increase in output per unit of labour – occurs.

On the other hand, quite apart from the aforementioned possibility of an increased rate of capital accumulation, technical progress might just as easily be "neutral", or even embodied primarily in labour itself. This cuts both ways, however, since although the maintenance of a fully-employed labour force might seem to enhance productivity in one sense, if the stimulus to improved labour productivity (or "human capital formation") depends upon the competitiveness of the labour market, then this could be reduced. In this regard it is likely that profit-sharing would be worse than wage subsidization, since the former depends on explicit collaboration between the firm and its existing employees. The theory of the labour-managed firm, as in the Yugoslav case, suggests strongly that such arragements would tend to lead to higher wages at the expense of employment. Wage subsidies are not entirely free of the charge of reducing incentives to human capital formation, but at the level of the firm the gap between the insiders and the outsiders would seem to be less.

Alternatively, it could be argued that technical progress is stimulated primarily by competition in the goods markets. When this is intense, firms have a strong incentive to improve the productivity of both their labour and capital inputs. If so, then it is evident that policies aimed at maintaining full employment, and hence demand, will be more conducive to progress.

If we drop the definition of "progress" in terms of pure material consumption, the argument in favour of full employment becomes even stronger. We may now wish to consider that progress involves not just a quantitative, but also a qualitative dimension which, although left out of the usual utility-function representation, contributes powerfully towards human welfare. Although many things could be included in this broadened definition (e.g. aesthetics, personal relationships, etc.) one of them must be the entitlement to productive employment, viewed not simply as an inevitable disutility, but as something satisfying in its own right. Indeed, that is at the heart of the earlier concern that persistent widespread unemployment could damage the social fabric. Hence, even if there are significant costs in terms of economic efficiency, employment creation might be the only way to ensure what we think of as our 'civilized' society.

However, I would like to adopt a definition – or at least a view – of "progress" that is somewhere between these extremes. In particular, taking a global and historical perspective on economic activity, it is clear that societies, and even whole "civilizations", experience periods of relative ascendancy and decline. The former stages are characterized by both artistic and cultural, as well as by economic expansion, while the latter stages are characterized by relative stagnation in both senses. I would argue that the essence of this process is the ability to achieve *transformation*. In the cultural sense this means the establishment of new art forms and criticism of social norms; in the economic sphere – with which I am chiefly concerned, although the two are linked – it means the ability to develop new products, to adopt new technologies, and to shift existing resources into these new areas. The Industrial Revolution is an example of such a transformation, propelling Europe, America and Japan into "first-world" status. However, as in every process of transformation, there were substantial costs borne by the displaced products, technologies and resources.

In fact, it is not unlikely that if the present-day system of universal political enfranchisement had been in place at the dawn of this Revolution, it would never have occurred. The hardships imposed upon vast numbers of dispossessed peasants and cottagers, and upon the equally vast numbers of low-paid workers in Blake's "dark, Satanic mills" would have led to the ousting of any incumbent government. Unfortunately for them, but very fortunately for us who are alive today, these people had little or no say in this process. Had they done so, it is possible (probable?) that Western Europe today would resemble parts of the so-called "Third World" (as in fact is the case with a few un-industrialized European nations).

The dilemma involved in progress is therefore clear: progress requires change, or as I have called it, transformation; however, transformation imposes burdens on sections of society, who, if they are significant in number or political power, may therefore be able to prevent transformation from occurring. The fact that future generations may benefit greatly from acquiescence is of little concern to those who may suffer immediate and substantial hardship. Viewed in this way, the unemployment problem thus arises because of the necessity for transformation (e.g. increased international competition). Part of this unemployment occurs because the economy is adjusting to change: so-called "frictional" unemployment. The remainder – which is now the major part – occurs instead because the economy is not adjusting: either so-called "structural" unemployment in which resources cannot be transformed, or "real-wage" unemployment in which resources (labour) resist change. This last is clearly the type of problem with which we have been concerned, and indicates the increased effectiveness of the majority of workers in preserving their real incomes and job security, largely at the expense of new entrants.

Employment creation policies should therefore be seen as attempts to alleviate the burdens imposed by transformation, and they should be assessed in terms of whether this alleviation promotes or inhibits that transformation. Ideally, such measures would exactly preserve real incomes while leaving all incentives to change unaffected. Maximal decline would conversely be the absence of any change with real incomes falling (at least in relation to other societies).

Traditional macroeconomic (Keynesian) policies are on this basis likely to inhibit progress, in the sense that although they are supposed to generate full employment, they do so by absorbing resources that have been displaced in the private sector. On the assumption that the public sector neither responds to economic incentives nor initiates new products or technologies – in short, that it is non-competitive – this perforce reduces the overall dynamism of the economy. Of course, as many have argued, public goods and socially–evaluated public projects may generate higher net returns than the private sector, but we leave this aside.

The New Classical doctrine can be construed as a fundamental belief in the net benefits of *laissez faire:* i.e. maximizing progress – the speed of transformation – for any given cost or burden, or minimizing the cost of transformation for any given degree of change. However, the growing perception of market rigidities, which we have viewed as a natural increase in resistance to change, has called this calculus into question.

Turning to our specific remedies, it is apparent that although profit sharing can provide a *one-off* shift from a situation of unemployment to one of full employment at unchanged real wages, its claim to *automatic* adjustment is unfortunately false. Otherwise, we would have something close to our idealized policy. Also, there appears to be some risk that after the implementation of such arrangements, the ability of employment to respond to subsequent shocks – i.e. to achieve transformation – would be lessened in comparison to a pure-wage system. On the other hand, wage subsidization is determined by *aggregate* labour market conditions, tailored to individual firms only by the requirements of short-run implementation. If this were not necessary (politically) then a uniform subsidy rate, albeit based on labour efficiency-units, could be applied indiscriminately. Variations in the subsidy rate thus perform the cushioning function for employment in each sector that profit sharing does not. In summary, a system of wage subsidization has what appears to be the potential to retain market signals while reducing the burdens of changes in real incomes. Hence, it would seem to be an effective means to promote progress.

As a postscript, it might be pointed out that two of the world's most successful economies evidence similarities to wage subsidies. In Germany the apprenticeship system, which encourages employers to take on new entrants, attracts direct subsidization, while in Japan the government gives extensive tax relief for companies to provide amenities for their workers. These include not only the usual pension and other perks, but in many cases living quarters and recreational facilities that constitute a significant part of the overall real income. These have of course developed along with both of these national economies rather than being implemented as economic policy. However, both countries are thought to be "practical" in the organization of their economic activities, and it is the case that in other Western countries considerations of practicality have forced an indirect policy of the type advocated here. For example, much of the nationalization of industry in Europe – and for that matter, government support in the U.S. – has occurred in order to save jobs and protect incomes in certain sectors. The argument here is that this is likely to be less efficient than a simple, direct subsidy for wages.

References

C.R.Bean, F.R.G. Layard, and S.J. Nickell (1986). The rise in unemployment: a multi-country study. Economica 53, Supplement.

C.Brown and E.Levin (1987). "Loading the dice in favour of less pay and more jobs", Financial Times, Feb.11.

P.R.G. Layard (1986). *How to Beat Unemployment.* Oxford University Press

D.Leach and H.Wagstaff (1986). *Future employment and technological change.* London: Kogan Page

I.McDonald and R.M. Solow (1981). Wage bargaining and employment. American Economic Review 71, 896–908.

J.Meade (1982). *Wage Fixing.* London: George Allen and Unwin

M.Weitzman (1983). Some macroeconomic implications of alternative compensation systems. Economic Journal 93, 763–783.

2.

Technological Change and Development
in Dual Economies

Indicative Labour and Capital Progamming
An Exercise on the Frontiers of Empirical Economics

by I. N. A. van der Walt and J. J. Swanepoel

1. Introduction

The aim of this study was to extend existing empirical knowledge of the marginal capital formation and employment multipliers in South Africa (RSA, 1984: 140–144). Specific attention has been given to the empirical application of the neo-classical net and gross production functions and the integration of these functions into the input-output model of Leontief. The integration of the net production functions and the calculation of the gross production functions have been achieved by using Samuelson's "Sweeping Theorem on Intermediate Products" (Chacholiades, 1978: 221–224). The final results are indicative labour and capital formation models which can be used for planning and programming purposes in South Africa.

This study is an exercise on the frontiers of empirical economics in which the mathematical and econometric contents of the neo-classical (net) production functions are extensively exploited. The mathematical basis of the empirical work is summarised in Section 2. The integration of the net production functions into the input-output model as well as the development of the indicative labour and capital formation models are purely of a mathematical nature. Section 3 explains how this integration was done. It is not possible to report on the results of this study in detail. However, the most important results for policy purposes are indicated within the relevant sections.

2. Net Production Functions

Derived Net Production Functions

For planning and programming purposes there is a long tradition of emphasising the relative scarcity of capital and the relative abundance of labour in the process of economic growth of developing countries. It is therefore not surprising that economic planners and programmers often concentrate on the investment criterion to *minimise* the incremental capital per unit output or the labour criterion to *maximise* the incremental labour per unit output. These two criteria can also be used simultaneously in order to identify the different production processes as either relatively capital or labour intensive or as both capital and labour intensive in relation to other production processes. The aim is to identify those production activities which need relatively more labour in order to develop a labour intensive strategy for industrial development in an economy where labour is the abundant factor of production.

By using the incremental capital and labour output ratios the relative intensities are established on a basis of *"need"*, i.e. how much capital and labour will be needed if the gross domestic product increases by a certain percentage (Thirwall, 1978: 114). No reference is made to how efficiently these factors of production are *"utilised"*. These ratios are therefore purely planning and programming instruments of limited economic significance. In order to achieve a greater economic significance the inverse relationships of the incremental capital output and labour output ratios are also essential. The inverse relationships identify the relative efficiency with which the factors of production are utilised. The aim now is to maximise both these relationships in order to achieve the greatest possible growth potential of the production structure as a whole.

At this point there are two conceptual problems as far as the incremental capital output and labour output ratios are concerned. *Firstly,* the minimisation of the incremental capital output ratio implies that the inverse relationship is maximised, meaning that the highest levels of productivity are sought. This argument is not necessarily true as far as the incremental labour output ratio is concerned. Maximisation of the incremental labour output ratio also means the minimisation of the factor's inverse relationship implying that the highest levels of labour productivity are of no importance. The incremental labour output ratio and its inverse may therefore be ignored by making the assumption that the minimisation of the incremental capital output ratio will automatically lead to the best utilisation of labour as a relatively abundant factor of production.[1] This assumption implies that there is concern for the relationship between capital and output whilst the relationship between capital and labour as such is ignored. This approach is therefore unable to establish the substitution of capital for labour or vice versa. In the absence of substitution an implicit assumption is also made that each factor of production contributes equally to the growth in output which is of course an abstraction from reality.[2] This assumption also holds in the case where the labour output ratio is not ignored but where both ratios under discussion are estimated separately, not taking cognisance of the elements of substitution.

Secondly, the inverse of the estimated relationships of capital and labour is nothing more than crude estimations of productivity in reality and when added together give an equally crude estimation of the returns to scale which are also of some importance in developing an industrial development strategy.

Given these limitations, these ratios are still beneficial to the economic analysis of the structure of production. These ratios reflect a priori information on the different parameter values of the net production function, which can be calculated by transforming the following incremental capital formation and labour output functions into a simple net production function, i.e.

$$K \quad = \quad A_1(t)\, Q^{q_1} \qquad\qquad ...(2\text{–}1)$$

and

$$L \quad = \quad A_2(t)\, Q^{q_2} \qquad\qquad ...(2\text{–}2)$$

to

$$Q \quad = \quad A(t)\, K^{(2q_1)^{-1}} \qquad L^{(2q_2)^{-1}} \qquad ...(2\text{–}3)$$

with

$$A \quad = \quad -\{A_1(t)/q_1 + A_2(t)/q_2\}/2$$

where Q is output, K is capital formation, t is a variable for technology and A, q_1 and q_2 are parameters respectively.

The three general sources of growth pertaining to output can be derived from equation (2–3) by taking the logarithms of the variables in the equation and differentiating the equation in respect of time, which gives (Thirwall, 1978: 53):

$$d \ Ln \ Q_t \ = \ d \ Ln \ T_t + (2q_1)^{-1} \ \cdot \ \frac{d \ Ln \ K_t}{dt} \ + \ (2q_2)^{-1} \cdot \ \frac{d \ Ln \ L_t}{dt} \qquad \ldots(2\text{--}4)$$

By taking the annual rates of change of the variables concerned the discrete form of equation (2–4) may be written as:

$$r_Q = r_T + (2q_1)^{-1} \ \cdot \ r_K + (2q_2)^{-1} \ \cdot \ r_L \qquad \ldots(2\text{--}5)$$

where r_Q, r_K and r_L are the annual rates of growth in output, capital and labour formation respectively. r_T is the contribution of technological progress to growth in output. The parameters $(2q_1)^{-1}$ and $(2q_2)^{-1}$ represent the respective partial elasticities (productivities) of capital and labour in relation to output. The returns to scale are represented by $(2q_1)^{-1} + (2q_2)^{-1}$ and the relative sources of growth are represented by r_T/r_Q (technological progress), $(2q_1)^{-1} \ r_K/r_Q$ (capital formation) and $(2q_2)^{-1} \ r_L/r_Q$ (labour formation).

Solow, *et.al.,* (Yotopoulos, 1976: 154–156) used equation (2–5) in an unique way by deriving the contribution of technology to growth in output from equation (2–5) as follows,

$$r_T = r_Q - (2q_1)^{-1} \cdot r_k + (2q_2)^{-1} \cdot r_k \qquad \ldots(2\text{--}6)$$

This method of deriving the contribution of technological development to growth proved to be beneficial as far as many econometric estimation problems are concerned. However, it is also important to note at this point that r_T cannot always be looked upon as the contribution of technological progress to growth alone but must mostly be seen as the contribution of all the factors ignored whilst estimating the different forms of the production function. This matter will be raised again at a later stage.

The estimation of equation (2–1) implies that capital formation (k) contributes a 100 per cent to the growth in output whilst equation (2–2) implies the same as far as labour is concerned. If the two estimated ratios are added together as in equation (2–3) the sources of growth derived from equation (2–5) equal 50 per cent for each factor of production. This property, due to the separately derived capital output and labour output ratios, proved to be unfortunate and it is not clear to what extent this limitation is acknowledged by those who use these ratios as policy making instruments. However, this property is also beneficial in econometric work in the sense that variables which experienced structural changes during the period of analysis can be identified. In these cases the sources of growth with regard to capital formation and labour may differ from the 50:50 ratio indicating that the data may be faulty or that the marginal neo-classical theory in terms of the production function is not applicable.

Table 1 shows the empirical results after the separately estimated capital output and labour output ratios of equations (2–1) and (2–2) were transformed to the production function of equation (2–3). However, technological development has been ignored in these estimations and derived from equation (2–6) whilst the relative sources of growth were then calculated according to equation (2–5). The results confirm that,

– the imposed property of an equal (50:50) contribution by each factor of production to growth in output is valid (Columns 9 and 10). There are only a few sectors of production with distortions in their variables which makes the use of incremental capital and labour output ratios debatable for purposes of neo-classical analysis. These sectors are indicated by an asterisk in Table 1.

Table 1

Sources of growth, elasticities and returns to scale of inverted marginal output rations, period 1946–1983 (constant 1975 prices)

Industries	Scale 1	Growth GDP 2	Elasticity Labour 3	Growth Labour 4	(3)x(4) 5	Elasticity Capital 6	Growth Capital 7	(6)x(7) 8	SOURCES OF GROWTH		
									% Labour (5)÷(2) 9	% Capital (8)÷(2) 10	Ignorance 100-[(5)÷(2)]+[(8)÷(2)]% 11
1. Agriculture, forestry and fishing	*	*	*	*	*	*	*	*	*	*	*
2. Coal mining	1,804	3,773	1,079	1,780	1,921	0,325	5,391	1,752	50,91	46,44	2,65
3. Gold mining	1,775	2,570	1,400	0,909	1,273	0,375	3,418	1,282	49,53	49,88	0,59
4. Diamond mining	1,881	2,986	1,531	0,975	1,493	0,350	4,265	1,493	50,00	50,00	0,00
5. Other mining	1,017	4,792	0,668	3,584	2,394	0,399	6,867	2,397	49,96	50,02	0,02
6. Processing of meat	0,938	9,416	0,570	8,319	4,742	0,368	13,238	4,872	50,36	51,74	-2,10
7. Dairy products	1,375	4,434	0,800	2,828	2,262	0,575	4,019	2,311	51,01	52,12	-3,13
8. Canning of fruits and vegetables	1,755	5,966	1,208	2,549	3,079	0,547	5,281	2,889	51,61	48,42	-0,03
9. Canning of fish	1,680	4,413	0,948	2,329	2,208	0,732	3,016	2,208	50,03	50,03	-0,06
10. Oils and fat	1,525	3,770	1,087	1,730	1,881	0,438	4,304	1,885	49,89	50,00	0,11
11. Grain mill products	2,126	6,003	1,506	1,946	2,931	0,620	4,903	3,040	48,83	50,64	0,53
12. Bakery products	1,304	4,400	0,775	2,852	2,210	0,529	4,260	2,254	50,23	51,23	-1,46
13. Sugar	1,371	5,654	1,049	2,563	2,689	0,322	8,529	2,746	47,56	48,57	3,87
14. Cocoa and confectionery	2,189	3,916	1,615	1,229	1,985	0,574	3,453	1,982	50,69	50,61	-1,30
15. Other food	1,560	5,908	0,963	3,108	2,993	0,597	5,038	3,008	50,66	50,91	-1,57
16. Animal feeds	1,166	7,042	0,842	4,185	3,525	0,324	10,929	3,541	50,06	50,28	-0,34
17. Distilling and wine industries	1,820	7,867	0,828	4,839	4,007	0,592	6,519	3,859	50,93	49,05	0,02
18. Malt liquors and malt	0,906	5,776	0,585	4,667	2,730	0,321	9,029	2,898	47,26	50,17	2,57
19. Soft drinks	1,521	5,147	1,100	2,157	2,373	0,421	6,225	2,621	46,10	50,92	2,98
20. Tobacco products	*	*	*	*	*	*	*	*	*	*	*
21. Processing of wool and cotton	1,527	10,744	0,933	5,715	5,332	0,594	9,002	5,347	49,63	49,77	0,60
22. Spinning and weaving	1,429	6,686	0,746	4,489	3,349	0,683	4,864	3,322	50,09	49,69	0,22
23. Made-up textile goods	1,163	6,916	0,675	5,035	3,399	0,488	7,087	3,458	49,15	50,00	0,85
24. Knitting mills (clothing)	1,328	8,104	0,554	7,622	4,223	0,774	5,173	4,004	52,11	49,41	-1,52
25. Other knitting mills	1,163	11,546(1)	0,595	9,680	5,760	0,568	9,914	5,631	49,89	48,77	1,34
26. Carpets and rugs	1,498	6,303	0,743	4,280	3,180	0,755	4,182	3,157	50,45	50,09	-0,54
27. Cordage, rope and twine	1,373	6,254	0,525	5,397	2,833	0,848	3,586	3,041	45,30	48,62	6,08

Table 1 (Continued)

Industries	Scale 1	Growth GDP 2	Elasticity Labour 3	Growth Labour 4	(3)x(4) 5	Elasticity Capital 6	Growth Capital 7	(6)x(7) 8	SOURCES OF GROWTH % Labour (5)÷(2) 9	% Capital (8)÷(2) 10	% Ignorance 100-[(5)+(8)]÷(2) 11
28. Other textiles	1,496	6,416	0,708	4,357	3,085	0,788	4,004	3,155	48,08	49,17	2,75
29. Wearing apparel	0,950	2,802	0,467	2,900	1,354	0,483	2,843	1,373	48,32	49,00	2,68
30. Tanneries and leather finishing	*	*	*	*	*	*	*	*	*	*	*
31. Leather products	1,300	5,096	0,600	4,478	2,687	0,700	3,445	2,412	52,73	47,33	-0,06
32. Footwear	1,817	3,298	1,149	1,452	1,668	0,668	2,563	1,712	50,58	51,91	-2,49
33. Wood and wood products	1,504	4,139	1,014	2,039	2,068	0,490	4,299	2,107	49,95	50,91	-0,87
34. Furniture	1,667	3,225	1,035	1,596	1,652	0,632	2,490	1,574	51,22	48,81	-0,03
35. Pulp and paper	1,442	9,566	0,778	5,903	4,593	0,664	7,481	4,967	48,01	51,92	0,07
36. Paper containers	1,810	6,993	0,980	3,543	3,472	0,830	4,185	3,474	50,01	50,04	-0,05
37. Other pulp and paper articles	1,223	6,183	0,833	3,712	3,092	0,390	8,021	3,128	50,01	50,59	-0,60
38. Printing and publishing	1,640	5,450	0,903	2,975	2,686	0,737	3,565	2,627	49,28	48,20	2,52
39. Fertilizers and pesticides	1,737	7,118	1,316	2,704	3,558	0,421	8,603	3,622	49,99	50,89	-0,88
40. Synthetic resins and plastic materials	1,615	7,898	1,188	3,337	3,964	0,427	9,586	4,093	50,19	51,82	-2,01
41. Paints and varnishes	*	*	*	*	*	*	*	*	*	*	*
42. Medicines	1,709	8,529	1,142	3,724	4,253	0,567	7,611	4,315	49,87	50,59	-0,46
43. Cosmetic and toilet preparations	1,880	8,374	0,945	4,434	4,190	0,935	8,469	4,179	50,04	49,90	0,06
44. Other chemical products	1,820	6,901	1,149	3,008	3,456	0,745	5,094	3,795	50,08	54,99	-5,07
45. Other basic ind. chemicals	1,617	8,567	1,238	3,535	4,376	0,379	10,845	4,148	51,08	48,42	0,50
46. Tyres and tubes	1,053	3,433	0,796	2,093	1,666	0,257	7,079	1,819	48,53	52,99	-1,52
47. Other rubber products	1,185	5,511	0,754	3,604	2,717	0,431	6,494	2,799	49,30	50,79	-0,09
48. Other plastic products	1,806	12,261)	1,027	5,947	6,108	0,779	7,797	6,074	49,82	49,54	0,64
49. Pottery, china and earthenware	1,186	6,048	0,660	4,551	3,004	0,526	5,428	2,855	49,67	47,21	3,12
50. Glass and glass products	1,754	7,100	1,157	2,793	3,232	0,597	6,411	3,827	45,52	53,90	0,58
51. Structural clay products	1,685	4,189	1,152	1,730	1,993	0,533	3,970	2,116	47,58	50,51	1,91
52. Cement	*	*	*	*	*	*	*	*	*	*	*
53. Other non-metallic mineral products	1,317	7,157	0,886	3,983	3,529	0,431	8,318	3,585	49,31	50,09	0,60

Table 1 (Continued)

Industries	Scale 1	Growth GDP 2	Elasticity Labour 3	Growth Labour 4	(3)x(4) 5	Elasticity Capital 6	Growth Capital 7	(6)x(7) 8	SOURCES OF GROWTH Labour (5)÷(2)% 9	Capital (8)÷(2)% 10	Ignorance 100-[(5)+(8)]÷(2)% 11
54. Iron and steel basic industries	1,028	7,744	0,656	5,878	3,856	0,372	10,313	3,836	49,79	49,54	0,67
55. Non-ferrous metal basic industries	1,717	13,136[1]	1,210	5,382	6,512	0,507	13,028	6,605	49,57	50,28	0,15
56. Hand tools and general hardware	1,181	6,184	0,909	3,436	3,123	0,272	11,391	3,098	50,50	50,10	-0,60
57. Furniture and fixtures of metal	1,195	5,166	0,887	2,859	2,536	0,308	8,331	2,566	49,09	49,67	1,24
58. Structural metal products	1,563	6,773	1,139	2,964	3,376	0,424	7,962	3,376	49,85	48,85	0,30
59. Other metal products	1,647	5,629	0,954	2,952	2,816	0,693	4,092	2,836	50,03	50,38	-0,41
60. Engines and turbines	1,608	7,623	1,037	3,663	3,799	0,571	6,730	3,843	49,84	50,41	-0,25
61. Agricultural machinery	1,111	3,511	0,912	1,873	1,708	0,283	6,349	1,797	48,65	51,18	0,17
62. Metal and woodworking machinery	1,608	7,623	1,037	3,663	3,799	0,571	6,730	3,843	49,84	50,41	-0,25
63. Special industrial machinery	1,595	6,581	1,075	2,985	3,209	0,520	6,484	3,372	48,76	51,24	0,0
64. Office and accounting machinery	1,608	7,623	1,037	3,663	3,799	0,571	6,730	3,843	49,84	50,41	-0,25
65. Other machinery, non-electric	2,081	13,140[1]	1,174	5,683	6,672	0,907	7,271	6,595	50,78	50,19	-0,97
66. Electrical industrial machinery	1,251	10,557	0,694	7,586	5,265	0,557	9,313	5,187	49,87	49,13	1,00
67. Radio and television	1,230	9,103	0,684	6,632	4,535	0,546	8,404	4,589	49,83	50,41	-0,24
68. Electrical appliances	1,229	8,900	0,688	6,425	4,420	0,541	8,287	4,483	49,66	50,37	-0,03
69. Other electrical apparatus	1,236	8,172	0,705	5,743	4,049	0,531	7,612	4,042	49,55	49,46	0,99
70. Ship building	1,151	9,903	0,812	6,058	4,919	0,339	14,841	5,031	49,67	50,80	-0,47
71. Railroad equipment	1,151	9,903	0,812	6,058	4,919	0,339	14,841	5,031	49,67	50,80	-0,47
72. Motor vehicles	0,942	7,952	0,547	7,243	3,962	0,395	9,936	3,925	49,82	49,36	0,82
73. Aircraft	1,151	9,903	0,812	6,058	4,919	0,339	14,841	5,031	49,67	50,80	-0,47
74. Other transport equipment	1,151	9,903	0,812	6,058	4,919	0,339	14,841	5,031	49,67	50,80	-0,47
75. Jewellery	0,955	6,792	0,631	5,365	3,385	0,325	10,487	3,408	49,84	50,18	-0,02

Table 1 (Continued)

Industries	Scale 1	Growth GDP 2	Elasticity Labour 3	Growth Labour 4	(3)x(4) 5	Elasticity Capital 6	Growth Capital 7	(6)x(7) 8	SOURCES OF GROWTH		
									% Labour (5)÷(2) 9	% Capital (8)÷(2) 10	Ignorance 100-[(5)+(8)]÷(2)% 11
76. Other manufacturing	1,506	6,540	0,821	3,985	3,272	0,685	4,779	3,274	50,03	50,06	-0,09
77. Electricity, gas and steam	1,372	6,884	0,849	4,066	3,452	0,523	6,588	3,446	50,15	50,06	-0,21
78. Water	1,372	6,884	0,849	4,066	3,452	0,523	6,588	3,446	50,15	50,06	-0,21
79. Building construction	1,248	5,222	0,829	3,127	2,592	0,416	6,463	2,689	49,64	51,49	-1,13
80. Civil engineering and other construction	0,613	5,319	0,393	6,720	2,641	0,220	12,150	2,673	49,65	50,25	0,10
81. Wholesale and retail trade	1,827	5,142	0,939	2,770	2,601	0,488	5,312	2,592	50,58	50,41	-0,99
82. Catering and accommodation	1,827	5,142	0,939	2,770	2,601	0,488	5,312	2,592	50,58	50,41	-0,99
83. Transport and storage	1,747	4,783	1,235	1,915	2,365	0,512	4,824	2,470	49,45	51,64	-1,09
84. Communication	1,191	6,133	0,805	3,856	3,104	0,386	7,887	3,044	50,61	49,63	-0,24
85. Financial institutions	0,855	4,355	0,413	5,338	2,205	0,442	4,955	2,190	50,63	50,29	-0,92
86. Real estate	0,855	4,355	0,413	5,338	2,205	0,442	4,955	2,190	50,63	50,29	-0,92
87. Business services	0,855	4,355	0,413	5,338	2,205	0,442	4,955	2,190	50,63	50,29	-0,92
88. Renting and leasing of machinery	0,855	4,355	0,413	5,338	2,205	0,442	4,955	2,190	50,63	50,29	-0,92
89. Health services	0,569	2,850	0,359	3,926	1,409	0,210	6,748	1,417	49,44	49,72	0,84
90. Other services, profit seeking	0,569	2,850	0,359	3,926	1,409	0,210	6,748	1,417	49,44	49,72	0,84
91. Other services, non-profit seeking	0,569	2,850	0,359	3,926	1,409	0,210	6,748	1,417	49,44	49,72	0,84
92. Goods and services not classified	1,340	6,527	0,890	3,643	3,242	0,450	7,298	3,284	49,67	50,31	0,02

Source: Industrial Development Corporation of South Africa.

1)   The growth rates of the Other knitting mills, Other plastic products, Non-ferrous basic metals and Other non-electric machinery industries are relatively high, due to the relatively undeveloped state of these industries during the initial years, followed by strong growth since the sixties.

- according to Column 1 most of the individual sectors produce to increasing returns to scale. There are a few exceptions to this rule, and the results of some of the service industries are worth mentioning in this regard,

- the elasticity (productivity) of labour (Column 3) is higher than the elasticity of capital for most of the production sectors (Column 6). Because each of these production factors contributes equally to output as a source of growth these elasticities may be an over- or underestimated result which can be rectified by the use of production functions which allow for differential sources of growth, and

- the coefficient of ignorance (Column 11), which includes technological progress, is relatively small and the assumption can be made that the influence of this coefficient on the general results, though not unimportant in economic terms, will be marginal.

Net Production Functions

In terms of a net production function aggregate output is written as a function of factor inputs and the prevailing technology, i.e.

$$Q = f(K, L, M, T, \gamma, \upsilon)$$
$$(K, L, M, T > 0; \gamma > 0; \upsilon > 0) \qquad \qquad ...(2–7)$$

where K is capital, L is labour, M is material inputs, T is technology, γ is a parameter of efficiency and υ is a parameter which quantifies the economies of scale.

Equation (2–7) can also be extended to include variables which are concerned with the quality of capital and labour. Though the importance of these quality variables is acknowledged the inclusion of these variables is looked upon merely as an extension of the investigation to date.[3] As a simple approach to the econometric estimation of the function, technical progress (or coefficient of ignorance) is derived from the mathematical properties of the function.[4] Other approaches for the identification of the technical progress may also be followed.[5] This study had more to do with capital and labour as sources of growth as such and found the derived parameter values for technical progress satisfactory for the purposes it was needed.

On an aggregate level imports must also be excluded from output in order to isolate domestic production activities more definitely. However, the identification of these imports for the different production sectors of the economy is problematic. The imports reported in the official statistics are on a single homogeneous product basis whilst the imports which have to be removed from the output of the production function consist of several products which are needed in the process of production as such. Though not impossible, the identification of these imports in the form of time series is a very costly and difficult task which sets limits as far as empirical economic research is concerned.

Material inputs M are excluded from the econometric specification of equation (2–7) because of the assymatric properties thereof. The use of these inputs are usually closely related with the level of gross output and their inclusion as an independent variable in equation (2–7) as well as their presence in gross output usually obscure the relationships of interest (Grilliches, 1971: 108).

When taking the problems of imports and material inputs into consideration, value added seems to be the best variable to represent output in the production function. The use of value added has advantages because the empirical results of the production functions for the different sectors of production can be directly related to the value added and import multipliers which are calculated with the input-output model of Leontief (Bulmer-Thomas, 1982: 183–187). The use of value added as a variable for output in the function also has certain implications for Samuelson's "Theorem on Intermediate Products" as well as for the gross production functions which were developed with this theorem and which have total production inputs as a basis. This matter will be clarified at a later stage.

The mathematical specification of the net production functions can therefore be written as,

$$Q = A \, K^{\upsilon\delta} \, L^{\upsilon(1-\delta)} \qquad \qquad \qquad ...(2-8)$$

with $\alpha = \upsilon\delta$, $\beta = \upsilon(1-\delta)$ and A = Antilog f (Cobb and Douglas, 1928 : 159–165). Where δ is α parameter for efficiency, α is the elasticity (responsiveness) of output with respect to capital (holding labour constant), and β is the partial elasticity of output with respect to labour (holding labour constant). Both a and b can also be seen as partial productivities whilst making use of the ceteris paribus assumption. The problem of multicollinearity is solved by restricting the function of equation (2–8) with respect to capital formation, resulting in the following specification.

$$Q = A \, (K)^{\upsilon} \, (L/K)^{\upsilon(1-\delta)} \qquad \qquad \qquad ...(2-9)$$

where K, which is the variable for capital formation, is transformed to a variable for returns to scale. An inspection for heteroscedasticity can also be made by using the method of indirect least squares. By weighing output with the variable for capital formation the function can mathematically be specified as,

$$Q/K = A(K)^{\upsilon-1} \, (L/K)^{\upsilon(1-\delta)} \qquad \qquad \qquad ...(2-10)$$

The problem of autocorrelation is unsolved but can be explained by the absence of a specified variable for technology. As was indicated previously the parameter for technology is derived from the mathematical specification of the equation (2–6). This approach was also followed in regard to the other production functions in this study.

The simple Cobb-Douglas production function assumes an elasticity of substitution of one. This assumption limits the use of the function for empirical purposes and is normally relaxed by making use of a constant elasticity of substitution (C.E.S.) production function which is mathematically specified as,

$$Q = \gamma \{ \delta K^{-\rho} + (1-\delta) \, L^{-\rho} \}^{-\upsilon/\rho}$$
$$(\gamma > 0; \; 1 > \delta > 0; \; \upsilon > 0; \; \rho \geq -1) \qquad \qquad ...(2-11)$$

where ρ is the parameter for the elasticity of substitution (Arrow, 1961: 225–250). Equation (2–11) is intrinsically non-linear and must be transformed in order to apply the least squares estimation method. For this purpose the method of Kmenta was followed by substituting an approximation based on a Taylor series expansion of the logarithm of the function around $\rho = 0$, which resulted in the following econometric specification of the function (Kmenta, 1967: 180–189)

$$Ln \, Q = Ln \, \gamma + \upsilon\delta \, Ln \, K + \upsilon(1-\delta) \, Ln \, L -{1/2}\rho\upsilon\delta \, (1-\delta) \, (Ln \, K - Ln \, L)^2 \qquad ...(2-12)$$

The right-hand side can be divided into two parts, one corresponding to the Cobb-Douglas production function and one representing a factor of correction if the elasticity of substitution deviates from one. The latter part will disappear if $\rho = 0$ reducing the function to the original Cobb-Douglas function.

The restricted version of this function which avoids the problem of multicollinearity resulted in,

$$Ln\ Q = Ln\ \gamma + \upsilon Ln\ K + \upsilon(1-\delta)(Ln\ L - Ln\ K) - \tfrac{1}{2}\rho\upsilon\delta\ (1-\delta)\ (Ln\ L - Ln\ K)^2 \qquad ...(2-13)$$

As in equation (2–10) the problem of heteroscedasticity can be solved by the method of indirect least squares.

Empirically, capital formation is measured in monetary values at constant prices while labour may be measured in physical numbers of workers. In this case the units of measurement differ and the elasticity of substitution *cannot be measured* in mathematical terms. This problem can be solved by redefining the units of measurement of K and L in the *correction factor* in terms of indexes. These indexes were calculated in such a way that their geometric averages in the *time series* sample were in fact equal and $(Ln\ \overline{L} - Ln\ \overline{K})^2 = 0$ (Grilliches, 1971: 10).

The elasticity of substitution as well as the returns to scale of the C.E.S. production function differ from one. However, these two parameter values remain constant for the period of analysis which is an abstraction from reality in those production processes where the elasticity of substitution is variable while the level of the returns to scale is also influenced. This problem can be solved by using of the transcendental logarithmic (translog) function which is established by defactorising the correction factor of the C.E.S. function (Christensen, 1973: 28-45), i.e.

$$Ln\ Q = Ln\ \gamma + \upsilon\delta\ Ln\ K + \upsilon(1-\delta)\ Ln\ L - \Omega_1\ (Ln\ \overline{K})^2 +$$

$$2\Omega_2\ (Ln\ \overline{K}) \cdot (Ln\ \overline{L}) - \Omega_3\ (Ln\ \overline{L})^2 \qquad ...(2-14)$$

If $\Omega_1 = \Omega_2 = \Omega_3$, this function reduces to a Cobb-Douglas function whilst the Kmenta approximation of the C.E.S. function holds when $-\Omega_1 = -\Omega_3 = \Omega_2^2$. A situation can also exist where $\Omega = 0$ or $\Omega_3 = 0$. In both these situations $\Omega_2 = 0$ because Ω_2 is the parameter which represents the product of both variables concerned and of which one is not relevant in the correction factor of the translog function (Mayes, 1981: 108), i.e.

$$Ln\ Q = Ln\ \gamma + \upsilon\delta Ln\ K + \upsilon(1-\delta)\ Ln\ L - \Omega_1\ (Ln\ \overline{K})^2 \qquad ...(2-15)$$
or
$$Ln\ Q = Ln\ \gamma + \upsilon\delta Ln\ K + \upsilon(1-\delta)\ Ln\ L - \Omega_3\ (Ln\ \overline{L})^2 \qquad ...(2-16)$$

Apart from a variable elasticity of substitution the change in the returns to scale for the sample period can also be measured by,

$$\upsilon \pm (2\Omega_1\ Ln\ \overline{K}\ or\ 2\Omega_3\ Ln\ \overline{L}) \qquad ...(2-17)$$

A positive or a negative sign in equation (2–17) indicates an increase or a decrease in the elasticity (productivity) of capital or labour respectively as well as the level of the returns to scale (Mayes, 1981: 109).

The problem of multicollinearity is solved by the restricted version of equation (2–14), i.e.

$$Ln\ Q = Ln\ \gamma + \upsilon Ln\ K + \upsilon(1-\delta)\ \{Ln\ L - Ln\ K\} - \Omega_1\ (Ln\ \overline{K})^2 +$$
$$2\Omega_2\ \{Ln\ \overline{K})\ (Ln\ \overline{L})\} - \Omega_3\ (Ln\ \overline{L})^2 \qquad \qquad ...(2-18)$$

The problem of heteroscedasticity can also be attended to by weighing output with capital formation in equation (2–18).

Finally, the sources of growth in the case of the Cobb-Douglas production function were calculated from equations (2–4) and (2–5). If the same procedure is followed by second order approximation of the C.E.S. function may be written as follows:

$$r_q = r_T + \upsilon\delta r_K + \upsilon(1-\delta)\ r_L - 1/2\upsilon\delta\ (1-\delta)\rho\ \{r_K^- - r_L^-\}^2 \qquad ...(2-19)$$

The last term gives the difference between the Cobb-Douglas and the C.E.S. function when $\rho \neq 0$ (Yotopoulos, 1976: 156).

There is empirical evidence indicating that the value of ρ does not differ markedly from zero over the relative short term and that long run time series tends to bias ρ upward due to the problem of business cycle variations. This bias is mainly the result of the misspecification of the C.E.S. functions with regard to technological change and capacity utilisation. Because ρ does not differ markedly from zero over the short term, Nelson argues forcefully that the difference between the Cobb-Douglas and the C.E.S. production functions for explaining the sources of growth is of little relevance (Nelson, 1965: 326–328). The upward bias in ρ over the long term is as far as this study is concerned relatively unknown because the method of Solow *et.al.,* was again used to calculate the source of growth as far as the ignored factors are concerned, i.e. from equation (2–19) it follows that:

$$r_T = r_q - \{\upsilon\delta r_k + \upsilon(1-\delta)r_L\} \qquad \qquad ...(2-20)$$

where r_T is the source of growth for the ignored factors. Though this approach can be criticised the results proved to be more realistic in terms of the econometric estimation of the functions.

Empirical Results

Aggregate Net Production Function for Industry

The annual aggregate net production function for the period 1946–1983 is of an unrestricted translog nature in which the index for labour is of less importance as far as the factor of correction is concerned, namely

$$Ln\ Q = -5{,}713 + 0{,}671\ Ln\ L + 0{,}555\ Ln\ K - 0{,}046\ (Ln\ \overline{K})^2$$
$$\quad\ (-2{,}188)\ (2{,}462) \qquad\quad (4{,}022)(-2{,}557)$$
$$\qquad R^2 = 0{,}99 \qquad\qquad\qquad DW = 0{,}356 \qquad\qquad ...(2-21)$$

All the test-statistics, with the exception of the Durban-Watson proved to be satisfactory. The Durban-Watson indicates the existence of autocorrelation due to the misspecification of the function with regard to technological development and capacity utilisation which were deliberately ignored. As far as capacity utilisation is concerned the necessary information on a ninety two sectoral basis does not exist in South Africa. Technology could have been incorporated into the production function with time (t) as a variable. However, the use of time as a variable, though generally accepted by econometricians in highly aggregated functions is much more complicated where a vast amount of disaggregated production sectors are concerned. If one adds the upward bias in ρ which may exist in production functions over the longer term matters are extremely simplified by accepting a low Durban-Watson and using equation (2–20) in which the correction factor is ignored, as well as (2–5) to establish the sources of economic growth econometrically.

Table 2

Relative importance of Capital and Labour Formation in Industry				
		Sources of Growth		
Year	Returns to Scale	Capital	Labour	Ignorance
1950	1,312			
1960	1,263	62,06	37,44	0,50
1970	1,190			
1980	1,120			

The results summarized in Table 2 indicate that industry produces in a situation of "increasing returns to scale", but that the scale has decreased from approximately 1,312 in 1950 to 1,120 in 1980, i.e. the effective utilisation of capital or labour or both in terms of output is decreasing. This decrease implies that the potential contribution of industry to the overall economic growth of the country is declining. If the elasticities in equation (2–21) are accepted on face value the function seems to identify capital formation as the main element responsible for the decrease in the level of the returns to scale. The effective utilisation of capital, and not necessarily labour alone, is in question and this may be for many reasons which the function is not able to explain. Capital formation is the most important source of growth as far as industry is concerned and contributed 62,06 per cent to the growth in output whilst the contribution by labour is estimated at 37,44 per cent for the period 1946–1983.[6]

Net Production Functions on a Sectoral Basis

Table 3 indicates the results of equations (2–20) and (2–5) respectively which were obtained from a wide range of functions within the explained family of C.E.S. production functions. The a priori indication from Table 1 that most of the production sectors produce in a situation of "increasing returns to scale" is confirmed by the results in Table 3. There are a few exceptions to this rule especially as far as the service industries are concerned.

Table 3: Sources of growth, elasticities and returns to scale of production functions, period 1946-1983 (constant 1975 prices)

Industries	Scale 1	Growth GDP 2	Elasticity Labour 3	Growth Labour 4	(3)x(4) 5	Elasticity Capital 6	Growth Capital 7	(6)x(7) 8	SOURCES OF GROWTH		
									% Labour (5)÷(2) 9	% Capital (8)÷(2) 10	% Ignorance 100-[(5)+(8)]÷(2) 11
1. Agriculture, forestry and fishing	1,750	2,513	0,705	-0,403	-0,284	1,045	2,835	2,963	-11,30	117,91	-6,61
2. Coal mining	1,230	3,773	0,809	1,780	1,440	0,421	5,391	2,270	38,17	60,16	1,67
3. Gold mining	1,304	2,570	0,808	0,909	0,734	0,496	3,418	1,695	28,56	65,95	5,49
4. Diamond mining	1,381	2,986	0,882	0,975	0,860	0,849	4,265	1,915	28,80	64,13	7,07
5. Other mining	0,971	4,792	0,572	3,584	2,050	0,399	6,867	2,740	42,78	57,18	0,04
6. Processing of meat	0,874	9,416	0,485	8,319	4,035	0,389	13,238	5,150	42,85	54,69	2,46
7. Dairy products	1,288	4,434	0,496	2,828	1,403	0,792	4,019	3,183	31,54	71,79	-3,43
8. Canning of fruits and vegetables	1,765	5,966	1,353	2,549	3,449	0,412	5,281	2,176	57,81	36,47	5,72
9. Canning of fish	1,741	4,413	1,221	2,329	2,844	0,520	3,016	1,568	64,45	35,53	0,02
10. Oils and fat	1,567	3,770	1,134	1,730	1,962	0,433	4,304	1,864	52,04	49,84	-1,48
11. Grain mill products	1,731	6,003	0,875	1,946	1,703	0,856	4,903	4,197	28,37	69,92	1,71
12. Bakery products	1,377	4,400	1,042	2,852	2,972	0,335	4,260	1,427	67,55	32,43	0,02
13. Sugar	1,309	5,654	0,926	2,563	2,373	0,383	8,529	3,267	41,97	57,78	0,25
14. Cocoa and confectionery	1,889	3,916	1,318	1,229	1,620	0,571	3,453	1,972	41,37	50,36	8,27
15. Other food	1,428	5,908	0,747	3,108	2,322	0,681	5,038	3,431	39,30	58,07	2,63
16. Animal feeds	1,400	7,042	1,230	4,186	5,149	0,170	10,929	1,858	73,12	26,38	0,50
17. Distilling and wine industries	1,509	7,867	1,060	4,839	5,129	0,449	6,519	2,927	65,20	37,21	-2,41
18. Malt liquors and malt	0,774	5,776	0,278	4,667	1,297	0,496	9,029	4,478	22,45	77,53	0,02
19. Soft drinks	1,859	5,147	1,081	2,157	2,332	0,378	6,225	2,353	45,31	45,72	8,97
20. Tobacco products	1,534	3,121	1,029	1,491	1,534	0,505	3,091	1,561	49,15	50,02	0,83
21. Processing of wool and cotton	1,615	10,744	1,217	5,715	6,955	0,398	9,002	3,583	64,73	33,35	1,92
22. Spinning and weaving	1,469	6,686	1,044	4,489	4,687	0,425	4,864	2,067	70,10	30,92	-1,02
23. Made-up textile goods	1,115	6,916	0,485	5,035	2,442	0,630	7,087	4,465	35,31	64,56	0,13
24. Knitting mills (clothing)	1,296	8,104	0,573	7,622	4,367	0,723	5,173	3,140	53,89	46,15	-0,04
25. Other knitting mills	1,155	11,546	0,699	9,680	6,766	0,456	9,914	4,531	58,60	39,24	2,16
26. Carpets and rugs	1,478	6,303	0,964	4,280	4,126	0,514	4,182	2,150	65,46	34,11	0,43
27. Cordage, rope and twine	1,642	6,254	0,432	5,397	2,332	1,210	3,586	4,339	37,29	69,38	-6,67
28. Other textiles	1,523	6,816	0,903	4,357	3,934	0,620	4,004	2,482	61,32	38,68	0,0
29. Wearing apparel	0,981	2,802	0,568	2,900	1,647	0,413	2,843	1,174	58,78	41,90	-0,68
30. Tanneries and leather finishing	1,882	2,302	0,389	1,904	0,741	1,773	1,045	1,560	32,19	67,77	0,04

Table 3 (Continued)

Industries	Scale 1	Growth GDP 2	Elasticity Labour 3	Growth Labour 4	(3)×(4) 5	Elasticity Capital 6	Growth Capital 7	(6)×(7) 8	SOURCES OF GROWTH		
									% Labour (5)÷(2) 9	% Capital (8)÷(2) 10	% Ignorance 100-[(5)+(8)]÷(2)% 11
31. Leather products	1,274	5,096	0,676	4,478	3,027	0,598	3,445	2,060	59,40	40,42	0,18
32. Footwear	1,475	3,298	0,587	1,452	0,852	0,888	2,563	2,276	25,83	69,01	5,16
33. Wood and wood products	1,379	4,139	0,803	2,039	1,637	0,576	4,299	2,476	39,55	59,82	0,63
34. Furniture	1,760	3,225	1,294	1,596	2,065	0,466	2,490	1,160	64,03	35,97	0,0
35. Pulp and paper	1,418	9,566	0,699	5,903	4,126	0,719	7,481	5,379	43,13	56,23	0,64
36. Paper containers	1,697	6,943	0,931	3,543	3,299	0,766	4,185	3,206	47,52	46,18	6,30
37. Other pulp and paper articles	1,386	6,183	1,123	3,712	4,169	0,263	8,021	2,110	67,43	34,13	-1,56
38. Printing and publishing	1,670	5,450	0,967	2,975	2,877	0,703	3,565	2,506	52,79	45,98	1,23
39. Fertilizers and pesticides	2,340	7,118	2,204	2,704	5,960	0,136	8,603	1,170	83,73	16,44	-0,17
40. Synthetic resins and plastic materials	1,831	7,898	1,607	3,337	5,363	0,224	9,586	2,147	67,90	27,18	4,92
41. Paints and varnishes	2,161	3,908	1,022	2,509	2,564	1,139	1,081	1,231	65,61	31,50	2,89
42. Medicines	1,635	8,529	1,024	3,724	3,813	0,611	7,611	4,650	44,71	54,52	0,77
43. Cosmetic and toilet preparations	1,856	8,374	0,829	4,434	3,676	1,027	4,469	4,590	43,90	54,81	1,29
44. Other chemical products	1,946	6,901	1,432	3,008	4,307	0,514	5,094	2,618	62,41	37,94	-0,35
45. Other basic industrial chemicals	1,361	8,567	0,881	3,535	3,114	0,480	10,995	5,254	36,35	61,33	2,32
46. Tyres and tubes	0,721	3,433	0,359	2,093	0,751	0,362	7,079	2,563	21,88	74,66	3,46
47. Other rubber products	1,223	5,511	0,871	3,604	3,139	0,352	6,494	2,286	56,96	41,48	1,56
48. Other plastic products	1,846	12,261	1,173	5,947	6,976	0,673	7,797	5,247	56,90	42,79	0,31
49. Pottery, china and earthenware	1,298	6,048	1,035	4,551	4,710	0,263	5,428	1,428	77,88	23,61	-1,49
50. Glass and glass products	1,953	7,100	1,476	2,793	4,122	0,477	6,411	3,058	58,06	43,07	-1,13
51. Structural clay products	1,578	4,189	0,806	1,730	1,394	0,772	3,970	3,065	33,28	73,17	-6,45
52. Cement	1,366	6,170	0,710	2,535	1,800	0,656	7,693	4,347	29,17	70,45	0,38
53. Other non-metallic mineral products	1,364	7,157	0,969	3,983	3,860	0,395	8,318	3,286	53,93	45,91	0,16
54. Iron and steel basic industries	1,184	7,744	1,014	5,878	5,960	0,170	10,313	1,753	76,96	22,64	0,40
55. Non-ferrous metal basic industries	1,625	13,136	1,065	5,382	5,732	0,560	13,028	7,296	43,64	55,54	0,82
56. Hand tools and general hardware	0,974	6,184	0,623	3,436	2,141	0,351	11,391	3,998	43,62	64,65	0,73
57. Furniture and fixtures of metal	0,871	5,166	0,378	2,859	1,081	0,493	8,331	4,107	20,93	79,50	-0,43
58. Structural metal products	1,385	6,773	0,891	2,964	2,641	0,494	7,962	3,933	38,99	58,07	2,94
59. Other metal products	1,582	5,629	0,848	2,952	2,503	0,734	4,092	3,004	44,47	53,37	2,16
60. Engines and turbines	1,542	7,623	0,910	3,663	3,333	0,632	6,730	4,253	43,72	55,79	-0,49
61. Agricultural machinery	1,433	3,511	1,250	1,873	2,341	0,183	6,349	1,162	66,68	33,10	0,22
62. Metal and woodworking machinery	1,542	7,623	0,910	3,663	3,333	0,632	6,730	4,253	43,72	55,79	-0,49

Table 3 (Continued)

Industries	Scale	Growth GDP	Elasticity Labour	Growth Labour	(3)x(4)	Elasticity Capital	Growth Capital	(6)x(7)	SOURCES OF GROWTH		
									Labour % (5)÷(2)	Capital % (8)÷(2)	Ignorance % 100-[(5)+(8)]÷(2)
	1	2	3	4	5	6	7	8	9	10	11
63. Special industrial machinery	1,427	6,581	0,775	2,985	2,313	0,652	6,484	4,228	35,15	64,25	0,60
64. Office and accounting machinery	1,542	7,623	0,910	3,663	3,333	0,632	6,730	4,253	43,72	55,79	-0,49
65. Other machinery, non-electric	1,996	13,140	0,908	5,683	5,160	1,088	7,271	7,911	39,27	60,21	0,52
66. Electrical industrial machinery	1,256	10,557	0,791	7,586	6,001	0,465	9,313	4,331	56,84	41,02	2,14
67. Radio and television	1,319	9,103	1,151	6,632	7,633	0,168	8,404	1,412	83,85	15,51	0,64
68. Electrical appliances	1,301	8,900	1,053	6,425	6,766	0,248	8,287	2,055	76,02	23,09	0,89
69. Other electrical apparatus	1,346	8,172	1,130	5,743	6,490	0,216	7,612	1,644	79,42	20,12	0,46
70. Ship building	1,092	9,903	0,721	6,058	4,368	0,371	14,841	5,506	44,11	55,60	0,29
71. Railroad equipment	1,092	9,903	0,721	6,058	4,368	0,371	14,841	5,506	44,11	55,60	0,29
72. Motor vehicles	1,032	7,952	0,877	7,243	6,352	0,155	9,936	1,540	79,88	19,37	0,75
73. Aircraft	1,092	9,903	0,721	6,058	4,368	0,371	14,841	5,506	44,11	55,60	0,29
74. Other transport equipment	1,092	9,903	0,721	6,058	4,368	0,371	14,841	5,506	44,11	55,60	0,29
75. Jewellery	1,093	6,792	0,852	5,365	4,571	0,241	10,487	2,527	67,30	37,21	-4,51
76. Other manufacturing	1,450	6,540	0,534	3,985	2,128	0,916	4,779	4,378	32,54	66,94	0,52
77. Electricity, gas and steam	1,364	6,884	0,787	4,066	3,200	0,577	6,588	3,801	46,48	55,21	-1,69
78. Water	1,364	6,884	0,787	4,066	3,200	0,577	6,588	3,801	46,48	55,21	-1,69
79. Building construction	1,233	5,222	0,816	3,127	2,552	0,417	6,463	2,695	48,87	51,61	-0,48
90. Civil engineering and other construction	0,650	5,319	0,430	6,720	2,890	0,220	12,150	2,673	54,33	50,25	-4,58
81. Wholesale and retail trade	1,385	5,142	0,923	2,770	2,557	0,462	5,312	2,454	49,73	47,72	2,55
82. Catering and accommodation	1,385	5,142	0,923	2,770	2,557	0,462	5,312	2,054	49,73	47,72	2,55
83. Transport and storage	1,704	4,783	1,250	1,915	2,394	0,454	4,824	2,190	50,05	45,79	4,16
84. Communication	1,207	6,133	0,818	3,856	3,154	0,389	7,887	3,068	51,43	50,02	-1,45
85. Financial institutions	0,870	4,355	0,455	5,338	2,429	0,415	4,955	2,056	55,77	47,21	-2,98
86. Real estate	0,870	4,355	0,455	5,338	2,429	0,415	4,955	2,056	55,77	47,21	-2,98
87. Business services	0,870	4,355	0,455	5,338	2,429	0,415	4,955	2,056	55,77	47,21	-2,98
88. Renting and leasing of machinery	0,870	4,355	0,455	5,338	2,429	0,415	4,955	2,056	55,77	47,21	-2,98
89. Health services	0,548	2,850	0,306	3,926	1,201	0,242	6,748	1,633	42,14	57,30	0,56
90. Other services, profit seeking	0,548	2,850	0,306	3,926	1,201	0,242	6,748	1,633	42,14	57,30	0,56
91. Other services, non-profit seeking	0,548	2,850	0,306	3,926	1,201	0,242	6,748	1,633	42,14	57,30	0,56
92. Goods and services not classified	1,226	6,527	0,671	3,643	2,444	0,555	7,298	4,050	37,44	62,05	0,51

The elasticity of labour is generally greater than the elasticity of capital. There are several sectors where the elasticity of labour indicates a situation of "increasing returns to scale" which is fortunate as far as the contribution of these sectors to the output potential of the production structure and the economic growth of a country as a whole is concerned. Only a few production sectors have relatively large elasticities as far as capital formation is concerned.

In most of the sectors of production the annual rates of growth for labour are lower than the annual increases in capital formation. In terms of equation (2–5) this argument implies that the elasticity of labour must be relatively *high* in order to allow labour to be the most important source of growth in output. However, in many of these sectors a relatively large elasticity may be related to a relatively big proportion of skilled and even highly trained manpower. *Vice versa,* in terms of equation (2–5) a relatively low elasticity for labour implies that capital formation is the most important source of growth in output, i.e. sectors of production which use relatively unskilled labour have capital formation as the most important source of growth. These relationships are particularly important in a developing economy such as that of South Africa with a relatively high proportion of unskilled labour with relatively high rates of unemployment amongst these people. An industrial development strategy aimed at increasing the production activities of those sectors of production which need relatively more unskilled labour (i.e. with relatively low elasticity) may be an obvious solution to the structural unemployment problem in South Africa, but it is also clear that such a strategy may be costly in terms of capital formation. *Secondly* a relatively low elasticity for labour formation may also imply that the returns to scale of the industry concerned are relatively low so that the strategy may also be costly in terms of growth in output and the economy as a whole. These conclusions clearly illustrate the conflict which may exist between an economic growth and an employment strategy.[7] In terms of economic growth an industrial development strategy can be developed simply by identifying those sectors with the greatest returns to scale which will include sectors of which either labour or capital may be the most important sources of growth. In this sense the economic growth strategy does not mean that the production structure will be bent towards one which makes more use of unskilled labour but rather towards one which tends to create more human capital through which the unskilled labour force is trained to higher levels of productivity.

Though it is empirically relatively easy to identify those production sectors which will facilitate a relatively unskilled labour or an economic growth strategy, the serious problem of policy instruments for these strategies still remains. At this point it must be noted that the discussion took place in a situation where Say's law is applicable, i.e. in a situation where supply creates its own demand. Policy instruments on the supply side of the economy mainly have to do with labour management and import substitution which recently proved to have become less contributory to relatively high levels of employment, economic growth and are expensive in terms of inflation and the in- and external competitiveness of production output in South Africa. The limited success of these policies is accepted in Europe as a fait accompli and there is a move to the relatively more successful market management or demand-side policies of countries in the Far East.

In order also to facilitate market management policies towards the development of an industrial development strategy in terms of employment and capital formation it is necessary to transform the production function approach followed so far to the demand-side of the production structure. This is an exercise on the frontiers of empirical economics which is by no means fully developed and in which relatively little research has been done so far.

3. Gross Production Functions

On the demand side of the production structure a specific final output is not only a result of the production function of the sectors of production under which it is classified but also the result of several intermediate inputs of which each has its own production function. The problem now is to incorporate these supply-side functions of sectors into a representative final product function on the demand side of the production structure. Samuelson suggested that this final product function(s) can be established through his "Sweeping Theorem on Intermediate Products", i.e.

$$\overline{V}_i = f\ (\overline{K}_i, \overline{L}_i) \qquad ...(2\text{--}22)$$

where $\overline{V}$, $\overline{K}$, $\overline{L}$ are total (direct and indirect) value added, capital and labour formation inputs respectively (Chacholiades, 1978: 221–224). In order to establish the time series of the variables in equation (2–22) for the econometric estimation of these functions an input-output table must be available for each and every year which is represented in the series. Such a situation does not exist in practice and a special approach is needed which can be achieved by the following procedure:

Firstly, by deriving the relevant ratios with the input-output model of Leontief, i.e.

$$\hat{v}_j \cdot (I{-}A)^{-1} \qquad ...(2\text{--}23)$$

$$(\hat{q}_1)_j \cdot \hat{v}_j \cdot (I{-}A)^{-1} \qquad ...(2\text{--}24)$$

$$(\hat{q}_2)_j \cdot \hat{v}_j \cdot (I{-}A)^{-1} \qquad ...(2\text{--}25)$$

where $(I{-}A)^{-1}$, v_j, $(q_1)_j$, $\cdot$ $(q_2)_j$ refer to the Leontief inverse, value added, capital-output and labour-output ratios respectively. The matrices of equation (2–23), (2–24) and (2–25) are identified for purposes of this study as value added, marginal capital and labour formation matrices respectively. The relevant ratios, also known as multipliers in input-output terms, are identified by the column sums of these matrices (O'Connor, 1975: 46–53).

Secondly, the respective capital- and labour-output ratios in equations (2–24) and (2–25) have to be transformed to include the properties of a constant or variable elasticity of substitution and returns to scale in those industries where these properties are applicable. This transformation is achieved in two steps namely,

– by *ceterus paribus* calculating these ratios from the relevant net production function elasticities by working backwards from (2–3) to (2–1), i.e.

$$(2 \cdot \hat{\alpha})_j^{-1} \cdot \hat{v} \cdot (I{-}A)^{-1} \qquad ...(2\text{--}26)$$

$$(2 \cdot \hat{\beta})_j^{-1} \cdot \hat{v}_j \cdot (I{-}A)^{-1} \qquad ...(2\text{--}27)$$

– and, finally by transforming equations (2–24) and (2–25) back again into the relevant production functions as was done initially in equations (2–1) to (2–3). The relevant elasticities are then identified by

$$\{2 \cdot \sum_{i} (2 \cdot \hat{\alpha})_j^{-1} \cdot \hat{v}_j \cdot (I-A)^{-1}\}^{-1} = \overline{\alpha}_j \ (i = j) \qquad \qquad ...(2\text{--}28)$$

$$\{2 \cdot \sum_{i} (2 \cdot \hat{\beta})_j^{-1} \cdot \hat{v}_j \cdot (I-A)^{-1}\}^{-1} = \beta_j \ (i = j) \qquad \qquad ...(2\text{--}29)$$

from which the gross production function can be written as

$$\overline{V}_i = \overline{A}_i \cdot \overline{K}_i{}^{\alpha_i} \cdot \overline{L}_i{}^{\beta_i} \ (i = j) \qquad \qquad ...(2\text{--}30)$$

The respective elasticities in equation (2–30) are the column sums of the marginal capital and labour formation matrices. The returns to scale are the sum of these elasticities whilst the relative intensities of utilisation are the ratios of each elasticity to the total elasticities of the two factors of production.

Thirdly, the sources of growth as shown in equation (2–5) can also be identified for equation (2–30), i.e.

$$r_{\overline{V}_i} = r_{\overline{T}_i} + \overline{\alpha}_j \cdot r_{\overline{K}_i} + \overline{\beta}_j \cdot r_{\overline{L}_i} \ (i = j) \qquad \qquad ...(2\text{--}31)$$

As indicated, time series for total (direct and indirect) value added, labour and capital formation do not exist so that the relevant growth rates for

$$r_{\overline{V}_i}, r_{\overline{K}_i}, \text{ and } r_{\overline{L}_i}$$

cannot be calculated. This places the demand-side analysis of the factors of production in terms of the production function in jeopardy especially when production sectors needed to be identified for increased growth in output in order to accommodate the present structural unemployment problem in South Africa. A selection process of industries which concentrate on relatively low total elasticity of labour in order to accommodate a low skilled labour strategy for industry may therefore easily end up as a strategy which is costly in terms of capital formation and economic growth mainly because recognition was not given to the relative rates of growth in the respective factors of production. This problem can partially be solved by the use of labour and capital formation programming and planning models, though it is still not clear how the relevant growth rates can be calculated.

Fourthly, the transformed marginal capital formation and labour output ratios of equation (2–26) and (2–27) may be used to construct these models, i.e.

$$\overline{V}_i = \hat{v}_j \cdot (I-A)^{-1} \cdot f_i \qquad \qquad ...(2\text{--}32)$$

for the calculation of total value added in terms of final demand (134),

$$\text{Ln } \overline{K}_i = \{2\hat{\alpha})_j^{-1} \cdot \hat{v}_j \ (I-A)^{-1}\} \cdot \text{Ln } \{\hat{v}_j \cdot (I-A)^{-1} \cdot f_i\} \qquad \qquad ...(2\text{--}33)$$

for total marginal capital formation and,

$$\text{Ln } \overline{L}_i = \{ (2\beta)_j^{-1} \cdot \hat{v}_j \ (I-A)^{-1}\} \cdot \text{Ln } \{\hat{v}_j \cdot (I-A)^{-1} \cdot f_i\} \qquad \qquad ...(2\text{--}34)$$

for total marginal labour formation. Due to the interrelationship between labour and capital in the production process the models of equation (2–33) and (2–34) must be simulated simultaneously in order to construct a reasonable indicative labour and capital formation programme. This programme can be developed within the present framework of the Economic Development Programme of South Africa from which a much clearer view can be built as far as capital and labour formation in South Africa are concerned.

The present study was able to identify the relevant elasticities indicated in equation (2–30) and though the study was able to show the importance of equation (2–31) it was not able to build the suggested labour and capital formation models of equation (2–33) and (2–34). The development of these models are very expensive and a task for a team of experts which were not available for this project.

Empirical Results

Table 4 indicates the results of the derived elasticities and the return to scale of the different sectors of industry as calculated by means of equation (2–30). The output of all the sectors were produced at a level of increasing returns to scale. The elasticity of labour is generally greater than that of capital formation. It seems as if the other basic chemical products utilises a highly skilled labour force while capital is also used in a most profitable way. Naturally this seems to be the opposite of what is happening as far as liquor products are concerned.

Table 4

Total (direct and indirect) returns to scale of industries as a whole as well as of the various production factors; normalised quantities in brackets (constant 1975 prices)					
		Returns to scale			
Industries	Industry as a whole	Labour		Capital	
1. Other basic industrial chemicals	3,827	2,487	(1,973)	1,340	(1,866)
2. Synthetic resins and plastics	3,431	2,841	(2,255)	0,590	(0,832)
3. Paints and varnishes	3,024	1,825	(1,448)	1,199	(1,670)
4. Engines and turbines	2,893	1,825	(1,448)	1,068	(1,487)
5. Other chemical products	2,742	1,887	(1,301)	0,855	(0,871)
6. Other plastic products	2,668	1,701	(1,350)	0,967	(1,347)
7. Cocoa and confectionery	2,664	1,684	(1,337)	0,980	(1,365)
8. Non-ferrous basic metals	2,560	1,639	(1,301)	0,921	(1,283)
9. Glass and glass products	2,525	1,805	(1,433)	0,720	(1,003)
10. Other rubber products	2,511	1,748	(1,387)	0,763	(1,063)
11. Metal and woodworking machinery	2,368	1,558	(1,237)	0,810	(1,128)
12. Paper containers	2,358	1,374	(1,090)	0,984	(1,370)
13. Fertilizers and pesticides	2,354	2,075	(1,647)	0,279	(0,389)
14. Bakery products	2,354	1,484	(1,178)	0,870	(1,212)
15. Canning of fruits and vegetables	2,322	1,538	(1,221)	0,784	(1,092)
16. Carpets and rugs	2,290	1,520	(1,206)	0,770	(1,072)
17. Furniture	2,274	1,582	(1,256)	0,692	(0,964)
18. Knitting mills (clothing)	2,260	1,205	(0,753)	1,055	(0,843)
19. Spinning and weaving	2,249	1,577	(1,252)	0,672	(0,936)
20. Animal feeds	2,233	1,174	(0,932)	1,059	(1,475)
21. Medicines	2,209	1,359	(1,079)	0,850	(1,184)
22. Processing of wool and cotton	2,208	1,458	(1,157)	0,750	(1,045)
23. Grain mill products	2,179	1,144	(0,908)	1,035	(1,442)
24. Cosmetic and toilet preparations	2,134	1,116	(0,886)	1,018	(0,418)
25. Tanneries and leather finishing	2,062	1,027	(0,815)	1,035	(1,442)

continued

Table 4 (continued)

Industries	Industry as a whole	Returns to scale Labour		Capital	
26. Footwear	2,071	1,044	(0,829)	1,027	(1,430)
27. Pulp and paper	2,027	1,064	(0,844)	0,963	(1,341)
28. Printing and publishing	2,026	1,174	(0,932)	0,852	(1,187)
29. Structural clay products	1,997	1,071	(0,850)	0,926	(1,290)
30. Pottery, china and earthenware	1,980	1,471	(1,167)	0,509	(0,709)
31. Oils and fat	1,949	1,168	(0,927)	0,781	(1,088)
32. Leather products	1,940	1,075	(0,853)	0,865	(1,205)
33. Tobacco products	1,933	1,171	(0,929)	0,762	(1,061)
34. Hand tools and general hardware	1,922	1,266	(1,005)	0,656	(0,914)
35. Other food	1,850	1,014	(0,805)	0,836	(1,164)
36. Dairy products	1,826	0,846	(0,671)	0,980	(1,365)
37. Other pulp and paper articles	1,821	1,362	(1,081)	0,459	(0,639)
38. Other knitting mills	1,815	1,174	(0,932)	0,641	(0,893)
39. Canning of fish	1,814	1,217	(0,966)	0,597	(0,831)
40. Soft drinks	1,806	1,232	(0,978)	0,574	(0,799)
41. Agricultural machinery	1,794	1,462	(1,160)	0,332	(0,462)
42. Other manufacturing	1,773	0,808	(0,641)	0,965	(1,344)
43. Iron and steel basic industries	1,767	1,416	(1,124)	0,351	(0,489)
44. Cement	1,739	1,008	(0,800)	0,731	(1,018)
45. Distilling and wine industries	1,722	1,114	(0,884)	0,608	(0,847)
46. Other textiles	1,720	0,906	(0,719)	0,814	(1,134)
47. Wood and wood products	1,711	0,994	(0,789)	0,717	(0,999)
48. Other non-metallic minerals	1,703	1,160	(0,920)	0,543	(0,756)
49. Motor vehicles	1,700	1,359	(1,079)	0,341	(0,475)
50. Cordage, rope and twine	1,690	0,847	(0,672)	0,843	(1,174)
51. Other metal products	1,679	1,111	(0,882)	0,568	(0,791)
52. Other transport equipment	1,677	1,147	(0,910)	0,520	(0,724)
53. Radio and television	1,649	1,389	(1,102)	0,260	(0,362)
54. Other electrical apparatus	1,663	1,312	(1,041)	0,351	(0,489)
55. Railroad equipment	1,662	1,214	(0,963)	0,448	(0,624)
56. Sugar	1,634	1,048	(0,832)	0,586	(0,816)
57. Structural metal products	1,631	1,160	(0,921)	0,471	(0,656)
58. Processing of meat	1,564	0,836	(0,663)	0,728	(1,014)
59. Other machinery, non-electric	1,545	0,965	(0,766)	0,580	(0,808)
60. Wearing apparel	1,544	0,949	(0,753)	0,605	(0,843)
61. Electrical industrial machinery	1,502	0,984	(0,781)	0,518	(0,721)
62. Made-up textile goods	1,500	0,803	(0,637)	0,697	(0,971)
63. Special industrial machinery	1,469	0,963	(0,764)	0,506	(0,705)
64. Ship building	1,409	0,940	(0,746)	0,469	(0,653)
65. Jewellery	1,384	0,945	(0,750)	0,439	(0,611)
66. Aircraft	1,333	0,879	(0,698)	0,454	(0,632)
67. Furniture and fixtures of metal	1,308	0,741	(0,692)	0,567	(0,964)
68. Electrical appliances	1,275	0,960	(0,762)	0,315	(0,439)
69. Tyres and tubes	1,054	0,582	(0,462)	0,472	(0,657)
70. Malt liquors and malt	1,046	0,426	(0,338)	0,620	(0,864)

Source: Industrial Development Corporation of South Africa.

4. Limitations

The limitations of this study are those which relate to the marginal production theory as well as the limitations of the interindustry model of Leontief in general. Firstly, this study accepts a situation of perfect competition in all the production sectors at a level of full capacity whilst no provision has been made in those sectors where over-employment may exist due to social considerations. Secondly, the transformation of the net production functions to gross production functions is a static one for a particular moment in time, that is, factors of substitution are not taken into account, whilst production output is seen to be homogeneous which are the assumptions made by the Leontief model and which is of course an abstraction from reality. The results of this study are therefore purely indicative and must be used with the greatest possible care.

5. Conclusion

This study indicates that the identification of an industrial development strategy in terms of the need for, and utilisation of, labour and capital is a very complicated issue. On the supply side the use of the net neo-classical production functions seem, with a few exceptions, to be of great help. On the demand side or in terms of a product basis, the gross production functions can be identified with the aid of Samuelson's "Sweeping Theorem on Intermediate Products". In practice, however, the calculation of these functions is an exercise on the frontiers of empirical economics. Though the elasticities of these functions can be derived with the input-output model of Leontief, the relevant total (direct and indirect) rates of growth in output, labour and capital formation are still unknown so that the sources of growth cannot be established. This places the identification of production sectors in terms of final demand for an industrial development strategy in question unless specific efforts are being made to use the suggested labour and capital formation models. In South Africa these models can be constructed within the framework of the country's Economic Development Programme.

Notes
The authors are particularly indebted to the Industrial Development Corporation of South Africa for financial assistance as well as Prof. G. L. de Wet, University of Pretoria, and Dr. D. Mullins, Central Economic Advisory Services, for useful suggestions.
[1]   The Harrod-Domar model for economic growth may be seen as an example of this statement.
[2]   This statement will also be empirically proved in Table 1.
[3]   See for example the work of Denison in this regard (Denison, 1967).
[4]   As indicated in paragraph 2.1.
[5]   See for example Kennedy and Thirwall on a survey in this regard (Kennedy, 1972: 11–73).
[6]   Madison who studied twenty two developing countries over the period 1950–1965 estimated labour as a source of growth at approximately 35 per cent and capital at about 55 per cent leaving a residual of 10 per cent (Thirwall, 1978: 67).
[7]   See for example Stewart I. in Streeten P. (Streeten, 1972, 321–346) for an excellent discussion on this matter.

References

Arrow K. J., Chenery H. B., Minhas B. S. and Solow R. M. (1961): "Capital-labour Substitution and Economic Efficiency", Review of Economics and Statistics, 43, 225–250.

Bulmer-Thomas V. (1982): "Input-output Analysis in Developing Countries: Sources, Methods and Applications", New York, John Wiley and Sons Ltd.

Cℓ.choliades M. (1978) : "International Trade Theory and Policy" New York, McGraw-Hill Co.

Christensen L. R., Jorgenson D. W. and Lau L. J. (1973) : "Transcendental Logarithmic Production Frontiers", Review of Economics and Statistics, 55, 28–45.

Cobb C. W. and Douglas P. H. (1928), "A Theory of Production", American Economic Review, 18 (Supplement), 139–165.

Denison E. (1967), "Why Growth Rates Differ: Post War Experience in Nine Western Countries", Washington, Brookings Institution.

Grilliches Z. and Ringstadt V. (1971): "Economies of Scale and the Form of the Production Function", Amsterdam, North Holland Publishing Co.

Kmenta J. (1967): "An Estimation of the C.E.S. Production Function", International Economic Review, 8, 180–189.

Mayes D. G. (1981): "Applications of Econometrics" London, Prentice Hall International.

Nelson R. R. (1965): "The C.E.S. Production Function and Economic Growth Projections", Review of Economics and Statistics, 47, 326–328.

O'Connor R. and Henry E. W. (1975): "Input-output Analysis and its Applications", London, Charles Griffin and Co. Ltd.

Kennedy M. C. and Thirwall A.P. (1972): "Technical Change: a Survey", Economic Journal, 82, 11–73.

Streeten P. (1972): "The Frontiers of Development Studies", London, The Macmillan Press Ltd.

Thirwall A. P. (1978): "Growth and Development with Special Reference to Developing Economies", London, Macmillan Press Ltd.

Yotopoulos P. A. and Nugent J.B. (1976): "Economics of Development: Empirical Investigations" London, Harper and Row Publishers.

RSA (1984): "Verslag van die Studiegroep oor Strategie vir Nywerheidsontwikkeling", Pretoria, Government Printers.

The Effect of Labourintensive Production on Progress

The Influence on the Human Factor and Psychological Implications
A South African Perspective

by Geert L. de Wet

1. Definitions

There are two concepts which must be clarified before one can determine whether policies directed towards increased labour intensity will deter progress or not.

It is not that these concepts are new or unknown. It is in fact because they are so well-known that one needs to state in what sense one is using them, because different people have different ideas about the meaning of a move towards labour intensity and by progress.

It is indeed difficult to define progress exactly, although we all have a general idea what the word means. In this paper we will in the first place talk about progress as being an increase in the number of people who earn an income, with the understanding that each's income is high enough to enable him to buy enough goods and services to survive.

Of course, the question immediately arises whether this is good enough[1]. Should income be high enough to survive, or should it be high enough to ensure some minimum standard of living? Where should this minimum be and who should determine it? Otherwise stated, according to what norm should this standard be determined? Will even this be high enough? Surely, the quality of life in a broader sense is also important. This means that the internal as well as external working conditions are to be taken into account. The internal working conditions refer to what is normally understood under the concept "working conditions", namely the direct conditions under which the day to day work is carried out. The external working conditions refer to the environment in which the worker finds himself. It comprises housing, natural surroundings, availability of services, the quality of these services, access to markets where goods and services can be bought, alternative employment possibilities etc. In short, it entails the entire life of the worker outside his employment. Apart from the opportunity to work, we will have to look into the internal as well as the external working conditions when determining what the effect of a move towards labour intensity on progress will be.

Under labourintensive production we generally understand that labour is used in abundance, relative to capital. Yet, the question arises where one crosses the line. What should be the ratio of labour to capital before one defines a production prosess as labour intensive? This is a most difficult question to answer.

In fact, for the purpose of this paper, this question will be evaded and we will refer to a process in which more labour is used, irrespective of what the dividing ratio is or should be. We will, therefore, refer to increased labour intensity, rather than to labour intensiveness.

2. A Point of Reference

The production process can be represented by the production function, showing how inputs combine to deliver outputs:

$$Q = Q(L,K)$$

when Q = total output

L = total labour employed

K = total capital employed (physical quantity).

The value of total production is found by multiplying the total physical output by the average price,

Value of output = pQ.

Labour's share in the value of total output is represented by

$$\frac{wL}{pQ}$$

where w is the average wage per worker.

Likewise, capital's share in the value of total output is represented by

rk/pQ

where r is the average cost of capital.

As a matter of identity, it must be that

wL + rK = pQ.

The direct aim of any move towards increased labour intensity is to increase L relative to K, that is to increase the ratio L/K. There must, of course, be a definite motivation for such a move.

Certainly, any deliberate move towards an increased use of labour, must imply an abundant source of unemployed labour. In other words, structural unemployment must exist. Such structural unemployment may be the result of wages being too high, relative to the cost of capital, as one may typically find in a developed economy, or the result of disguised unemployment coming to the surface in a developing economy.

3. The modus operandi of Increased Labour Intensive Production and the Probable Immediate Risks Attached to it

In a planned economy, the central planners would simply select from the available technology a technique of production which will use more labour than before.

They have the choice of using less, the same, or more capital than before, depending on the ability to generate new capital in a short period of time at a rate faster than the normal rate of depreciation. If it is possible to accumulate new capital rapidly, the need for more labour intensive production methods does not really exist. We will concentrate, therefore, on the case where the central planners are unable or unwilling to accumulate new capital at a sufficient pace and are compelled to work with the same or even a slowly declining stock of capital. For analytical purposes, we can work with the case where the stock of capital remains unchanged. The central planners then move from

$$Q_1 \quad = \quad Q_1(L_1, K)$$
$$\text{to} \quad Q_2 \quad = \quad Q_2(L_2, K)$$
$$L_2 \quad > \quad L_1.$$

Let us assume that the share of capital in production is also distributed amongst the labourers, since we include management, supervisors and/or highly skilled labour in L. The real income per capita is therefore equal to Q/L. The first interesting question is now whether Q_2/L_2 is smaller, equal to or greater than Q_1/L_1.

If we have $Q_2/L_2 > Q_1/L_1$, there is no problem and the move has been worthwhile. There is a possibility, however, of

$$Q_2/L_2 < Q_1/L_1.$$

In this case the question arises whether the change towards increased labour intensity has been worthwhile. Of course, even if the unemployed workers are left unemployed, one will still have to feed them.

The real question therefore is, if L_2 also denotes the total of labour available, whether

$$Q_2/L_2 > Q_1/L_2.$$

If this is indeed the case, it is certainly better to move towards more labour intensive production methods. Yet, one has to admit that although it is probable that $Q_2 > Q_1$, it is also possible that $Q_2 < Q_1$, in which case it will at a first glance be better to leave part of the labour force unemployed. Such a possibility arises if the change in production technique decreases the average productivity of labour significantly, which is not inconceivable. In fact, it is quite possible that the increase in the number of labourers, given the stock of capital, may reduce the average performance of all the workers, unless great care is taken by the supervisors or "management"[2]. The absence of a profit motive may increase this possibility even more.

In this case, where $Q_2/L_2 < Q_1/L_2$, we are now left with the subjective question whether it is in the general interest to have some people unemployed and care for them through the proceeds of the employed at a higher average real income, or have them participate in production at a lower average real income. One clearly has to compare the negative psychological effects of being unemployed, to the negative effect of seeing average real income dropping. From a pure output point of view there is clearly no choice, but from a broader social point of view the choice may become very difficult.

The question whether progress has been achieved becomes rather ambiguous. Productivity and the role of everyone involved in the average output per worker, is a very important factor when increased labourintensive production methods are considered.

The problems attached to increased labour intensity may be equally pressing in a market economy. Whether the structural unemployment is the result of labour having become relatively expensive for reasons other than its relative scarcity or whether it is the result of disguised unemployment being revealed in a developing sector of the economy as is typically the case in dualistic economic systems, there is but one way to persuade the market to use labour more intensively – labour must become relatively cheaper.

In a market economy, the share of capital will not be distributed evenly amongst the labourers. In fact, only a small portion of the wider labour force, namely the entrepreneurs, will receive the share of capital. We need to slightly redefine the production function to read

$$Q \quad = \quad Q(L,E,K)$$
where E denotes entrepreneurship.

Let L_1 and L_2 once again denote the amount of labour used before and after the increase in labour intensity, and Q_1 and Q_2 the corresponding output levels. Since we operate in a market economy, Q_2 must be greater or equal to Q_1, if we assume the price level to remain constant at p, or the change will not be considered at all.

In fact, the market will simply not sanction the change. The initial share of labour in total output will be w_1L_1/pQ_1. The unemployed labour, L_2-L_1 may, of course, receive assistance from the government through taxing the initial share of labour, capital and entrepreneurship.

Taxation itself may be counterproductive in a market economy, leading to a steady decrease in total output as resistance against a high tax burden grows. Initially this may lead to even higher tax rates as the government attempts to force the collection of the resources necessary to finance its collective programme. At some or other stage, the vicious circle of increasing tax rates and declining output will become evident. Quite apart from other considerations, this may itself be a driving force to bring about more labour intensive production methods. Yet, even if tax rates are reduced so that the incentive to increase production exists once again, the use of increased labour intensive production techniques can be effected in a market economy only if relative wages decline. Thus we need, if r and p remain unchanged, $w_2 < w_1$.

It may be that $\dfrac{w_2L_2}{pQ_2}$ is greater than $\dfrac{w_1L_1}{pQ_1}$

or it may not be the case. This will be determined by the relevant elasticities. However, whether the aggregate share of labour in the value of total output increases or decreases, is really irrelevant.

As stated above, the share *per labourer* or the per capita income of labour, will have decreased, since this is the only way to increase the number of labourers employed in a market economy, given the stock of capital and given the approximate level of output. This is where the difficulty starts. In a smoothly adjusting market, competition amongst labourers will bring about the necessary decline in the wage rate. Yet, the very existence of structural unemployment implies that market failures already exist, so that the necessary decline in the wage rate will not materialize automatically. This may be the result of trade union or other employee-organisation pressure, or it may be the result of the existence of a dualistic economy, imperfect knowledge and broad social pressures in the form of minimum wage levels, irrespective of labour productivity. Whilst more labour intensive production methods may not be coming forth, the pressure for the more intensive use of labour at *unchanged* or even higher wages, will certainly create all sorts of conflict, pressure and even unrest. The producers may respond by using even less labour intensive production methods as a means of evading the growing labour and social unrest. Labour will almost certainly respond by becoming more aggressive and more demanding. In the end a government may be forced to intervene by either directly undertaking the production of private goods and services or indirectly undertaking such production through some or other agency at various levels. These agencies may be local governments or so-called public corporations. Functionally such action incorporates elements of central planning into the economy.

The fact, however, that labour was in the first instance not productive enough relative to its wage rate, to be automatically employed through the market mechanism, spells trouble for the results of such government action on progress. The average productivity of labour will certainly decline, consequent to the introduction of labour with a low marginal productivity.

This means that Q_2/L_2 will be lower than Q_1/L_1. Yet, since the average wage rate will be the same, or even higher because of broad social pressures, profit levels will come under pressure and inflationary tendencies will emerge. Even if profit levels are not entirely maintained, some increase in the general price level will almost certainly materialize as profit levels are at least partially maintained. The only way in which this can be prevented, will be if the monetary authority allows no increase in the money supply at all. Yet, normally this will technically and politically be difficult to achieve[3], whilst the circumstances under which increased labour intensity is forced onto a market economy, will make monetary discipline politically even more difficult. We are thus faced with

$$\frac{w_1 L_2}{p_2 Q_2} \qquad \text{as compared to} \qquad \frac{w_1 L_1}{p_1 Q_1}.$$

Since $Q_2/L_2 < Q_1/L_1$, it follows that

$$\frac{L_2}{Q_2} > \frac{L_1}{Q_1} \qquad \text{so that} \qquad \frac{w_1 L_2}{p_2 Q_2} \qquad \frac{w_1 L_1}{p_1 Q_1}$$

is sufficiently higher than p_1.

So long as pressure exists to keep increasing the number of labourers employed at the same or higher wages, a tendency for prices to increase will also exist. This is nothing more than the inflationary wage-price spiral at work. The exact consequences of inflation are difficult to predict. It is generally accepted, however, that continued inflation will in the end retard progress. In fact, apart from the ultimate negative effect it may have on real output, it will certainly have very serious effects on the general psychological climate in the economy. Real investment, real durable consumption and savings will directly be impeded because of the gradual decline in confidence in the stability of the system. Labour as a group and business as a group will become increasingly more anxious and aggressive. It will almost certainly spill over into political instability in some or other way.

4. The indirect Results of a Drive Towards Increased Labour Intensity

From the argument in the previous section, it should be clear that increased labour intensive production methods will most probably be forced onto the economy. The very need to consider such policies will never arise in a smoothly operating market economy, since the necessary marginal wage reductions will take place continuously. Yet, in either a centrally planned economy or a market economy with market failures, the central planners or the government is likely to step in and attempt to force it down. The likely effect on progress is ambiguous. More labour will be employed and this may have a positive psychological effect insofar as it is psychologically preferable to be employed. Yet, a decline in average productivity is bound to take place and this will mean a decline in average per capita income for the previously employed workers, which may affect them psychologically negative.

In a centrally planned economy the result will be more or less immediate. In a market economy where it is forced down onto the economy on account of market failures, the decrease in average per capita income may temporarily be avoided through an artificial resistance to a decline in relative wages. Yet, inflation will set in and force the necessary wage adjustment to occur. The broader psychological effects of inflation are uncertain, but will undoubtedly be in the negative spectrum of possibilities.

Let us now explore the indirect effects of increased labour intensive methods of production, especially when it is taking place on a large scale and a significant number of people are involved. These effects relate to the external environment. Since the drive towards increased labour intensity is likely to be a forced one, it is highly unlikely that adequate attention will be paid to these external factors before they take on threatening proportions and the negative effect on society becomes dangerous. However, even in a smoothly operating market, these developments will often not be avoided since they usually occur outside the market. This will probably be the case anywhere, but I will analyse it according to my own observations in South Africa.

Housing and living conditions

A primary cause of any pressure to increase the labour intensity of production, is found in the surfacing of disguised unemployment as an economy or part thereof gradually develops. Rapid urbanization usually follows as the unemployed leave the developing areas and seek work in the developed areas, which are found in and around the big metropolitan areas.

Such influx takes place in an uncoordinated way and the people involved have to find their own accommodation. This they find in some instances with relatives who are already employed and settled. Yet, in the majority of cases the people have no fixed accomodation and they simply start to squat in unoccupied open areas. This may cause tension in the community as the old inhabitants of the area may simply not like an accumulation of squatters on their doorsteps. This tension, intensified by whatever countersteps the government may take, will have negative psychological effects on the old inhabitants as well as on the newcomers. However, the squatters will certainly suffer other more serious negative effects. Slum townships, devoid of even the most basic of services develop out of the squatting. The self-respect of the people living in these areas must necessarily suffer. They moved from an underdeveloped economy, but an economy in which they fitted into a definite social and economic order. In the slum areas they find themselves uprooted in an unstructured society and they become aware of their poverty. Although the majority of them may still retain their integrity, the circumstances favour the development of social decline and criminal tendencies amongst at least a minority of the people. In an ordered society such elements can be dealt with effectively, but it is very difficult to do this in slum townships. In many instances the resistance from the side of the inhabitants who are already residing in the vicinity, as well as from the local or other form of government, prohibit a rapid upgrading of the new squatter camps. Invariably there will initially be attempts to remove the squatters, before the situation is eventually accepted.

Even then it will still take time before an active upgrading of the new township is started. The whole process may take years. People who are in the first place not trained to work in the world they have entered, find themselves in an external environment which dampens their self-respect and in the end their productivity as well. Instead of progress, we find mass poverty, aggravated by the inflationary tendencies referred to in the previous section.

The demonstration effect

The unemployed from the developing sector, whose presence sparks off the pressure for increased labour intensive production and who are mostly living in poor conditions in squatter camps, suffer also from the demonstration effect. They are living in a new world where they see the results of development. They see the high material living standards of the well-to-do. They see the wide variety of consumer goods which are offered on the market. They must, without any doubt, aspire to share in these fruits of a developed economy. Yet, they must be terribly frustrated because they cannot. Many of them can't find jobs. Those who do, find the real value of their wages eroded by inflation. The psychological impact of this situation may easily lead to political revolt, through the ballot if they have the vote and if they do not have the vote, possibly in a violent manner. Attempts to redistribute income through taxes and subsidies, will most probably lower the work incentives of the wealthy producers.

In the end, the living standards of the poor will not increase substantially, since the high taxes set in motion a process which results in higher inflation. Eventually even subsidies will not improve their situation rapidly enough to overcome their negative psychological experiences. In fact, subsidization itself may be to the psychological detriment of the subsidized themselves. The only way in which these people can really be helped, will be through a process which increases their marginal and average productivity. When this happens, increased labour intensive production can actually increase the per capita availability of consumer goods and in this way a real increase in the standard of living will come about.

Inadequate training and educational facilities

In order to increase the marginal and average productivity of labour, it will be necessary, at the very least, to increase their level of skill. This, of course, may not be enough. Management also needs to readjust in order to increase the productivity of labour. However, the level of skill of labour is a primary factor. The situation which demands an increase in their level of skill, will unfortunately probably not help much towards achieving it. As is the case with housing, training and educational facilities are simply not provided when the unemployed move from the developing to the developed areas. The same attitude which initially causes the community to deplore their arrival, will retard the provision of schooling, training and other educational facilities.

Even if no resistance is present in the developed areas towards accepting the new people, communities are simply not geared to provide the necessary infrastructure to increase the level of skill of the newcomers. One usually finds a long time lag before the need is identified, because the influx of people does not take place in one big move. The need grows gradually and even if it is gracefully acknowledged, social programmes need to be rebudgeted and restructured. It is not very easy to train grownups, especially if they have no or very little formal school background. To be most effective, one has to start with pre-school children. Yet, they live in poor external circumstances and grow up in houses where an atmosphere of illiteracy reigns and few or no educational stimuli exist[4]. Increasing the level of skill of developing people remains technically a difficult and slow process. In the meantime the pressure to employ the newcomers increases, productivity declines and progress suffers.

Working conditions: transport

It is difficult to say generally what will happen to working conditions in the workplace. In modern times these may not be of too low a standard. Yet, one aspect of working conditions which often tend to be depressive, is the transport situation. The squatter camps which gradually turn into slum townships are often rather far removed from the places where the people eventually find work. The transport system will definitely be of a kind not tailormade for the convenience of the newly arrived job seekers.

They will be faced by long distances to be travelled when commuting from their living places to their places of work and back. It will mean long hours on trains and buses, people having to get up as early as four o'clock in the morning and getting back as late as ten or even eleven o'clock at night. Apart from the long distances, the transport facilities are often hopelessly overcrowded. This also lengthens the time spent on the commuting system. Employers are often not aware of this situation. In the meantime someone who is psychologically already rather insecure, finds himself engaged in only three activities, work, commuting and sleep. He spends only a few hours during the night at home, and spends almost as many hours travelling to and from his job as he spends at his job. To spend almost one's entire year in this way may be fine enough for the highly skilled workaholic in a top management position. He does it by his own choice. It is, however, an unpleasant experience for the unskilled worker who is forced to do it without much of a choice, simply because he lacks the level of skill to be able to escape this vicious circle.

This depressing vicious circle of sleep – commute – work, forced upon people because of long distances and poor transport facilities is fortunately not always present. There are instances where the distances are not so long or where factories and other businesses are erected near the newly-sprung townships. In other instances, as is the case, for example, with the mining companies in South Africa, good housing is provided at the place of work. However, when people find themselves squatting in places far from their jobs, and many people are in this unfortunate position, the experience must be extremely demoralizing.

It must, without any doubt affect their productivity and motivation rather negatively.

The final effects

The move towards increased labour intensive production methods results economically in a low-productivity-high-inflation environment. Socially it may easily create circumstances regarding the external living conditions of the workers which are psychologically degrading. Movement from the developing sector in a dualistic economy is especially likely to produce these results. This will eventually also affect those who are not immediately involved. The broad social and political system will come under pressure as all forms of unrest start to breed out. People living in such degrading circumstances are in the first place likely to become dissatisfied with the socio-political structure in view of the demonstration effect. Around them they view people who are living in quite different circumstances. They aspire to move into that world, so closely nearby, but the vicious circle of low productivity and a low level of skill, prevents them from doing so. Apart from their own natural reaction to the situation, they become targets of all sorts of groups and cranks who want to change the system for their own purposes. The end result may very well be no progress at all!

The conditions and situation described and analysed above, refer to the situation when disguised unemployment is revealed in a dualistic economy and the pressure for increased labour intensive production methods in the developed sector mounts.

The same pattern will probably be discernable in an already developed economy, where structural unemployment resulted from too aggressive actions on the part of trade unions and other employee-organisations. The intensity of the resulting poverty may not be as strong as is the case in a dualistic economy, but the direction of influence on the human mind will be the same. The probability that in the end we will see very little progress is still very high.

5.   What Action to take?

The question arises whether any move towards increased labour intensity should be resisted because it seems to be doomed at any rate? The answer is certainly in the negative. Whenever structural unemployment exists, something must be done. In a developed economy, action is necessary because the political influence of the unemployment will be dangerous. In a dualistic non-western type system, the immediate political influence of the unemployed may not be pressing, but in the end the developing unrest and general dissatisfaction will also force action upon the community. In the end the moral question remains whether a society can tolerate mass unemployment from an ethical point of view. Even if the unemployed are subsidized through welfare programmes, it is unlikely that the economy will be able to carry the unemployed indefinitely. Thus, something will have to be done.

The best alternative would, of course, be for wages to be flexible, so that surplus labour will automatically be employed through adjustments in the market mechanism. Yet, whether the market mechanism does the trick or whether active policy has to be employed to increase the labour intensity, the problems regarding the external living conditions of the unemployed are likely to be present. Simply providing work through increased labour intensive production methods will not automatically mean progress. As was shown above, through the external circumstances it may very well retard progress and even breed revolutionary tendencies. Increased labour intensity may affect the worker psychologically positively insofar as he benefits from having a job. However, care will have to be taken that the negative psychological effects flowing from the external circumstances described above, do not completely outweigh any positive effects.

6.   The South African Experience

South Africa entered the 1950's as still a relatively quiet agricultural-mining country, although the secondary industry had already started to increase in importance after World War I. However, in the period 1947–1951, agriculture and mining still accounted for 28 per cent of total economic activity and agriculture alone constituted 17 per cent of total production. Yet, towards the middle of the 1960's, the relative share of these two primary producing sectors in total production had declined to 23 per cent, that of agriculture alone had declined to 11 per cent, whilst manufacturing already accounted for 21 per cent of total production[5].

This change reflected the industrial revolution which took place in the first two decades after World War II in South Africa[6]. In this same period and largely the result of the same forces of development, the underdeveloped rural areas in South Africa were opened up. Disguised unemployment surfaced and a huge influx of people from the developing sector of the economy towards the developed metropolitan areas started to take place[7]. At first attempts were made to check the flow of people from the developing to the developed areas, through a policy of so-called border industries. The South African government deliberately attempted to create employment opportunities on the borders of the so-called homelands by an active policy of decentralization of especially the growing secondary industry. However, this policy had limited relative success. Although impressive industrial complexes were established at the borders of the homelands, which also constitute the borders between the developed and the developing areas in South Africa, the employment seekers were many more than the number of jobs created. Thus, the influx into the developed sector continued[8].

It is interesting to observe that ways and means were sought all along to implement increased labour intensive production methods. In the meantime a large number of people moved from the developing homelands into the developed metropolitan areas. Huge new townships sprang up, like Soweto near Johannesburg and Guguleto near Cape Town. In fact the older cities in South Africa are today surrounded by so-called Black Townships. They all sprang up as squatter camps and sleeping quarters. Only since the midseventies, after the Soweto unrests, have attempts been made to upgrade the conditions in these townships, through, for example, the establishment of the Urban Foundation by the private sector.

The need and pressure for increased labour intensive production methods increased, but since the beginning of the 1970's the trade union movement has started to gain momentum. Black trade unions were legalized at the same time that active steps were taken to narrow the so-called wage gap between wages earned by Whites and those by Blacks[9]. This did not help towards increasing the labour intensity of production. In fact, a steady move towards increased capital intensity has since taken place. At the beginning of 1987 the unemployment rate amongst Blacks, the people who moved from the developing to the developed areas, amounted to 18 per cent of the total Black population [10].

Conditions in the growing Black townships were uninspiring. Many people commuted over long distances, whilst basic services in many of these townships have only recently been provided. Until the 1970's the official policy had been that these townships were of a temporary nature only and that they would vanish once the flow of people were redirected towards the homelands. Formal school facilities for the Blacks were until very recently almost non-existent in the developed areas, except in the case of private schools and schools run by church groups. These, however, catered for only a small number [11]. The vicious circle of poverty, a low skilled level and low productivity leading to an unsuccessful attempt at increased labour intensity is vividly illustrated by this history.

The official approach has changed over recent years. Apprenticeships were recently opened to Blacks and vigorous attempts are made to increase the formal educational facilities. However, the backlog is so big and financial cost is so high, that it will take a long time to put these people on the educational level which one would normally expect to find in a developed economy[12].

The permanency of their presence was recently recognized when influx control was abandoned in 1986 with the scrapping of the infamous pass laws. However, restrictions on the economic ability of Blacks, such as the group areas act, still remain in force, although it is generally accepted that this will also be abandoned in the near future.

In the meantime the poor living conditions which many Blacks experience, their formal educational disadvantage and the growing unemployment figure, together with political restrictions, have helped to create a situation in which unrest has reached such proportions that special, extremely unpopular emergency measures are needed to maintain law and order[13].

From an economic point of view, the lesson is clear. Employee-organisations did not assist in making wages flexible enough so as to bring about a smooth movement towards increased labour intensive production methods. Resistance against the influx of people from the developing areas was incorporated into a formal policy of racial segregation. This retarded the natural development of economic ability and capacity amongst the unemployed moving from the developing areas to the developed sector. Consequently, their productivity did not increase enough to render labour intensive production methods profitable. External living conditions were poor. Instead of economic progress, the average real rate of growth in South Africa declined ever since the beginning of the 1970's whilst political and social unrest mounted. This, of course, threatens to retard progress even further.

Notes

[1]   Jones B, *Sleepers, Wake! Technology and the future of work,* Wheatsheaf books, Brighton, 1982, p.150.

[2]   Ibid., p.152.

[3]   De Wet GL, *Monetary control as seen by the De Kock Commission: an assessment,* South African Journal of Economics, Vol 54, No 1, Maart 1986.

[4]   De Wet A, *Learning disabilities in pre-school children,* Unpublished M-thesis, Medunsa, Pretoria, 1986.

[5]   South African Statistics 1968, Buro of Statistics, Pretoria, p.13.

[6]   Stadler JJ, *Some aspects of the changing structure of the South African Economy since World War II,* South African Statistics 1968, Buro of Statistics, Pretoria, p.7.

[7]   *Focus on Key Economic Issues,* Mercabank, Johannesburg, Nr. 9, *The Homelands,* July 1974 and Nr 19, *Urban Blacks,* Nov 1977.

[8]   Ibid.

[9]   Departement van Mannekragbenutting, *Verslag van die Kommissie van Ondersoek na Arbeidswetgewing,* Staatsdrukker, Pretoria, 1979–1981.

[10] *Focus on Key Economic Issues,* Mercabank, Johannesburg, Nr 40, *The Influence of political reform on the economy,* May 1987.

[11] Ibid., Nr 27, *Employment through Education,* November

      1980.

[12] Ibid., Nr 40, *The influence of political reform on the economy,* May 1987.

[13] Ibid.

The Development of Economic
Thought in the Economic Culture of South Africa

by N. J. Schoeman

1. Introduction

Generally speaking, economic culture includes the sum total of attitudes and values of the society towards economic affairs. These attitudes and values result from peoples' philosophy of life and is at the same time subject to the influence of ideological propaganda. Within a society, different ideological views and philosophies can exist simultaneously. This is merely the result of the divergent and sometimes contradictory economic motives of the society or parts thereof. Therefore different economic cultures can exist within the borders of the same country. In this process they are influenced by each other with the result that as long as these dynamics continue, economic perspectives will be subject to change.

The history of these changes constitutes an important key to the nature of the South African economic system, which indeed is characterized by its plurality, in that different cultural groups exist and participate in the economic process. Each of these cultures represents a variety of languages, social relations, politics and religions. In effect all of these find expression in different economic philosophies and contribute to the economic results of the system. The three main cultural groups that will be dealt with are the Afrikaners, the English and the Africans.

Subsequently an effort will be made to project the most likely outcome of the development of economic thought in South Africa.

2. Heterogeneity of the Cultural Society in South Africa

The Afrikaner Culture

Basically the Afrikaner is regarded as an extension of western civilization and in that context has his roots in the classical Greek, Roman and Jewish civilizations. The Cape of Good Hope, a Netherlands colony founded in 1652, was populated by a Dutch speaking community. They were confronted by a bare and hostile continent where none of the familiar infrastructure existed. Their numbers were supplemented by the French Hugenots who arrived in South Africa in 1688. However, the economic history during the first century and a half is no flattering description of the evolution of the Afrikaner culture. In comparison with settlements elsewhere in the world during the same period, a striking shortage of economic dynamics existed in the Cape Colony.

The population was too small to develop its own cultural dynamics away from the homeland. From an economic point of view the situation deteriorated. During the nineteenth century the economic culture of the Afrikaner did not improve substantially. The main economic activity comprised farming, but with few developed markets, poor technology, a shortage of capital and insufficient infrastructure, harvests were used mainly to feed the cattle, whilst surpluses were used in barter trade. After the invasion of the Cape Colony by the British, a large number of colonists left and moved northwards in an effort to obtain political freedom and probably also better land for their farming activities.

Increasingly they fell prey to cultural starvation which gradually resulted in an unaware-
ness of the cultural dynamics of the outside world.

However, the exploitation of South Africa's rich mineral resources (especially diamonds
and gold) which started in the second half of the previous century, caused a dramatic
about turn, not only in the economy, but also in the political and spiritual lives of the Afrikaner people. Europeans flooded the country in an attempt to share in the newly dis-
covered richess. Cities shot up all over the previously deserted highveld areas. Markets for agricultural products were established and the demand for unskilled mine workers in both diamond and gold mines grew.

Initially the Afrikaner was totally isolated from the financial benefits of the economic revolution which had been taking place overseas. Neither economic motives nor principles
were developed such as to enable the Afrikaner to reap the benefits of the changing society. However, it was not long before the prosperity of the rest of the white population
became such a challenge to the Afrikaner that a vast number left their agricultural activities in the rural areas and migrated to the urban areas.

History reveals that this was a bitter experience for most Afrikaner families, resulting in
serious poverty and loss of self-esteem. They were merely objects and not subjects taking part in the economic system of the time. An average low level of education and lack
of experience in a dynamic economy contributed to the fact that they were employed
as unskilled workers with consequent low wages and salaries.

Nevertheless, despite the poor conditions prevalent amongst the urban Afrikaner the
migration from rural areas increased steadily. The Afrikaner had one immaterial, but
very meaningful asset left, namely his religion. The Dutch Reformed Church took the
lead in establishing a number of organizations to improve the socio-economic conditions of their parishioners. Much attention was paid to the improvement of educational
and training facilities in order to make the Afrikaner more competitive and self-respect-
ing. The Afrikaner soon realized that his only chance of survival was to save himself
from being destroyed culturally and of being absorbed totally in the cosmopolitan urban
society, dominated by the British and Jewish cultures.

Eventually this development programme began to bear fruit. Although the majority of
Afrikaners diverted to the public sector, a number of them managed to make in-roads
into the business world and gave good account of themselves. Due to their traditional
attitude towards the importance of savings and their conservative economic lifestyle,
huge amounts of savings were mobilized towards Afrikaner dominated institutions such
as banks, building societies and insurance companies. These then provided in the financial needs of prospective Afrikaner property owners and entrepreneurs, thus contributing to their economic ability.

Due to their numerical dominance in white politics, the Afrikaner played an important
role in the structuring of a political system in South Africa. Their main aim was to insure
political freedom for all cultural groups and the infamous policy of separate development developed as a main instrument in this respect, although it is presently being dis-
mantled. The Afrikaner is still acknowledged as one of the most influential cultural
groups on the South African scene.

Although a great deal of the entrepreneurial functions are still in the hands of other white
groups such as the English and the Jewish oommunities, the Afrikaner is acknowledged
as a respectable partner and a most capable employee. In many cases management
has been taken over by the Afrikaner. The Afrikaners' experience during the past cen-

tury contributed to their being absorbed into and becoming indispensable participants in a sophisticated and dynamic South African economic society.

The English Culture

The increase of the English South African population resulted from the second British conquest of the Cape Province in 1806. However, the largest increase occurred after the opening of diamond and gold mines, especially after the second Anglo-Boer war. A large group of British immigrants, the 1820 settlers, occupied land on the eastern border of the Cape Colony serving as a buffer between the black population on the eastern side of the country and the rest of the Cape Colony with its administrative centre in Cape Town.

However, most of them soon realized that the South African climate with its severe periods of drought and heat together with attacks from black tribes who raided their cattle and plundered their harvests, did not permit much success in the agricultural sector. Eventually more than two-thirds of them migrated to urban areas where their entrepreneurial skills and managerial qualities were in high demand. Soon most of the economic activities were solely in the hands of the English, supplemented by a considerable number of Jews and also a few other nationalities such as Germans, Poles and Dutch.

In the towns and cities the predominantly English population maintained the traditions of the European economic culture. However, adaptions had to be made continuously, in order to comply with the lack of economic infrastructure and the different environment. Their social aspirations were not focussed upon the South African soil, though. England remained their home country and they preferred to be governed by the political structures of their homeland.

Nevertheless, they created an economic environment based upon mining, industrial production and the provision of services within a fairly sophisticated market economy highly integrated in foreign trade. This economy differed largely from the rural agricultural economy where Afrikaners were the main participants augmented by large numbers of black employees on their farms. Although no functional clash occurred between these two economic systems, the Afrikaner economy was too stagnant to meet the growing needs of the population.

The outcome of the latter form of dualism inevitably led to a drastic change in the economic motives and principles according to which the Afrikaners acted. During the first half of the twentieth century the spending pattern in South Africa was determined mainly by British norms of consumption and capital formation. The pattern of household expenditure on food, clothes, sports, etc., was also British. Furthermore, the principles of law governing production and trade, as well as the establishment of labour unions, chambers of commerce, public finance and monetary policy were also gained from the British system.

No doubt the motives and principles of the economic system in South Africa were substantially influenced by the British economic culture. By the time the British immigrants came to South Africa, Britain was well-known for its economic liberalism, individual freedom and trust in technical progress. Today these lines of thought serve as the cornerstone of the development of a new social and economic order in South Africa.

The African Culture

The African culture in South Africa, as in the rest of Africa, has always been characterized by a traditional economic system directed at subsistence and therefore only the provision of basic needs. In spite of 300 years of contact with western cultural groups the situation has remained unchanged for a large part of the African community. One possible important explanatory factor in this regard, is the fact that the black population in South Africa comprises nine different language groups which in turn entail an even greater number of various sub-cultures, differing with regard to economic motives and principles. This phenomenon can be attributed to a number of social, economical and political factors of which the following four may be regarded as rather important:

1.   Although the African languages are rich in figurative speech, they admit a few possibilities for quantifying economic ideas. This makes it difficult to reason and calculate in modern economic style.

2.   Religion plays an important role in cultural activities, with many African people still believing in the existence of ancestral spirits, which supposedly rule their daily lives and whose traditions they ought to obey. They are ill at ease with any form of economic activity which differs from the traditional lifestyle. Rational thought and the objectivity which is necessary for the proper functioning of a dynamic economic system are consequently often still largely dormant.

3.   The third important barrier in the way of black economic development has traditionally been their attitude towards labour. Whilst the men were responsible for the herding of cattle, women were responsible for cultivating the crops. The fact that black men did not want to work on the sugar plantations in the Natal Province was the main reason for the influx of Asian people from India at the beginning of this century. Today, mines still have to attract a large number of migrant workers from outside the borders of South Africa, because of the negative attitude of South African blacks towards working underground.

4.   The fourth barrier, and by far the most controversial one, is the political structure in South Africa. The past few decades saw increasing urban migration by rural and thus economically underdeveloped Africans. They were lured by expectations of better working conditions, higher wages and therefore a higher standard of living. In fact, the growth which took place in the mainly British and Jewish-owned industrial, mining and trade sectors, depended largely on the availability of cheap and unskilled labour. White people feared that the availability of cheap labour would endanger their jobs. In an attempt to deal with these fears as well as the urbanization problem, new political structures were established which excluded non-white participation. A variety of discriminatory laws and regulations were enforced on the African community. Such laws made provision for influx control, separate residential areas, work reservation and income discrimination against non-white races. Whatever their merits, such discriminatory policies were a major factor inhibiting African's participation in the economic system and the concurrent evolution of economic thought.

Despite these inhibiting factors a strong African society was established gradually in the urban areas. A middle class evolved with a higher degree of education, urban civilization, self-confidence and self-respect. Confronted by westernised economic ethics, their historic cultural ties weakened and their traditional economic principles and motives changed in favour of a more enlightened acceptance of market-orientated principles and motives of rational thought.

An increasing demand for educational facilities exists. Simultaneously, a new group of African leaders emerged who are increasingly involved in a bargaining process, especially via the labour unions, to enlarge the Africans' share in the South African economy. With most of the discriminatory regulations now abolished, the African cultural groups are moving into the European centre of the economy and are contributing to the Africanization of the economic culture in South Africa.

3. Projected Developments in Economic Thought in South Africa

The evolution of economic culture has presently reached a critical stage. Although educating the economic society is by no means completed, all groups are now represented by capable leaders who contribute substantially to economic and political processes in South Africa. It can not be denied that these processes are mutually dependent and highly integrated.

The optimal economic future of South Africa is envisaged as an essentially private and competitive free enterprise system. Therefore it is important that the nature of the existing system does not change radically towards a centrally planned socialist democracy. The present state of political tension causes widespread suspicion of, and opposition to, the prevailing economic system. This antagonism causes vaguely articulated but strongly held support for socialism. The socialistic philosophy is regarded as the logical alternative to the rules of economic behaviour which prevail in South Africa. Socialism is thus seen by many blacks as the true harbinger of economic security, freedom and prosperity.

Had these perceptions amongst Africans been well founded, their entry into the political process would lead to a destructive confrontation between the ideologies of individualism and socialism. This would be aggravated by social differences between the new entrants and the traditional economically active part of the population. Should this happen, African participation in South African politics would become virtually impossible. Only by sharing in the welfare produced by a fairly free economy, will Africans be persuaded to support the principles of a free market and to base their case for the total removal of statutory discrimination on these principles rather than on those of socialism. It seems vitally important to remove the prevalent misunderstanding about the nature of the market versus socialist ideologies. Like the Afrikaner, Africans will eventually realize through their participation in the economic system that market economy is the product of human nature. This implies that the political-economic system patronising market economy is based on a more realistic and consequently superior understanding of human nature. Due to the plurality of the South African society this concept is of utmost importance in the decision making process.

In these special circumstances, it is foreseen that political structures and economic policy which take cognisance of the reality of individualism will give rise to the development of a society in which people will be bound together in voluntary associations, such as trade and industry. In such a society each participant serves his own ends, but in fact all contribute to the improvement of the order which is the unforeseen spontaneous result of individual actions. This view supports a government policy of limited intervention in these spontaneous processes.

In conclusion, it should be mentioned that this process of interaction which started more than 300 years ago is, as will be the eventual outcome thereof, characterised by numerous problems unique to the South Africa situation. In fact, due to their cultural and historical nature, most problems are so unique that they can only be dealt with by South Africans. In this respect, the South African community deserves the support and appreciation of the rest of the world. Ironically, progress regarding the activation of economic moments in the economic world of Africans, is largely underestimated by world opinion. In an attempt to further political objectives, the principles of free enterprise are being placed under suspicion. In the rest of Africa Marxism is the rule rather than the exception. Today it constitutes a real threat to the future of the South African economic system.

Despite apparent international hostility, South Africans today are closer to each other and have mutual understanding of their problems and aspirations. A probably unequalled transformation of economic thought has been taking place amongst the various cultural groups. From an economic point of view one can only hope that South Africans will find the strength to continue with the progress which has been made, despite the growing outcry for economic isolation and political destruction.

References

[1] Assocom "Removal of discrimination against blacks in the political economy of the Republic of South Africa", compiled by Bepa, University of Pretoria, 1985.

[2] Lombard, J. A., "On economic liberalism in South Africa", Bepa economic papers no.1, 1979.

[3] Lombard, J. A. and Stadler, J. J., "The economic system of South Africa", Haum, 1967.

[4] Schoeman, N. J., "The evolvement of economic motives and principles in the culture of the Afrikaner with special reference to secondary education", unpublished thesis, Pretoria, 1980.

3.

Socialist Market Economies – A Third Way?

The Difficulties in Reforming Soviet Type Economies

Red China's new economic policies in the light of Eastern European reform experiences

by Dieter Loesch

Introduction

We in the West are apparently so convinced that our economic and political systems are highly superior to Socialism that any announcement of intended reformatory measures in socialist countries is interpreted as the beginning of a one sided process of convergence. i.e. an approximation of "real existing socialism" to the western market economy and a system of pluralistic democracy. The response in the west to such reform announcements or to the first tentative steps towards reform is often so euphoric and so inspired by wishful thinking that one could gain the impression, that centrally administrated and/or centrally planned socialism no longer exists – neither in Eastern Europe nor in the People's Republic of China.

A. The Chinese reform model: plan-commodity economy

What is true is that China (and the USSR) have introduced policies of economic reform. In China these new policies were implemented between 1979 and 1984. The concept underlying the Chinese reforms was explicitly labelled as *plan-commodity economy* (i.e. a planned economy supplemented by a number of market elements), not as *market socialism* or *socialist market economy.*

The Chinese plan-commodity economy is characterised as a planned economy which utilises the market as an auxiliary factor. The central plan is still regarded as the dominant (system-constitutive) institutional factor of the economic system, whereas the market mechanism is viewed as an instrument which relieves central planners of the burden to work out too many microeconomic target figures, serves as a corrective of erroneous central planning decisions and has positive allocative and stimulative effects.

Nevertheless the market system has gained ground in the Chinese economy. There are markets for consumer goods and services, for agricultural and mineral resources and capital goods. There is even a financial market. Central planning, on the other hand, is now primarily confined to determining the basic proportions and directions of economic development.

B. The neoliberal thesis of instability and suboptimality of mixed economies

In many respects therefore, the Chinese economy can be characterised as a mixed economy, i.e. an economy which is neither a pure planned nor a pure market economy. In neoliberal economic literature such mixed economies are regarded as *instable* and/or *suboptimal* economic systems. *W. Röpke,* for example, stated: „Marktwirtschaft oder Kommandowirtschaft, ein Drittes kann es hier sowenig geben, wie eine Tür nicht anders als offen oder geschlossen sein kann."[1] (Market economy or command economy, another alternative does not exist, just as a door is either open or closed.) And *W.*

Eucken argued that each society or government has to choose between the two alternative systems: market economy and „zentralwirtschaftlicher Lenkung wesentlicher Teile des Wirtschaftsprozesses...“[2] (central administration and control of vital economic processes). The neoliberals are convinced that – as a result of the incompatibility of the two main determinant elements of the system – plan and market – mixed economies have a built-in instability, which brings about tendencies of system transformation towards a centrally administered bureaucratic economy. At the same time the neoliberals contend the suboptimality of mixed economies, e.g. *F. A. Hayek,* who says in his famous book The Road to Serfdom: „Mischungen von Planwirtschaft und Wettbewerbswirtschaft sind schlechter als jede für sich.“[3] (Mixtures of the planned economy and the competitive economy are worse than each of both on its own).

If the neoliberals are right,[4] the present Chinese economic system

–   will sooner or later be transformed whether via a restoration of the old centrally administered economy or via a continuation of reform policies and a further expansion of markets together with a step-by-step reduction of the central planning elements, and

–   will sooner or later prove to be suboptimal by revealing undesired effects on performance.

The neoliberal contentions of suboptimality and instability of a mixed economy primarily refer to market economies with steadily increasing government intervention. The theoretical arguments on which these contentions are based are relatively weak, since although all economies of modern industrialised countries being more or less influenced by government policies no western economy has so far developed into a state socialist system via transformation of the kind described by the neoliberals.

C.   The experiences of decentralisation reforms in the Eastern European socialist countries

Paradoxically, the instability and suboptimality hypothesis relating to mixed economies was corroborated to a greater extent by the reform experiences of socialist countries.

Figure 1 shows (in a very simplified form) the development of the economic systems of the five major Eastern European socialist countries between 1955 and 1985, the sectors 1, 2 and 3 representing the *centrally administrated* Soviet Type Economies (1), the *decentralised or parametric model of socialism* (2) and *market socialism* (3). The curve demonstrates the state of the economic system at a certain date; the crosses symbolise system-immanent corrections. i.e. smaller institutional changes intended to "perfect" („vervollkommnen") the traditional Stalinist system.

The figure makes clear that there are three different types of system development in socialist economies:

(1)   During the 30 years period between 1955 and 1985 the *USSR, GDR and Czechoslovakia* made just one single major effort to decentralise the centrally planned and bureaucratic administered system in the sixties. The reforms initiated in the GDR in 1963 were implemented until the middle of the decade, when restoration of the former Status quo ante already began: by 1970 the main features of the former centralised system had been restored. In the *USSR* decentralisation policies began later (1965) and came to an end earlier. In *Czechoslovakia* the reform period was also very short;

Figure 1

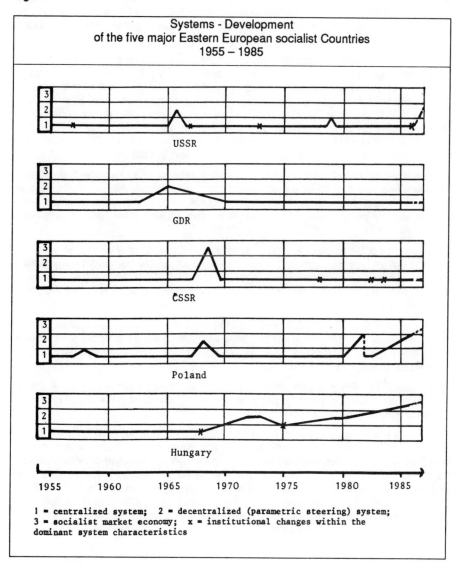

Systems - Development
of the five major Eastern European socialist Countries
1955 – 1985

USSR

GDR

ČSSR

Poland

Hungary

1955   1960   1965   1970   1975   1980   1985

1 = centralized system; 2 = decentralized (parametric steering) system;
3 = socialist market economy; x = institutional changes within the
dominant system characteristics

unlike the aforementioned cases, the CSSR not only set out to achieve a decentralised model of socialism, but went a great deal further within only a few months and opted for market socialism. This was reason enough for the Soviet Union to stop the reform via military intervention.

(2)   In *Poland* two reform attempts failed and the failure of a third is not unlikely. First efforts were already made to reorganise the only recently established Stalinist Soviet Type Economy via decentralisation measures during the late fifties, but without any success. A second reform attempt was made, with the same negative result as in the GDR and the USSR: the anti-reformist trend gathered momentum after only a short period of decentralisation policies. Finally a new attempt at reform was made by Poland in 1980. This was abruptly stopped by the declaration of martial law in December 1982, but continued after its abolition and was still on the way in 1985.

(3)   In *Hungary* the reform started in 1968. The main elements of a decentralised system were implemented up until the beginning of the seventies. After a short phase of stagnation and slight restoration the reform impetus returned; although the parametric system was not yet completed distinct steps towards a socialist market economy have been made, since the beginning of the eighties.

In summary, it is fair to claim that all experiences made up to now with attempts to reform the Soviet Type Economies (i.e. the centrally planned and bureaucratically administered economy) indicate the foundering of the so called reform concept (i.e. the decentralised, parametric steering system). *Empirical evidence, therefore, supports the instability thesis:*

In the cases of the USSR, GDR, and Poland the mixed decentralised system proved to be extremely instable, since conservative elements gained the upper hand after a very short period of its existence and long before it was completely established. *Reform was followed by restoration.*

In the cases of Czechoslovakia and Hungary the reform model proved to be instable in that the reform moved beyond the parametric model of socialism in the direction of market socialism; *the reform was reformed.*

As regards the thesis that decentralised socialism is not only instable but also brings about suboptimal results, empirical evidence is not so clear-cut. For nowhere in Eastern Europe has the reform system worked long enough to allow us to draw conclusions regarding to its performance. In the light of a more detailed analysis, a great deal supports the supposition that the instability of the reform system results from its unsatisfactory performance – more specifically: the undesired side effects of the reforms on the one hand and its scanty and disillusioning efficiency effects on the other.

D.   Is the Chinese plan-commodity system unstable and/or suboptimal?

Let us now return to the case of the *People's Republic of China.* If China also progressed from an economic system which can be characterised as a Soviet Type Economy, there is a high probability that its present plan-commodity (mixed) economy will not bring about the expected positive efficiency results. In the medium term, therefore, it will either be rereformed to bureaucratic socialism or via further expansion of the reform policies really will in fact be transformed to the status of market socialism.

The third possibility is that China will succeed in establishing a stable and efficient mixed economy as it is officially claimed.

The question which attracts our attention during this first part of our conference is:

Which of these projections is the most probable?

In order to find an answer to this question, we have to analyse the reasons for the foundering of the decentralised socialist system in Eastern Europe as well as examine whether conditions in the People's Republic of China differ from those in Eastern European socialist countries to such an extent that we can expect the reform model to be successful there (i.e. stable and efficient) over a longer period of time.

1. The instability of the reform model

Empirical regularities in the past are of no use for projections of future developments if there is no theory explaining the underlying causalities. As previously indicated, the neoliberal arguments for their instability thesis (the so called oilfilm theory) are not convincing, at least not for our problem, when seeking to explain the empirically verifiable instability of the socialist reform model. For they only set out to explain why the installation of non-compatible elements in the framework of capitalist market economies tend to culminate in state controlled systems produced by a vicious circle of cumulative interventions. What is needed, therefore, is an explanatory theory for the empirically proved instability of a decentralised socialist economy.

Figure 2 shows the feedback effects of economic policy measures. There are not only desired (positive) effects but also inevitable undesired (negative) side effects. The success of the adopted economic policies, therefore, depends on

– the adaquacy of the measures to achieve intended goals,

– the degree of counterproductive side effects,

– the time lags between the policy measures and the positive effects on the one hand and the negative effects on the other, and

– the intensity of the intended effects in relation to that of the unwanted effects.

Bearing this in mind we can now define the conditions for successful decentralisation policies in socialist countries as well as the reasons for their failure:

– If the desired outcome is no more than weak and/or only takes effect with a relatively long time lag, whereas

– the undesired side effects are intense and/or come into effect almost immediately,

then the probability that the decentralisation policies will be dropped or at least changed as a result of these feedbacks is very high, particularly if the support for reform within government circles, relevant interest groups and the population as a whole has only been weak.

Figure 2

The Feedback Effects of economic policy Measures

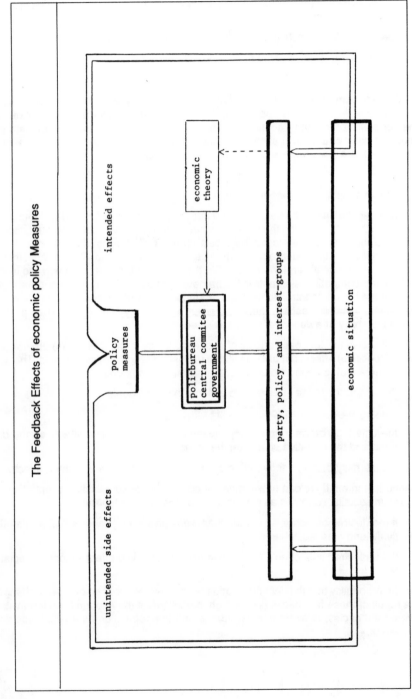

intended effects

economic
theory

policy
measures

politbureau
central commitee
government

party, policy- and interest-groups

economic situation

unintended side effects

2.   Reform and efficiency of the economy

The experiences Eastern European socialist countries have made with reforms have provided empirical proof that "decentralisation", i.e. the creation of a so called parametric steering system, does indeed not cure the lack of efficiency of socialist economies – at least not in due time. In some cases, therefore, the long time lag between the implementation of decentralisation reforms and their efficiency effects, may explain why reforms were interrupted before they could lead to the desired results.

But why is this time lag so long? Or is the time lag problem not the crucial aspect? Are other reasons for the inappropriateness of decentralisation when trying to improve the efficiency of the socialist economy more significant? If this question is analysed at a more theoretical level it can be shown that the desired results of reforms do not arise as a result of inconsistencies of the economic system during the reform period. Due to the interdependencies of the subsystems of the economic mechanism, changes within the sphere of one of these subsystems necessarily have effects on others, which may cause undesired if not disastrous results in these spheres. (The liberalisation of the price control system, for example, may lead to inflation!) Moreover if partial reforms are not sufficiently coordinated it is possible that the reform as a whole will not work at all. A good example for this is that in most of the Eastern European countries the introduction of the system of economic accounting (khozraschet) and of profit as a main economic indicator for firms was not followed in time by reforms in the area of price formation and price control – which meant that the wider scope for independent decisions for managers did not alter their unsatisfactory market-orientation.

Apart from the problem of coordinating and timing partial reform measures, the supposition can not be rejected that the concept of decentralised socialism suffers from a fundamental inconsistency: namely between planning and the market, albeit not of the kind the neoliberals believed. Planning and market are by no means incompatible if their spheres are clearly separated. But it is precisely this clear separation of the market and of planning spheres which is lacking in the concept of decentralised socialism, since this concept is based on the belief "that the extension of the role of the market must be paralleled by the strengthening of central control to prevent the worst features of the market mechanism from raising their ugly heads"[5]. In the reform concept, therefore, the elements of central control and of market incentives to decision making at the micro-level of the economy necessarily interfere with each other in such a way that the inefficiency of the traditional planned economy is at best somewhat offset by the reform system.

3.   The contradiction between efficiency and equity[6]

Where for these reasons the desired and expected efficiency effects of the decentralisation policies will usually only be poor, there are also unwanted but inevitable side effects. These result from the fundamental "dilemma of socialism", namely the contradiction between the efficiency conditions of the economy on the one hand and the realisation of main socialist welfare (or equity-)goals, based on the ethical principles of solidarity and security, on the other (see figure 3).

114

Figure 3

Contradictions within the socialist Results-Behavior-Structure Matrix

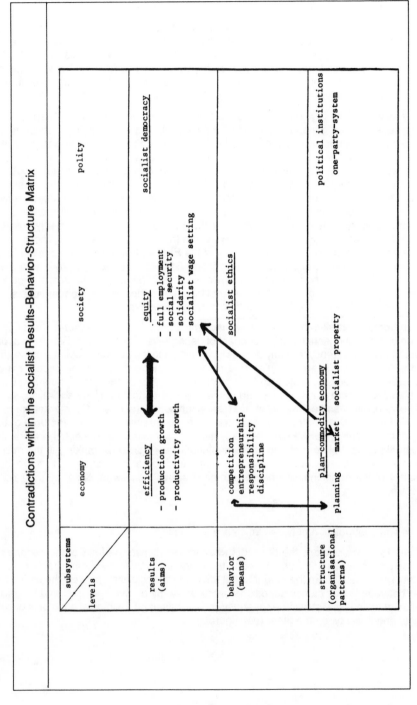

It was Janos *Kornai,* a Hungarian economist, who clearly pointed out this dilemma. His line of argument in a brief[7]:

For efficiency reasons the economy needs

–   an incentive system "which stimulates better performance from all individuals participating in production";

–   "there must be fast and flexible adjustment to the current situation and external conditions";

–   "non-efficient production activities must be terminated";

–   "decision-makers must display entrepreneurship through their initiative, disposition for innovation, and risk-taking"...

These conditions for efficiency inevitably conflict with the following equity goals:

–   full employment (no fear of unemployment)

–   social security

–   solidarity (instead of competition)

–   socialist wage-setting ("to everybody according to his labour" and "equal pay for equal work").

One could add another socialist principle, not mentioned by *Kornai:*

–   equal distribution of income.

It can easily be demonstrated, how these efficiency criteria clash with the equity goals of socialism. For example, we know from our own experience how exaggeratedly far reaching social security measures have disincentive effects on economic effort of individuals; or, if unprofitable firms do not run the risk of bankruptcy, managers are not forced to economise on inputs (including labour) in order to produce at the highest possible quality standard, innovate products or production technology etc.

It follows from this conflict between equity and efficiency, that decentralisation reforms which really create efficiency maximising institutional structures inevitably cause "negative side effects in the sphere of equity": furthermore, it is to be expected that most of these side effects (e.g. unemployment) will precede the improvement of standard of living via higher efficiency of the economic system.

All this leads to the following *conclusion:* Even if reforms are successful in the economic sphere, the associated counterproductive effects in the sphere of social policies are likely to cause restorative policies; the *instability argument* proves to be valid. Or, in response to the first effects on equity goals, the government introduces further reforms to eliminate the obvious defects of the new system. These corrections may be successful in the social sphere but have adverse effects on efficiency; this corroborates the suboptimality thesis, particularly if permanent change of the not yet established institutional framework generates too much uncertainty.

Let us now come back to our initial question: Is the Chinese plan-commodity economy an unstable and/or suboptimal system?

–   Chinese reforms seem to have brought about rather impressive efficiency effects, especially with regard to the growth of production in agriculture, but also of industrial production and exports. However, these effects are neither spectacular in an international comparison nor with regard to the success stories of former growth periods of the Chinese economy (if these are at all true!).

– What is more, inflation increased considerably, the national currency was severely devaluated and foreign exchange reserves decreased, whereas there was a substantial increase in foreign indebtedness.

– In the sphere of equity goals income differentiation as well as corruption, have increased considerably.

Notwithstanding the increasing number of critics and the growing opposition to the present system which comes from both the conservative as well as from the progressive sides (the one preferring restoration and the other further decentralisation) the ruling elites seem to be determined to adhere to the plan-commodity system.

Conclusions (Theses for the discussion)

(1)   At first glance the Chinese reform system has up to now been relatively stable; changes in the short or medium term seem very unlikely.

(2)   This, however, should by no means be regarded as a falsification of the instability/suboptimality argument; it should be recalled that the reform started in 1979 and was only completed about three years ago.

(3)   The main reason for the relative stability of the Chinese reform system (compared with former reform experiences of socialist countries) is undoubtedly the adherence of the leadership to the reform course and the fact that China still seems to have a much more totalitarian political system than all Eastern European socialist countries (at least since the XX. party congress of the CPSU).

(4)   In view of this strong and rigid political system and the Chinese hierarchical tradition it seems very unlikely that China will set out along the road to market socialism.

(5)   On the other hand, the longer the present system continues to exist the more unlikely becomes restoration of bureaucratic socialism. But what then? I personally believe, that in the medium term China will neither experience further major reforms of its economic system nor record spectacular economic success. Smaller changes in both directions – further reform as well as restoration of bureaucratic elements – will constantly take place. So paradoxically the present Chinese system will perhaps prove as well relatively stable (i.e. that the plan-commodity system will not be replaced neither by a return to the bureaucratic model nor by market socialism) as unstable (i.e. that within the framework of the present system experiments will go on).

Notes

[1] Wilhelm Roepke: Civitas humana, Grundfragen der Gesellschafts- und Wirtschaftsreform, Geneva 1946, p. 281;

ibid.: Die natürliche Ordnung. Die neue Phase der wirtschaftspolitischen Diskussion. In: Kyklos, Vol. 2 (1948), p. 212.

[2] Walter Eucken: Die Wettbewerbsordnung und ihre Verwirklichung, p. 22.

[3] Friedrich A. von Hayek: Der Weg zur Knechtschaft, Munich 1971, p.3.

[4] Cf. Wilhelm Roepke: Die Gesellschaftskrise der Gegenwart, 4th ed., Erlenbach, Zurich 1942, pp. 260; Alfred Mueller-Armack: Wirtschaftslenkung und Marktwirtschaft, Hamburg 1947, pp. 76. – Kritisch hierzu (aber in Form der These von der „Dominanz der Teilordnungen" zustimmend) Egon Tuchtfeldt: Zur Frage der Systemkonformität wirtschaftspolitischer Maßnahmen. In: Zur Grundlegung wirtschaftspolitischer Konzeptionen, edited by Hans Jürgen Seraphim: Schriften des Vereins für Socialpolitik. N.F. Vol. 18, pp. 203, especially pp. 223; Josua Werner: Probleme einer gemischten Wirtschaftsordnung. In: Zeitschrift für die gesamte Sozialwissen-schaft, Vol. 117 (1961), pp. 39.

[5] I. Wilczynski: The Economics of Socialism, 4th ed., London 1982, p. 27.

[6] Jonas Kornai: The Dilemmas of a Socialist Economy: The Hungarian Experience, Dublin 1979.

[7] Ibid.: p. 4.

Development and Problems of Reform
in the Chinese Economic System

by Rolf Dittmar

1.   Three years after the death of Mao Tse-tung (1976), the Chinese leadership introduced a policy of opening up the country, and this had, when compared internationally,
unique effects in the country's domestic, foreign and economic policy; at a time when
the world economy was still recovering from the adjustment process caused by the second oil crisis, it guided the Chinese economy into a long-term upswing.

In the area of *domestic policy* – compared with the previous state of affairs – there has
been a considerable *liberalisation* over the last ten years.

As regards *foreign policy,* since the end of the seventies development has been marked
by efforts to improve relations *with basically all countries.* Precedence was given here
firstly – due to economic considerations – to the Western industrialised countries. Since
about 1984 a readiness to open up to the socialist countries as well has manifested itself. The guiding thrust of the foreign policy is *independence from foreign powers.* This
requires that a certain distance is maintained towards the imperial superpowers of the
USA and the USSR; as far as Japan is concerned, the problems of the bilateral past
still make themselves felt and cause a sceptical attitude despite – or perhaps because
of – the intensive economic relations.

Economically the People's Republic of China has enjoyed a period of persistent upswing since the beginning of the 1980s, on average resulting in a real growth over the
last six years of the order of 10 percent p.a. The standard of living of the population has
since risen to a previously unknown degree – more than the growth rates of the economy as a whole would lead one to expect. In particular, the sharp rise in food production to the beginning of the 1980s and the great stress laid in 1980/81 on the "readjustment" of the economy, which shifted the emphasis from heavy to light industry, have
brought with them a marked improvement in the supply of consumer goods.

In addition, the supply, especially in the cities, has been improved by imported goods.

It is remarkable that the upswing in the Chinese economy occurred at a time when the
world economy was still recovering from – let alone overcoming – the adjustment processes caused by the second oil crisis.

2.   There are *various* reasons for this generally impressive development in the
Chinese economy. On the one hand, during the ten years of "total chaos" (the cultural
revolution), a considerable *backlog demand* had *accumulated* – accompanied by a *col-
lapse in economic productivity.* On the other hand, China benefited at the beginning of
the 1980s – despite suffering itself from a chronic shortage of available energy – from
its independence from the world energy markets. The current growth is borne by the
internal economy, although it is also fostered by the purchase of modern machinery and
equipment abroad, which has expanded and improved the economic production potential.

3.   Strictly parallel with, and scarcely distinguishable from the policy of opening up,
the reform of the economic system has been underway since the end of the 1970s. This

economic reform is – more often than is appropriate – mentioned as a cause of the positive economic development.

The reform is concentrated in the main on three areas: agriculture, foreign trade and industry.

The earliest area affected was *agriculture.* Since 1979, the collective agricultural system has gradually been replaced by the introduction of the contract system. Individual households are now granted certain areas for use on a lease basis, and the production of certain products is regulated from year to year on a contractual basis. In addition the area for private cultivation has extended. For produce which exceeds the level of production stipulated in the contract, and also for produce from private plots, private farmers' markets are permitted, at which these surpluses can be sold according to market laws. Regarding the prices, the state restricts itself to monitoring abuses.

This "privatisation of agriculture" has taken place on a lease *basis,* and there is still no *private ownership of land.*

The reform of agriculture is now regarded as largely complete. During the first years of the reform in particular, significant rises in productivity could be achieved by mobilising and improving the use of previously idle workers, without any large new investment being necessary. The significant harvest results have largely been achieved without mechanisation, if the substantial increase in the numbers of small tractors in private ownership is disregarded, for these are overwhelmingly used for transport purposes in rural areas.

In the coming years, agricultural production is expected to level out appreciably, as the arable land has decreased and the productivity reserves of idle workers have been substantially taken up. Increases in productivity will be more dependent on new investment in the future than hitherto.

Over and above this, the infrastructure for marketing a further sharp increase in agricultural production is not at present to be found: there are chronic bottle-necks in distributing, storing and processing agricultural produce. These bottle-necks are to be eased through cooperation with abroad.

In the next few years the emphasis on quantitative growth will be shifted to improving the quality of the produce with the aim of exporting more agricultural produce.

The agricultural reform has as a whole improved the situation of the approx. 800 million workers in the country. Admittedly substantial disparities in the development and distribution of incomes have formed; farmers near towns (the availability of free markets) have particularly been able to achieve a sharp improvement in their income. This brings with it risks for the further development of the social climate.

In the *foreign economy* sphere the situation has changed decisively in that trade with foreign countries is today given an active role in the expansion of the domestic economy, whereas before imports had a "bit part" (only what was regarded as absolutely necessary and could not be manufactured on the domestic market was imported, and all that was exported was what was necessary to pay for the imports). As a consequence of the new foreign trade policy, links have since been built up on the foreign trade front, although the incorporation of the Chinese economy into the world economy is still only in its initial phase.

At the beginning of the 1980s a clear decentralisation of the foreign trade apparatus was undertaken. Those foreign trade organisations responsible for individual areas of industry and goods increased their field of operation at regional level by a further development of their network of branches in the provinces. At the same time, *decision making* in business was moved to provincial or municipal level. In addition, the number of associations and enterprises permitted to engage in foreign trade has increased considerably.

This development had the advantage that the Chinese foreign trade potential could clearly be better exploited by extending the available possibilities for engaging in foreign trade. What was negative was the fact that this development, especially in 1984/85, resulted in a strongly unfavourable Chinese trade balance, because goods were imported, largely without the coordination and control of the centre, for regional prestige projects, and also in near-consumption areas, which had not been agreed with the centre (e.g. building up fleets of taxis, which were subsequently used inefficiently). This also led to measures towards a partial recentralisation of foreign trade being introduced during 1984. 1987 has shown another trade surplus, so that now more will be purchased abroad again.

One important new element in the shaping of foreign trade relations was the decision taken at the end of the 1970s to permit foreign investment in the form of joint ventures. In connection with this, one should mention the setting up of special economic zones within the territory of the People's Republic of China (so far there are four in the southeast of the country), through which predominantly foreign capital and technology is to be brought into the country with the aim of producing exportable goods.

The core of the reform policy in the coming years will be *industrial reform* (because of the concentration of industry in the cities, this is also known as the "city reform"). This refers to a decision by the 3rd plenum of the XII CC of 20.10.84 and was only introduced in its essential form in 1985. As a precursor to the industrial reform, trials were carried out in selected firms, at first in the Sichuan province (at the beginning of the 80s), and in the following years these were extended to a total of approx. 100,000 firms (c. 1/4 of Chinese state companies).

In the early 1980s a *readjustment* of the economy preceded the industrial reform, shifting the emphasis from heavy to light industry. The result of this restructuring has been that since 1982 agriculture, heavy industry and light industry contribute to the national product of the People's Republic of China in roughly the same proportions.

The reform is based on two *principal decisions:* the first of these is a greater decentralisation of *decision-making powers.* The authority to make and implement decisions is shifted from the centre to the provinces and cities and also the firms. It is true that the principle of central planning is to remain, but the provinces do receive more opportunities to take part in the input phase and are involved in the execution of plans to a greater extent. For executing regional projects the decision-making powers at the decentralised level are extended. According to the other principal decision, the economy is divided up into three sectors on the basis of the planned economy, and they are subject to planning to varying extents:

–   The key economic areas (particularly energy and raw materials, heavy industry, especially the armament industry, and basic foodstuffs) remain subject to mandatory planning; prices here are fixed by the state.

- The large part of light industrial production, and especially consumer goods, is subject to planning by directives, which allow some flexibility both regarding the quantities and quality produced as well as the price, within a fixed limit.

- In the case of services regarded as having lower priority, small-scale business and also the industrial production of high value consumer goods (so-called luxury items), the market takes on the main guiding function.

4. The *main features* of the industrial entrepreneurial reform are:

Reinforcing the independence and entrepreneurial responsibility. "Breaking the iron rice bowl" must have the consequence for the enterprises that they themselves bear the responsibility for their own performance.

Delegation of responsibility within enterprises has been minimal up till now. On the one hand, practically all enterprise matters were directed from above, i.e. from outside, and on the other there has previously been no hierarchy within the enterprise to make clear what responsibility each worker has (including disciplinary possibilities). In additon, work modes were determined by the influence of the party secretary in each enterprise, and he received his instructions via party channels.

A major element of industrial reform is the introduction of *performance-related pay.* It is true that the roots of this were formed a few years back; a start was made in the introduction of performance-related bonus payments at the beginning of the 1980s. However, these payments soon came to be treated more and more as a fixed part of the wage packet and were paid out to practically every worker – irrespective of his performance. The payment of actual performance-related premiums in industry remains insignificant at present.

With regard particularly to the intended reinforcement of enterprises' responsibility, *reform of the price system* is becoming increasingly urgent. The large majority of prices has so far been set without any relation to cost and profit margins, and has partly been linked with considerable subsidies. Free pricing has so far existed only in a few areas (small-scale businesses, free markets: although, this pricing is not totally free, as on the one hand, as a result of fixed prices which do not bear a relation to costs, the actual costs do not enter into the price-setting process as input, and on the other there exists the possibility of abuse monitoring by the state.) The price reform should help dismantle the subsidies.

A key factor in the success of an enterprise determining its own operations would be a *market oriented system.* Beyond market- and performance-related pay, this requires that the enterprise can itself determine the hiring and firing of workers. The first steps have been taken in this direction. Since the whole social security system, including housing, is linked to the enterprises, far-reaching changes are only likely in the long term. New appointments have generally been made on the basis of fixed-term contracts since last year. This would therefore complete the breaking of the iron rice bowl.

In the course of the reform of the tax on businesses, the existing assessment system is to be replaced by a tax imposed on enterprises, which leaves post-tax profits largely to the discretion of the enterprises. Previously all profits had to be handed over to the state, which then sanctioned financial allocations for investment by the enterprise.

The further expansion of the banking and financial system is of key importance, less specifically for the industrial reform than for the development and modernisation of the economy. The banks will be involved to a greater extent than hitherto in financing the construction of the economy. For this, alongside a further specialisation, a quantitative and qualitative rise in banking services is required. The state monetary and financial policy is faced above all with the task – which has become increasingly difficult – of maintaining a course aimed at stability, whilst ensuring a structural and regional financial burden-sharing corresponding to the demands which have changed due to shifts in authority.

A central point of the economic policy, and therefore at the same time an important factor in the industrial reform, has been and remains the need further to ease the economic bottle-necks in energy, transport and communications.

5. Problems of the economic reform: evaluation

The economic situation of the last five years and the sharp rise in the standard of living in the Chinese population has popularised the government's policy of opening up. The necessary basis of trust in the population for further reforms has been created.

Problems inherent in the system arise when an attempt is made to *link together elements of the planned and market economies.* Where the planned economic system is retained in principle, market rules can only effect those individual sectors opened up by the state for this purpose, and even here only to a limited extent, because the links with the overall plan which remain in force place restrictions on room for manoeuvre available within the market. This holds true for example for the supply of raw materials and spare parts.

The *decentralisation of the economy,* so important for the reform policy, *sometimes* has *negative* effects, because due to the lack of an efficient information and communications system the centre is often no longer in a position to coordinate and monitor economic decisions.

There has so far been no comprehensive ruling on sharing the state income between the central administration and the provinces.

The reform of the *price system* has scarcely made any progress, and – as a result of the recent student unrest – it is to be further spun out. Whilst it is indispensible, the introduction of cost-based prices will lead to price rises, which can again unleash additional inflationary tendencies.

In order to strengthen the foreign trade side, the legal preconditions for foreign capital investment in the People's Republic of China were further improved recently by the 22 point programme of October 1986, with the aim of strengthening a persistent import of capital. The limits to the involvement of foreign firms in the People's Republic of China are set less by the legal framework conditions than by the actual way the joint ventures fit in to the system of the planned economy. It is doubtful whether improving the legal framework conditions alone will have sufficient effect.

With regard to an evaluation of *further growth possibilities* in the Chinese economy, *aspects of the economic reform are only partly relevant.* There is still room for efficient use of manpower, so that with the assistance of individual incentives and organisational changes even without the integral application of a market economy system, large reserves of productivity can be opened up. To this extent the achievement of the strategic aim (quadrupling global economic output by the year 2000) seems, given the fact that demand in the Chinese population is unlikely to be met, quite possible.

In conclusion one can say that the People's Republic of China is one of the few developing countries introducing its reforms whilst keeping the realities clearly in view. Bold decisions, such as making the People's Bank of China a central bank, will be a step towards macroeconomic management of the economy. Previous results show that this releases the growth potential which has opened up a path for China towards a greater integration in the world economy.

China: Trade and the Drive to Modernization

by Richard L. Brinkman

It is somewhat ironic that "Although Communism is essentially international, early Socialist and Communist writers neglected the theory of foreign trade. Marx, Engels and later Lenin dwelt on the political aspects of trade between nations, but they did not attempt any rigorous analysis of the economic principles underlying international trade." [Wilczynski (1965): 67]. Foreign trade per se was viewed a vehicle for foreign domination. Foreign trade was a means for exploiting others or being exploited by them and, consequently, to be avoided as policy. The historic experience of the Soviet Union's and China's low trade over income (T/Y ratio) percentage was not only a function of their large size as nations but was also evidently a function of deliberate policy.

The lack of applying the logic of the science of economics to the problems of trade might be attributed to Mao's allegedly admitted layman's knowledge in this area.[1] It should also be noted that in the earlier phase of Mao's development he sought Western ideas and philosophy but ultimately chose rejection based in part on the West's penchant for colonialism and exploitation. Marx was introduced to Mao and China as a result of the Russian Revolution of 1917[2]. With the victory of the People's Liberation Army in 1949 and independence there developed, uncharacteristically for China, an external dependency directed toward the Soviet Marxian model. This turn of events, which generated an illusion of a monolithic and permanent structure, was unexpectedly short-lived.[3]

After a period of retrenchment, parochialism and intensified institutional crumbling, China has emerged with a more cosmopolitan and open policy. This is manifest in the innovation of a more eclectic and practical implementation of the Marxian matrix. We now find an extraordinary reversal of policy in China oriented toward the introduction of a matrix of Marx plus the market. To some this might all be viewed as extraordinary in the sense of the unexpected. In this article, however, we will argue that such a course of events might be considered very much predictable and can be based upon the logic inherent in the long–term processes of economic development and culture evolution.

Our position is not deterministic. That is we do not subscribe to the view that certain given conditions will inevitably give rise to certain preconceived ends. But rather that given the logic and theory inherent in the processes of economic development and culture evolution that certain procedures and policy ought to take place. And that what is now taking place in China is consistent with a continuity of the ongoing processes of economic evolution. The Chinese Revolution really constitutes a manifestation of a specific culture's drive to modernization. Events of twentieth century China constitute the institutional crumbling of antiquated feudal traditions to make way for the modern era characterized by industrialism. We speak here of increasing economic capacity to the level contained in modern economic growth. The focus of our discussion will be directed on a general level, to the interrelation of the processes of culture evolution and economic development. From this perspective the main problem in China's drive to modernization resides in the area of social organization and the need for institutional adjustment. The problem of institutional adjustment relates to making China's culture permeable to modern science and technology consistent with the historical goals and values of that culture.

Such an adjustment can not be conceived for China in isolation. Though big in many ways, China is not an island unto itself. Given that China contains as a nation the world's largest population and ranks sixth in overall GNP, such a large economic entity cannot be ignored and viewed apart from a global perspective. As China pursues modernization along with a concomitant policy of trade expansion, there is bound to be a significant impact upon other nations of the global community. Though of obvious significance, this paper is not primarily concerned with the effect of China's trade expansion on other nations.[4] But rather we are concerned primarily with analysis and theory relevant to showing how trade expansion will serve to ameliorate the forces of modernization. In order to demonstrate the positive aspects of trade expansion on China's drive to modernization let us first attempt to clarify the meaning of "modernization."[5]

The Scientific Epoch and Modern Economic Growth

Currently economic policy in China appears to be dominated by drive toward the well-known "Four Modernizations" focusing on the areas: 1. Industry; 2. Agriculture; 3. Defense; and, 4. Science and Technology. Apparently this policy direction was originally annunciated by Chou En-lai in 1964 and further reinforced by him in 1975 at the Fourth National People's Congress. In 1978 the "Four Modernizations" were put forward as a program evidently under the leadership of "China's quintessential pragmatist" Deng Xiaoping. Consequently, it might be said that the "...real patron saint of the post-Mao policies was Chou En-lai and the real prime mover pushing for their rapid implementation was Deng.."[6] "Modernization is at the core ... it is the essential condition for solving both our domestic and our external problems ... economic development is primary." [Deng (1983): 225]. But what is meant by "modernization" and "economic development"? And further, what is the process through which these objectives are achieved? To answer such questions we must dip into the empirical record of the historical past.

Prior to World War I industrialization and modernization were confined to the specific cultures of Western civilization. Outside of Japan the process had yet to spread to Asia. The empirical results of modern economic growth have been documented by many. The record of increased productivity, high and sustained rates of economic growth, higher levels of GNP/capita and energy control, reduced illiteracy and increased industrialization, constitute a myriad of benefits. These basic economic results are reasons enough why the less developed country (LDC) world desires modernization, let alone the associated enhanced military and political power. The empirical record as to specifics of statistics and quantification is perhaps subject somewhat to question, but this area is not that much subject to debate. What provides for a broad spectrum of interpretations and debate manifest in a very large literature concerns explanation, causation and theory. From this vast sea of knowledge we will focus primarily on the work of the Nobel laureate, Simon Kuznets. Though thought of more as an empiri-cist, rather then as a theoretician, per se, to our view Kuznets' contributions to theory and explanation are also of great significance and are interrelated to the empirical.[7]

Modern economic growth (MEG) was introduced for the first time during the Industrial Revolution which took place in Great Britain, circa 1750–1850. To Kuznets: "A country's economic growth may be defined as a long-term rise in capacity to supply increasing diverse economic goods to its population..." [Kuznets (1973): 247]. Historically this capacity has been altered and provided for by epochal innovations. The basic innovation of the modern period was that of a science-fed technology [Kuznets (1966): 1–16]. The

Industrial Revolution, characterized by the empirical record of modern economic growth was spawned in the milieu of a scientific epoch. It is debated in the literature as to whether or not craftsmen or scientists served as the primary force behind the nascent technology of the Industrial Revolution.[8] And while to our view evidence appears in support of Kuznets' position of a science-fed technology, the resolution of the issue is really of no import for our purposes for by the end of the nineteenth century, almost all agree that MEG had as its fountainhead science-fed technology.[9]

But why did science as the basis for modern technology prove so dynamic and transform culture with such revolutionary acceleration? How then might one integrate the anthropologists conception of culture with Kuznets' modern economic growth?[10] While not explicit, to our view Kuznets implies in his analysis the useage of the concept of culture, not all of culture but the "core of culture" contained in the technics of economic production and social organization. To Kuznets, MEG is a distinct type of economic growth contained in an epoch characterized by the "...spreading application of science to the processes of production and social organization..." [Kuznets (1966): 487; Eckstein (1977): 231]. And the application of knowledge to the practical ends of production and social organization is also presented in the literature as a conception of technology. To connect such technology to culture we submit that the material and nonmaterial aspects of technology constitute the artifacts and institutions stored by culture. Not all of culture but rather that technology as applied knowledge constitutes the "core of culture."

Homo sapiens in interacting with culture and the physical environment originates new knowledge which when applied appears as a material technic such as the steam engine. But steam engines do not function in isolation of human behavior but rather require concomitants of social organization as social technology. The social institution serving as a concomitant to the steam engine was the factory system. Therefore the production of textiles required a technology as a gestalt of material and nonmaterial parts, as an organic whole. Of importance, in this conception, technology is both social as well as material. But the steam engine and factory system are also integral to the anthropologists (scientific) conception of culture.

Knowledge is consequently Janus-faced and appears on the one hand in its application as technology and in its store as culture. To change one is consequently to change the other. To change technology is also to transform culture in that such technology substantively comprises culture. In the context of the scientific epoch the exponential advance of knowledge is manifest in an accelerated technology which proved revolutionary in the transformation of culture.[11]

Is the concept of economic growth synonymous with that of economic development? If an economy or culture grows does it also develop? While the processes of growth and development are interrelated they are not synonymous. For example, transportation technology has provided humankind with an exponential growth rate as measured in miles per hour. Starting form approximately four miles per hour, as a measure of foot travel, the rise has been exponential to the current level of twenty-thousand miles per hour given the technology of rockets.

The resulting exponential growth curve was not the result of the simple process of growth and replication of a given structure (foot travel) but rather was the result of structural transformation of transportation technology. The developmental process, as technological advance, results in structural changes which enable growth to proceed on an exponential continuum.[12] Foot travel as the given structure of transportation technology places a ceiling or limit on capacity to grow as measured in miles per hour. The high level of growth as measured by twenty-thousand miles per hour was not achieved as a growth process of replicating more and more feet and/or running faster, but rather was the result of a developmental process of transformation.

Concerning culture overall, rather than the specifics of transportation technology, we argue similarly that growth is limited by a given structure of culture in the context of the stages of economic development. Growth as quantitative replication, as more and more bows and arrows, leads no where but ultimately to stagnation. Ongoing growth of a culture (civilization) requires a transformation of one stage of economic development to the next. A culture bound by agriculture and a pre-Newtonian base of science experiences a ceiling on its capacity for economic growth.[13]

Consequently, if China desires modernization, as exemplified by modern economic growth, it must transform its culture, via the process of economic development, to that of industrialism. Industrialism delineates a stage of economic development as one which is dominated by a scientific epoch and characterized by the application of that science to economic production and social organization. The transformation of culture to the stage of modern economic growth is predicated on the innovation of a scientific epoch or by the same token a science-fed technology. Consequently, the direction of the current pragmatic leadership in China is very consistent with the inherent logic of the development process exemplified by Western experience. Deng Xiaoping has stated "The crux of the four modernizations is the mastery of modern science and technology..."[14]

Apparently what is required for China is institutional adjustment at the macro and micro level of social organization to promote culture permeability to modern science and technology. The current problem of China is consequently relegated to the primary area of social organization. But our discussions have been directed to a general theory of the processes of growth and development. How then does international trade serve as a part of the whole and potentially a positive force to promote modernization?

Comparative Advantage: The Statics of Economic Growth

The task before us now is to relate international trade to China's drive to modernization and economic development. Is it correct as J. S. Mill has stated: "The opening of foreign trade ... sometimes works sort of as an industrial revolution in a country whose resources were previously undeveloped..."[15] Historically, British classical and neoclassical economists have focused on international trade and its relation to growth and development. Given the insular nature of the British economy and the relative small size and resource base, it would be predictable and obvious that attention would be directed to the external sector of international trade. "Dominating all the issues" ...the ultimate question"... Can foreign trade have a propulsive role in the development of a country." [Meier (1968): 214,VII]. In addressing this issue let us first look at the matrix of comparative advantage as originally formulated by Torrens and Ricardo. Our analysis will be directed to current neoclassical analytical tools in the framework of general equilibrium theory.

Basically what is traded, and to which trading partner, is determined by relative cost advantages. Though the lawyer (industrial country) has an absolute advantage in both areas of production vis-a-vis the secretary (agricultural country) both the secretary and the lawyer (and by analogy both nations) would be better off through specialization and exchange. As a result of free trade and specialization both countries would be better off, though not necessarily to an equal degree, in terms of increased economic efficiency and total production. Therefore, whether or not either country has an absolute advantage or disadvantage, based upon relative costs, or comparative advantages, there are gains to be derived from trade. Both countries would benefit from specialization, free trade and international exchange.

Submitting this simplistic analogy to nations and then further translating the logic through the implementation of the rigorous analytical tools of neoclassical economics is a relatively simple matter. To the uninitiated, however, analytical tools such as the Edgeworth-box diagram, transformation curves, domestic terms of trade, international terms of trade, reciprocal demand and the Marshallian offer-curve analysis might indeed represent a complexity of abstraction. Given neoclassical methodology, it is easy to get lost among the trees and lose sight of the forest. Nonetheless as we will try to show, the actual conception of the economic process imbedded in neoclassical theory is relatively simple, that is, once one breaks through the barrier of esoteric abstraction. We will now briefly present the salient features of the neoclassical pure theory of trade.[16]

In the paradigm of neoclassical theory, the Bowley-box diagram is used to derive the "efficiency focus" which serves as the basis for a given nation's production possibilities curve. And given the assumption of constant costs the transformation curve provides the basis for the domestic terms of trade. If increasing costs are assumed then the point of tangency of the transformation curve with an indifference curve determines the domestic terms of trade. The domestic terms of trade, as determined between two products such as cloth and wine, become the basis for assessing comparative costs. In this framework the Heckscher-Ohlin model focusing primarily on the quantity of factor inputs serves as the basis for determining each country's relative costs, that is the domestic terms of trade. Underlying the analysis of course are the important assumptions of homogeneous production functions (identical technology and given for all nations), perfect competition, internal mobility and external immobility of the basic factors of production, as well as full-employment of resources.[17]

Up to this point our discussion related to the derivation of the production possibilities curve. Of crucial and basic importance to the framework is the assumption that a shift of the production possibilities curve in an outward direction constitutes economic development. "We can now extend the analysis the development problems by first interpreting a country's development in terms of an outward shift in its production frontier." [Meier (1968): 22,216]. Thus an outward shift of the transformation curve as more and more cotton or wine as increases in real income, constitutes economic development. In a no-trade world, trade assumed to be invariant, such a shifting of the transformation curve is based upon increases in domestic resources or technology. To show the effect of trade, neoclassical trade theory then assumes ceteris paribus that resources and technology are held constant; trade is then introduced as the variable resulting in development. Given the conception of economic development as an outward shift in the production frontier, the challenge is to then demonstrate how trade serves to fulfill this function.

At this point we note that: "the theory of comparative costs is not, of course, a complete theory to explain international trade." [Wilczynski (1965): 63]. In order to explain the derivation of the international terms of trade it is necessary to introduce the concept of reciprocal demand formulated by J. S. Mill and innovated into the literature as the Marshallian-offer-curve analysis. Whereas the domestic terms of trade are primarily derived from the Heckscher-Ohlin framework the international terms of trade are in turn based upon the equilibrium position as the intersection of the offer curves of the two trading nations. The new international terms of trade constitutes an improvement in the rate of exchange over the domestic terms of trade and, consequently, both nations are better off. And to be noted, the new international terms of trade constitutes the same result "as if" each nation's production possibilities frontier had moved when in actuality it did not [Meier (1968): 20]. The analysis, simply stated: "therefore, whenever, domestic price ratios are different from world price ratios there is a gain from trade. This gain...is taking advantages of any differences between domestic price ratios and world price ratios. This is the essence of the argument for free trade." [Chow (1985): 282]

Theory is one thing, however, reality is another. "The foregoing analysis indicates only what could be or ought to be – not necessarily what has been or is. Indeed, the historical experience of numerous poor countries reveals considerable growth in their foreign trade, but only a slow rate of domestic development."[18] Is comparative advantage relevant to third world countries as D.H. Robertson once claimed: "...the specializations of the 19th century were...above all an engine of growth." [Robertson (1938): 5]. In this connection J. R. Hughes comments: "...the failure of international trade to serve as an engine of growth ... hence Mills' hypothetical history of economic development through international trade strikes us as roseate, naive." [Hughes (1970): 6–7]. Simon Kuznets also states: "...the realization that the nineteenth-century theory of international division of labor, with its promise of the inevitable and rapid spread of modern economic civilization to all corners of the earth, is hardly tenable." [Kuznets (1968): 3,80].

What went wrong, has the pure theory of trade served as a "beam in our eyes" and precluded the correct policy direction in order to promote world-wide economic development and integration, as Gunnar Myrdal maintains? Fundamental to the theory and its lack of relevancy relates to its static assumptions. "The chief criticism is that comparative advantage is essentially a static concept that ignores a variety of dynamic elements." and that it represents a "cross-sectional" view rather than a framework for structural transformation.[19] The concepts static and dynamic constitute kaleidoscopic words and are subject to differing interpretations.[20] A static process in our interpretation results in changes within a structure as reproduction (growth) whereas a dynamic process entails transformation (development) of a structure. And it is the advance of science and technology which provides for the dynamics of structural change.

The static neoclassical matrix contains a fundamental conceptual error in assuming economic growth to be synonymous with development. Outward shifts of the production frontier exemplify and demonstrate quantitative economic growth not qualitative structural changes inherent in the processes of economic development. For the LDC world, specialization in form of increased agricultural and raw material production was really at the opportunity cost of foregone industrialization. The consequence of free trade and international specialization resulted in a North (industrial) and South (agricultural) dichotomy for the global economy. The free trade policy of the nineteenth century in actuality served as an "engine of growth" for the LDC world and an "engine of development" for the nations that had engaged modernization. If such an analysis is correct it would appear that free trade and static comparative advantage would retard rather than enhance China's drive to modernization.

Certainly not all would agree with the analysis and conclusion offered above. Gregory Chow feels that neoclassical theory is relevant and that free trade would serve a positive function in China's economic development. In our analysis we have tried to focus attention on the need for institutional adjustment. Social organization in China must become permeable to modern science and technology. At first glance, Chow might appear in agreement: "As important as technology, if not more so, is the kind of economic institutions that a country adopts to produce its products."[21] But the actual matrix of neoclassical theory used by Chow essentially ignores the institutional issue. Institutional adjustment, as a variable of analysis, is outside the paradigmatic boundaries of neoclassical economics. To our view, social institutions can serve as social technology and consequently are relevant to the dynamics of economic development. The development process is essentially the process of technological change.

However, by invoking the Heckscher-Ohlin framework as is done by Chow and many other neoclassical economists, "...Technology is assumed to be identical in different countries..." and, consequently, "It might be suggested that the Heckscher-Ohlin theory as presented here has limited applicability because of its assumption that the same technology is available to each country." [Chow (1985): 282,284]. To assume that since modern technology is essentially "public knowledge" and somehow, therefore that technological differences do not represent a problem is to assume away the problem. The problem facing China is precisely that of a technological gap and that there are vast differences in the levels of technology for an LDC nation such as China and the modernized nations of Western civilization and Japan. Technology as the dynamic agency of structural change is avoided by neoclassical theory.[22] Consequently, to designate the production-possibilities curve as a transformation curve is really a misnomer in that nothing really is transformed.

To argue as H. Myint does that the negative features of static comparative advantage can be overcome by using the "vent-for-surplus" explanation as the basis for policy is less than sufficient.[23] For international trade to provide an outlet for unemployed labor and resources does indeed constitute a positive function, but this simply places an economy on the "efficiency locus" as the full-employment of resources. This however does not address the issue which we have tried to delineate as being central. The vent-for-surplus argument does not explain technological change and structural transformation which constitutes the crux of development. Given vent-for-surplus assumptions increased trade may not be costless (zero opportunity costs) if it is at the opportunity cost of foregone industrialization.

Where does all this leave us? Are we now supporting an anti-trade position and arguing that an expansion of trade is inimical to China's drive to modernization? To critique a theory (static comparative advantage) does not necessarily negate the reality of the situation as to the actual effects of trade on economic development and culture evolution. That Ptolemy presented a wrong theory of the cosmos did not stop the earth from spinning around the sun. Nor might we say that we even view static comparative advantage as negative to the process of economic evolution. Let us now try to demonstrate why we disagree with Wilczynski when he states: "the task set in this article is to show the irrelevancy of the theory of comparative costs in the centrally planned economies of the Communist type..." [Wilczynski (1965): 63].

Comparative Advantage: The Dynamics of Economic Development

China's problem is not how to become a more efficient secretary, in the statics of economic growth, but rather how to engage the dynamics of development and transform a secretary (an agrarian society) into a lawyer (industrial society). Secretaries lack the status, power, and high levels of income characteristic of lawyers. The same problems pertain to agricultural countries in comparison to the industrial. And while the globe cannot nurture a population satiated with lawyers, the global economy can and should be characterized by modernization for all nations. In all of this it is obvious that economic development entails a complexity far greater than the simplistic conception as an outward shift in the production possibility curve. Gunnar Myrdal's conception "...as the upward movement of the entire social system...", and which we view as the complex whole of culture appears more relevant to the reality of the process of economic development.[24]

Nonetheless this is not to infer that static comparative advantage lacks rele-vancy to the processes of economic evolution. Economic evolution it should be noted relates to the processes of both economic growth and economic development. Economic growth involves the quantitative processes of reproduction and replication of what is, be it rabbits, automobiles or rice. Economic development represents flux and transformation, as qualitative changes in structure in the movement from railroads to automobiles or an agrarian society to industrialism. But both processes, as growth and development, are integral to evolution. Consequently the economic growth characteristic of static comparative advantage is of merit and integral to the overall process of economic evolution. If more rice production as economic growth generates a "staple trap" and forgone industrialization then specialization and increased exports would obviously have produced negative results. However in a positive sense, export revenue from specialization and expanded production, as economic growth, could be used through economic planning to promote the dynamics of modernization through importing capital equipment, foreign experts and technology. Static comparative advantage in this instance would have promoted positive results.[25]

But of course comparative advantage need not be static and fixed in terms of a given resources and only "attributed to differences in the quantities of inputs available..." "Comparative advantage changes as technology changes... In the process of economic development and technological change, a country's comparative advantage changes." [Chow (1985): 282,294]. Comparative advantage can therefore be analyzed in the dynamics of economic development. Given the logic of static comparative advantage, a nation at a given moment of time would or should forego the production of certain commodities based upon comparative cost disadvantages.[26] Enter A. Hamilton, F. List, and R. Prebisch, the "infant industry" argument, and the need for government intervention and planning to promote industrialization and modernization. Industries can be "targeted" and promoted. Would the predilection of free trade and static comparative advantage as policy have led Japan to engage and achieve the phenomenal successes it did in the areas of automotive and steel production. What is amazing is not simply that Japan is the leading automotive and steel producer in the world today but that the economic miracle was achieved in the span of approximately two decades. It should be noted and emphasized that the modus operandi of the Japanese economic miracle was not the negation of market signals and economic effiency. But rather, that government intervention was directed toward the promotion and enhancement of market signals, trade expansion and economic efficiency.[27] And relevant to our query, did trade expansion serve as an albatross around the neck of the Japanese economy? The very title of MITI as the Ministry of International Trade and Industry indicates that trade and industry go together. Trade expansion served as a salubrious solution to Japan's intensified drive to modernization. International trade and industrial expansion can and do go together, but how and why is this so?

Whereas orthodox theories of the past tended to stress the movement of goods and the immobility of factors, modern theories of trade emphasize and analyze capital mobility, technological change and product-life-cycle models.[28] In historical perspective it might be said that Ricardo's static comparative advantage unfortunately shunted the train of trade theory on to a siding and off the dynamic tracks as constructed by A. Smith in the mold of the "productivity doctrine".[29] The productivity doctrine basically states that international trade, "...as a dynamic force which, by widening the extent of the market and the scope of the division of labor, raises the skill and dexterity of the workmen, encourages technical innovations, overcomes technical indivisibilities and generally enables the trading country to enjoy increasing returns and economic development."[30] The productivity doctrine appears more relevant to the British example of "export-led growth" (development). In this instance an expanding market size promoted endogenous technical advance within Great Britain and in the form of invention and discovery. The steam-engine technology, per se, was not diffused into the British economy from abroad but was representative more so of endogenous technological advance. In this sense the expanding market size and benefits of economies of scale served to promote the dynamics of endogenous technological change and modernization for Great Britain.[31]

The "productivity doctrine" is consequently more relevant to Great Britain as the nation in the vanguard of general culture evolution. Such a nation, serving as the epicenter of modern economic growth, endogenously invents and creates the nascent and early technology of modernization. And while the LDC countries will also benefit from the "productivity doctrine" and endogenous invention and discovery they would benefit more so from cultural diffusion. Therefore, for countries such as China the problem is more so how to absorb and become permeable to the vast store of accumulated modern science and technology already on hand and in existence [Viner (1958): 64; Haberler (1968): 109, 110]. While China could undoubtedly achieve modernization through isolation and endogenous invention and discovery, such a path would have very long-run dimensions. However, if the desire is for rapid modernization, and in a reasonable short-run time span, the sine qua non for such a policy objective would be trade expansion. Haberler states: "...even more important than the importation of material goods is the importation of technical know-how, skills, managerial talents, entrepreneurship. ... Trade is the most important vehicle for the transmission of technical know-how." [Haberler (1968): 109, 110].

In this regard and in relation to our focus on culture evolution, it might be said that trade serves as an umbilical cord of culture diffusion. In the literature of classical economics this is referred to as the "indirect benefits" or "educational effects" of international trade, and/or what Myrdal refers to as the "noneconomic".[32] In our conception of the process of economic development, the advance of knowledge serves as the essence and fountainhead of the process. Humankind exhibits the capacity and proclivity to advance knowledge exponentially. And given the assumption of culture permeability, such knowledge in its application accounts for the dynamics of technological advance and in the process transforms and advances culture as well. If such a theory of development is correct, "A deficiency of knowledge is a more pervasive handicap to development than is the scarcity of any other factor." [Meier (1968: 220]. Therefore, in summary, trade expansion in the matrix of static comparative advantage may or may not lead to positive results. By comparison, the matrix of dynamic comparative advantage is highly supportive of the conclusion that trade expansion will serve to promote, not retard, China's drive to modernization. Trade concerns more than just the movement of goods and therefore can serve as a primary agency whereby science and technology are diffused from one culture (nation) to another.

China: Trade and Telesis

In our analysis in addressing China's drive to modernization we have focused on social organization and the need for institutional adjustment. The conception of modern economic growth has been incorporated in this paper "... as a thorough transformation of a country's economic and social framework."[33] The question concerns which form of institutional adjustment will best serve China to introduce and innovate modern science and technology? In the complexity of the whole of the process of economic development we have tried to delineate a part and to explain the positive function of trade expansion. In the matrix of a dynamic comparative advantage trade expansion can serve as the basis for the culture diffusion of modern science and technology. Modern science and technology, in turn, are necessary for China in order to address its two basic and fundamental problems in the areas of: 1. population growth; and, 2. economic development.

That China has endured and survived the tremendous population increases of the post-World War II period is miraculous. In the period of a lifespan of one generation the population of China has increased from approximately 500 million, to approximately that of 1.0 billion in the 1980's. Some 500 million people, the approximate combined total population of the United States and Western Europe, was added and poured into the territorial confines of one nation. As an awesome contemplation, could the United States have withstood within its territorial borders an addition to its population to the magnitude of 500 million, within such a short time span, without chaos and breakdown? And bearing in mind that China is a less developed country and therefore lacking in the basic infrastructure associated with transportation, communication, educational facilities, hospitals, fuels, housing, and on. It is amazing to note, therefore, that during that time span the Chinese, however, have: "...essentially solved to the problems of food and clothing and have become essentially self-sufficient in grain." [Deng (1984): 383]

Such population increases obviously cannot continue. Population growth rates must be attacked directly and this is being done today in China. But also population growth rates must be addressed indirectly and this is also being done through the drive toward modernization. As the experience of the West demonstrates, the process of economic development, itself, tends to move society toward a ZPG (zero population growth). Therefore through the modernization process and economic development, China's population will be more easily controlled and a lessening of the population pressure will also further enhance economic development. And as part of that overall complexity, international trade will provide for a very important function. Trade expansion will aid in promoting the culture diffusion of modern science and technology.

But is rapid economic development an unmitigated good in itself, as the above seems to infer? Might not the spread of modern science and technology and accelerated economic development be at the opportunity cost of other values held to be of greater importance and merit? If the science and technology to be diffused is captive and controlled by Western civilization in its genesis will not the use of that science and technology, by other nations, lead to a transformation of their cultures along the lines of Western values and institutions?[34] Will trade expansion and the diffusion of modern science and technology serve as a Trojan horse and contain within a means of subverting Chinese culture and long-term future goals? Given the current political realities of China, the charge of "bourgeois liberalization" cannot be ignored as an argument against trade expansion. But does the argument hold?

To begin with if a nation desires modernization this by definition means that culture transformation will and must take place. But this relates to the holistic conception of culture as offered by Tylor. The alternative as no culture transformation would be manifest in economic stagnation and no economic development. And this, obviously, no one wants. But if the whole of culture must of necessity be transformed is not to say that all parts, as specific technics, must be transformed identically for all nations. It does not follow that all specific aspects or parts of the whole of culture, as to values and given social institutions, must be replicated as identical structures for all cultures engaging modern economic growth? The nations of Western Europe, the U.S., the U.S.S.R. and Japan have engaged modern economic growth and have consequently experienced an evolution and transformation of culture. But in addition these countries reveal a spectrum of varying social institutions and values rather than homogeneity.[35] The resulting specific structures, both material and social, can and should be unique to China's culture and civilization. In fact not only has Japan's success been spectacular in terms of innovating modern science and technology, but at the same time, equally impressive has been Japan's retention of its genetic pool as well as certain specific values and attributes of nonmaterial culture.

Also it would appear difficult to argue, at least from the Chinese vantage, that cultural diffusion from the West is necessarily always negative. The Marxist-Leninist tradition, for example, was not an endogenous product of Chinese culture but obviously had its origins in culture diffusion. What China needs to import is processual, a method, rather than specific institutions or aspects of Western culture. The problem is how to use the systematic knowledge, inherent in the meaning of a scientific epoch, to solve China's problems of modernization and economic development.[36] The resulting specific structures, both material and social, can and should be unique to China's culture and civilization. Therefore though the process be the same for nations in the contest of a scientific epoch the resulting specific structures both material and social need not. It appears that the current leadership in China, while practical and realistic, has not foresaken the "four cardinal principles" as the long-term goals of modernization and development.[37] This hardly constitutes an endorsement of "bourgeois liberalization" but rather constitutes an argument for long-run cultural integrity toward China's socialist revolution.

Now that China has achieved independence and sovereignty, the matrix of dependency theory also appears of less relevancy.[38] But it is also hard to conceive of increased self-reliance and enhanced independence and sovereignty as being a function of self–sufficiency as autarky. Self-reliance can also be viewed as "relying on one's own capabilities which may naturally include intensive trade relations with the outside world."[39] Self-reliance will be enhanced through economic growth and development which in turn require modern science and technology. And for the LDC world, "...such countries really have no alternative if they wish to gain access to the rapidly changing international stock of knowledge ... the nature of the international technological transfer process is such that complete independence, amounting to a form of cultural autarky is no longer possible or desirable..." [Street (1979): 241].

Jacob Viner also has drawn attention to the fact that rich countries have an accumulated "stock of scientific and technical knowledge ... available for borrowing" by the poorer countries. And of interest, even Viner grants the fact that "this knowledge will not flow to them automatically..." [Viner (1958): 64]. And given the complexity of culture evolution, which we have stressed, "Rapid technology absorption is not a simple process." [Barnett (1981): 196–206]; it would then logically follow that the process be managed or planned. It is in this context that the concept *telesis,* as "planned progress" is meaningful and relevant.[40] The position which have attempted to develop is that trade and telesis go together. Trade is not the whole of the developmental process but functions as a crucial and important part.

Trade expansion and a more open policy will help to provide China with the much needed modern science and technology through the agency of culture diffusion. In this process of trade and telesis it would appear that an electric and pragmatic approach is very much in order. And this is indeed what is being done. "Despite the problems and uncertainties, however, it seems clear that China's shift to a new, more flexible and pragmatic approach to national economic development is historic, and over time should enhance the prospects for sound, sustainable development." [Barnett (1981): 120]. For in the last analysis, if it works let us use it: "It does not matter if the cat is black or white, as long as it catches mice."[41]

Notes

[1] Cheng (1982), "...Mao frankly acknowledged that he was a layman in economics..." p. 29; however to Joan Robinson and others, the paradigmatic blinders sometimes inherent in economic analysis might not always be of an advantage: "The purpose of studying economics is not to acquire a set of ready–made answers to economic questions but to learn how to avoid being deceived by economists." Galbraith (1973): 11.

[2] Mao (1967): 413; Cheng (1982): 30.

[3] "...relatively few people – whether historians, political scientists or others, predicted the split, and those who did failed to foresee that it would come so soon." Barnett (1981): 3.

[4] It is not only Henry Kissinger and the members of the business community in the U.S. who note the obvious economic importance of China, see also Okita (1979); Shinohara (1984), and on.

[5] The literature in this area is somewhat open–ended, briefly note the following and the many bibliographical references contained therein: Barnett (1981): 120–268, passin; Buxbaum (1982); Eckstein (1966), (1977): 233–276; Maxwell (1979): 259–278; Prybyla (1981): 217–248; and especially Chow (1985): 1–40, 275–302, and bibliography 302.

[6] On the "four modernizations": Deng (1984): 101–116, 145–150; Phillips (1984); Baum (1980); Barnett (1981): 12–121; Chow (1964): 73–74; Sigurdson (1980);

[7] Kuznets' contributions are prolific, we briefly refer to (1973) (1968) and (1966). For Kuznets' relation to institutional economics, note: Street (1979): 227–257; and, Brinkman (1981).

[8] For a general discussion of this chicken and egg controversy plus references to the literature, note: Brinkman (1981): 292ff; 314 #65; Johnson (1967): 228; Landes (1965): 293, 559: Kerker (1961: and, Kuznets (1966): 9–11, #3 for a balanced view.

[9] Singer (1958): V–VI, 663–681, and "...certainly since the second half of the nineteenth century, the major source of economic growth in the developed countries has been science–based technology..." Kuznets (1966): 10.

[10] We speak here of the E. B. Tylor conception, "as that complex whole which was formulated in 1871.

[11] This conception interrelating technology and culture constitutes an almagam and synthesis of the contributions of S. Kuznets (economics), L. A. White (anthropology) and W. F. Ogburn (sociology) among others, note Brinkman (1981).

[12] That ongoing growth on an exponential continuum requires continuous structural change is associated with the "principles of similitude" and "Structural differention", note Bell (1973): 172–74. Introducing such structural change in analysis relates to T. Parson, as well as the exponential and "logistic surges" of W. F. Ogburn and H. Hart.

[13] While Kuznets is critical of Rostow's stages, in this instance we would expect Kuznets and Rostow to be in agreement.

[14] Deng (1984): p.102, and also, "Without modern science and technology, it is impossible to build modern agriculture, modern industry or modern national defense. Without the rapid development of science and technology, there can be no rapid development of the economy." p.102

[15] Mill (1911): 351; Meier (1968): XII, for a passage frequently quoted in the literature.

[16] For an excellent general discussion note Meier (1968); and, Chow (1985): 275–302, in relation to China. This represents the standard textbook treatment or what T. S. Kuhn would categorized as "normal science" in economics.

[17] Even granting that these assumptions do not prevail for the real world, most economists still adhere to and accept the Heckscher-Ohlin model.

[18] Meier (1968): 222; and also providing the basis for the heterodox critique of Myrdal and Prebisch among others.

[19] Chenery (1979): 272; Myint (1958): 318; Haberler (1968): 105, 106; Viner (1958): 61; and Meier (1968): and to which "comparative statics" do not suffice to resolve, "short of a truly dynamic analysis." pp. 4, 225.

[20] Note Machlup (1963) in which he concludes: "Probably more often than not we should be able to do without the terms Statics and Dynamics." p.42.

[21] Chow (1985): 2. Also whereas Chow apparently separates technology and social institutions, our conception of technology is that both material and social technics are integral.

[22] For example, Chow's treatment: "One characteristic of this book is that it is brief on institutional details ... would make the book too lengthy. Readers wishing to learn about Chinese economic institutions can refer to the Almanac of China's Economy..." (1985):2.

[23] Myint (1958); Caves (1968); and on the "staple theories" of economic growth of Harold A. Innis and others, for discussions note: Landes (1980); and, Watkins (1963).

[24] Myrdal (1968): 1868–69, (1973): 182–196 on the view that growth is not synonymous with development, a view also held by J. Schumpeter and many others.

25 Subject to question if the assumption is altered to: "... a far more realistic one in today's world – that foodstuffs and raw materials are in permanent oversupply." ..."traditional development theories and policies are losing their foundations." Drucker (1986): 774,775. Prebisch might have been correct after all, "But then no one, including myself, believed him." p. 775, 77.

26 "The task of foreign trade is to anticipate and promote the development of socially desirable industries, even where there are cost disadvantages" Wilczynski (1965): 76. Dynamic comparative advantage is a function of technological change (culture evolution) rather than to the quantities of resources that are available.

27 This constitutes the misconception of the "industrial policy" debate, that intervention is anti-market. MITI, and economists such as L. Thurow and R. Reich, in the tradition of Keynes, argue in behalf of governmental intervention in order to improve upon, not negate, market signals.

28 For early discussions in this area, note: Vernon (1966), and Wells (1968).

29 Myint (1958): 318; Meier (1968): 219; Haberler (1968): 106–107.

30 Myint (1958): 318–319; Smith (1937): 415.

31 And in this context Young (1928) and many others, who also note that increased market size in "Not area or population, alone, but buying power..." p.533.

32 The focus here is on J. S. Mill, note Meier (1968): 220, but analysis of "indirect benefits" also introduces the social and cultural into economic analysis. Neglect by neoclassical economists according to Haberler is explained by the fact that: "...these factors do not lend themselves will to precise mathematical treatment." (1968): 108.109.

33 Kuznets (1966): 462; "In China's case, economic development involves a seminal institutional transformation ... Cheng (1982): XVII.

34 On "Science and the Struggle Between Two Lines", cf., OECD (1977): 203–216, for commentary by A. D. Barnett and F. Godement.

35 This had led Kuznets to refer to modern economic growth as being characterized by a "scientific epoch" rather than "industrial capitalism" (1966): 9.

36 In neoinstitutional economics, the basic problem of institutional adjustment is addressed by formulating and advancing instrumental-value principles, note: Tool (1979) in the Dewey-Ayres tradition..

37 "Uphold the Four Cardinal Principles" Deng (1984): 166–191.

38 "In sum, science and technology tend to become universally available, and they offer an escape from the hopeless dependency and incessant foreign exploitation." Street (1979): 3.

39 Sigurdson (1980):4; Snead (1975); Li (1975); and, OECD (1977).

40 According to Webster's Dictionary: "Progress intelligently planned and directed; the attainment of desired ends by the application of intelligent human effort to the means."

41 This cat analogy appears with frequency: Pye (1986) :207; OECD (1977): 206, reportedly asserted by Deng in 1962 one cannot help but contemplate what Peirce, James and Dewey would have thought of all this, Pye: (1986): 220, 226.

References

Barnett, A. Doak. 1981. *China's Economy in Global Perspective* Washington, D. C.: The Brookings Institution.

Baum, R., ed. 1980. *China's Four Modernizations: The New Technological Revolution*. Boulder: Westview Press.

Bell, Daniel. 1973. *The Coming of Post–Industrial Society.* New York: Basic Books.

Brinkman, Richard L. 1981. *Cultural Economics*. Portland: The Hapi Press.

Buxbaum, D. C., C. E. Joseph and P. D. Reynolds. 1982. *China Trade: Prospects and Perspectives*. New York: Praeger.

Caves, Richard. 1968. "Vent for Surplus' Models of Trade and Growth" pp. 211–230 in J. D. Theberge, ed. *Economics of Trade and Development.* New York: John Wiley.

Chenery, Hollis. "Comparative Advantage and Development Policy", pp. 272–308 in *Structural Change and Development Policy,* New York: Oxford University Press.

Cheng, Chu-yuan. 1982. *China's Economic Development: Growth and Structural Change.* Boulder, Colorado: Westview Press.

Chow, Gregory. 1985. *The Chinese Economy.* New York: Harper & Row.

Deng, Xiaoping. 1984. *Selected Works of Deng Xiaoping* (1975–1982). Beijing; Foreign Languages Press.

Drucker, Peter F. 1986. "The Changed World Economy." *Foreign Affairs* (Spring): 768–791.

Eckstein, Alexander. 1977. *China's Economic Revolution.* Cambridge: Cambridge University Press.

Eckstein, Alexander. 1966. *Communist China's Economic Growth and Foreign Trade.* New York: McGraw Hill.

Galbraith, John Kenneth. 1973. *Economics and the Public Purpose.* Boston Houghton Mifflin.

Haberler, Gottfried. 1968. "International Trade and Economic Development." pp. 103–112. J. D. Theberge, ed. *Economics of Trade and Development.* New York: John Wiley & Sons.

Hughes, Jonathan. 1970. *Industrialization and Economic History.* New York: McGraw Hill.

Johnson, E.A.J. 1967. "Industrialization and Economic Growth: Problems in Methodology." *Journal of Economic Issues* (September): 219–230.

Kerker, Milton. 1961. "Science and the Steam Engine." *Technology and Culture* (1961): 381–390.

Kuznets, Simon. 1973. "Modern Economic Growth: findings and Reflections." *the American Economic Review* (June): 247–258.

Kuznets, Simon. 1968. *Toward A Theory of Economic Growth.* New York: W. W. Norton.

Kuznets, Simon. 1966. *Modern Economic Growth.* New Haven: Yale University Press.

Landes, David S. 1980. "The 'Great Drain' and Industrialization: Commodity Flows from Periphery to Centre in Historical Perspective," pp. 294–327 HD82 I 45 Vol.2 in R.C.O. Mathews, ed. *Economic Growth and Resources.* New York: St. Martin's Press.

Li, Xin. 1975. "Self-Reliance Is a Question of Line" *Peking Review.* (August 8).

Ma, Shu-yun. 1986. "Recent Changes in China's Pure Trade Theory." *The China Quarterly.* (June):291–305.

Machlup, Fritz. 1963. *Essays on Semantics.* Englewood Cliffs: Prentice Hall.

Mao Tse–tung. 1967. *Selected Works of Mao Tse-tung.* Vol.4, Peking: Foreign Languages Press.

Maxwell, Neville. *China's Road to Development.* New York: Pergamon Press.

Meier, Gerald M. 1968. *The International Economics of Development.* New York: Harper and Row.

Mill, J. S. 1911. *The Principles of Political Economy.* London: Longmans.

Myint, H. 1958. "The Classical Theory of International Trade and the Underdeveloped Countries." *Economic Journal.* (June): 317–37.

Myrdal, Gunnar. 1973. *Against the Stream.* New York: Pantheon.

Myrdal, Gunnar. 1968. *Asian Drama: An Inquiry into the Poverty of Nations.* New York: Pantheon.

Okita, Saburo. 1979. "Japan, China and the United States: Economic Relations and Prospects." *Foreign Affairs.* (Summer).

Organization for Economic Co-operation and Development (OECD). 1977. *Science and Technology in the People's Republic of China.* Paris: OECD.

Phillips, David. 1984. *China's Modernization: Prospects and Problems for the West.* The Institute for the Study of Conflict, No.158.

Prybyla, Jan S. 1981. *The Chinese Economy: Problems and Policies.* Columbia, S. C.: University of South Carolina Press.

Pye, Lucain W. 1986. "On Chinese Pragmatism in the 1980's" The China Quarterly 106 (June): 207–234.

Robertson, D. H. 1938. "The future of International Trade" *The Economic Journal.* (March): 1–14.

Shinohara, Miyohei. 1984. *Industrial Growth, Trade and Dynamic Patterns in the Japanese Economy.* Tokyo: University of Tokyo Press.

Sigurdsen, Jon. 1980. *Technology and Science in the People's Republic of China.* New York: Pergamon Press.

Smith, Adam. 1937. *An Inquiry into the Nature and Causes of the Wealth of Nations.* New York: Random House.

Snead, William G. 1975. "Self Reliance, Internal Trade, and China's Economic Structure." *China Quarterly.* (June): 322–8.

Street, James H. 1979. "Technological Fusion and Cultural Independence: the Argentine Case." in J. H. Street and D. James, ed., pp.227–245. *Technologied Progress in Latin America: the Prospects for Overcoming Dependency.* Boulder: Westview Press.

Tool, Marc R. 1979. *The Discretionary Economy: A Normative Theory of Political Economy.* Santa Monica: Goodyear.

Vernon, Raymond. 1966. "International Investment and International Trade in the Product Cycle." *The Quarterly Journal of Economics.* (May): 190–207.

Viner, Jacob. 1958. "Stability and Progress: The Poorer Countries Problem." pp. 41–65 in D. Hague, ed., *Stability and Progress in the World Economy.* London: Macmillan.

Watkins, Melvin. 1963. "A Staple Theory of Economic Growth." *Canadian Journal of Economics and Political Science.* (1963): 141–158.

Wells Jr., Louis T. 1968. "A Product Life Cycle for International Trade." *Journal of Marketing.* (July): 1–6.

Wilczynski, J. 1965. "The Theory of Comparative Costs and Centrally Planned Economies." *The Economic Journal.* (March): 63–80.

Young, Allyn. 1928. "Increasing Returns and Economic Progress." *Economic Journal.* (December): 527–542.

Gorbachev's Economic Reforms:
A structural or a technical Alteration?

by Helmut W. Jenkis

The Eastern and Western world are diametrically opposed to each other not only politically and militarily but also economically and socially. In the socialist lands the Communist one party system is dominant; in the West it is political pluralism, in *Comecon* the planned economy prevails, and in the Common Market and the USA it is the market economy, of course, not in the form it took in the nineteenth century. From a social point of view the Eastern bloc guarantees full employment at a lower standard of living, in the market economy the higher standard of living is accompanied by structural, cyclical unemployment. Both systems claim to be superior to the other.

It is noteworthy that the General Secretary of the Central Committee of the Communist Party, Mikhail Gorbachev[1], in his declaration of January 15, 1986, presented[2] not only a three step plan for the elimination of all atomic weapons as far as 2000 A.D., but he had also made fundamental statements on the domestic structure of the Soviet economy and society in a political report of the Central Committee of the Communist Party of the Soviet Union on the XVII *Parteitag*, February 25, 1986,[3] which has been interpreted in the West as democratising, and an approach, therefore, to the Western system.

In connection with the extensive pronouncements of Gorbachev, we are simply interested in the economic assertions and those on the democratization of society. After a sketch of these proposals we shall determine whether it is simply a question of "technical" or structural changes which can lead to a convergence of the systems. Finally, the question will be pursued of how the satellite states might behave.

I. The Socio-Economic Development and Democratization of Society

In his report, Gorbachev describes the world of today, that is the basic trends and conflicts.[4] At the end of these statements, he emphasizes that at the center of social progress stands man with his interests and problems.

The struggle is concerned with providing dignified material and spiritual conditions of life for all peoples and the secure habitation of our planet. Gorbachev ends this chapter with these words:[5] "In this area we challenge the capitalist system to a *competition*, to a competition within the conditions of a permanent peace." This challenge suggests the superiority of socialism and the planned economy relative to the Western democracies and their market economy.

The question has already been raised here of why social and economic development should be accelerated and society democratized when it is presented as superior.

1. The Acceleration of Social and Economic Development[6]

Gorbachev begins his social and economic statements with the following demands: "In the first place it is a matter of the increase in the speed of economic growth. Of course, not only for that reason. ... The strategy of acceleration assumes here a perfection of social relationships, a renewal of the form and methods of working of political and ideological institutions, a deepening of social democracy and a determination to overcome laziness, stagnation and conservatism, that is, all those things which restrict social progress." (p. 61) It is noteworthy that Gorbachev demands competition with the market economies, of course, at the same time as he demands the overcoming of laziness and stagnation.

As the key to a new qualitative condition of Soviet society arises out of the acceleration of political development, this is being demanded by Gorbachev. Twenty-five years have passed since the adoption of the *Third Programme*. Production has achieved impressive success and had reached the American economy in many areas, but in the seventies the speed of economic growth declined noticeably.

In this way the goals set in the Programme of the Communist Party for the development of the economy and even more lowly goals set in the ninth and tenth Five Year Plan would not be attained. The social programme provided for these years could not likewise be completely realized (p. 63)...

Considerable backwardness was admitted in machine construction, in mining, in electrical engineering, in iron metallurgy, in chemistry, as well as in investment. The attainment of the most important goals of effective growth and of the raising of the standard of living was not achieved. (p. 64)

From this fact, Gorbachev draws his conclusions for the future:

The *most important task of the Party* consists in removing the unfavorable trends in economic development for "without accelerated economic growth the social programme will remain only a pious wish,..." (p. 65f). National Income is to be almost doubled before the end of this century. This is only possible by a *far-reaching modernization of the economy* on the basis of the latest scientific and technical knowledge. Quality and effectiveness are to take the place of quantitative indices. In the current Five Year Plan more than 200 billion roubles – more than in the preceding ten years – are being made available for modernization and new technical equipment. Of definite significance is the building of machinery by which the productivity of labour will be raised and the quality of the product improved. In this way, 12 million labourers will be saved and more than 100 million tons of fuel. This modernization will definitely be determined by the *EDV-Technik* to which science will devote special attention.

It is especially important in order to silence the malcontents not to concede that the core of the problem is being replaced by palliatives instead of a cure. (p. 71) ... Apparently some of our comrades have not recognized the depth and importance of the problem before which they have been put. (p. 72)

Science and Research must apply themselves more vigorously to the needs of the economy, on the other hand, production must accept scientific and technological accomplishments, that is, to overcome the conservative behavior of the leaders of enterprises and those in the ministries. It is a "holy duty" to lead every scientist, engineer, designer or industrial leader into fundamental research in the field of production.

Without the slightest delay *the provision of food for the individual* is to be solved. Advances are to be recorded, yet the overcoming of backwardness is still too slow in agriculture. "In agriculture it depends on a decisive change, so that the provision of food can be notably improved already in the twelfth Five Year Plan. ...Can we accomplish that? We can and we must do it." (p. 76). The crucial point will lie in the area.of the economic methods of governing the economy, the enlargement of independence and in the raising of responsibility in the kolkhozy and sovkhozy. These cannot be reached only through intensive use of technology, but also by better methods of harvesting, transportation, storage and manufacture. This transition to new methods will be authoritatively determined by the leadership and the administration of the economy. These proposals amount to "offering the economic methods of the administration of the economy a great deal of room in which the independence of the kolkhozy and sovkhozy can grow considerably and raise their responsibility for the final outcome." (p. 78). In this citation it becomes clear that Gorbachev is thinking not about a change in structure – return to private agriculture with private property – but wants to create a higher degree of flexibility within the collective system and collective property. It is, therefore, a technical, not a structural reform. To this belongs that which can be cultivated and economized by the plan, can be relatively freely sold. That it is not a question of a transition to a greater degree of market activity, the following quotation verifies: "It is planned to complete a transition to more perfect methods of planning on the basis of progressive norms." (p. 79) ...

> It depends on pushing forth a strong bolt into the mismanaged economy and the ideology of the parasites, and to end with an appeal to the so-called objective circumstances which have become a part of the kolkhozy and sovkhozy, a cloak for their insolvency, including their disinclination to work better. ... As you see, Comrades, the conditions for economizing in agriculture change fundamentally. (p. 80)

According to Gorbachev, the solution of new problems without a thorough change over of the mechanism of the economy and without a flexible system of administration is impossible. Of course one can agree with the following demands, for example, the setting of goals, yet in our opinion it is a question of a pseudo-normative empty formula: "The leadership and direction of the economy needs – and this is well-known – a continuous improvement. Yet the situation at present is so arranged, that it is not a matter of being restricted to a partial alteration; a radical reform causes distress." (p. 81). One would like to learn which concrete steps are to be undertaken, how the leadership and direction of the economy can be improved. Then one would also like to know why this steering function will or cannot be left to the market.

The Central Committee of the Communist Party and its *Politbüro* have stated as follows the main direction of the transformation of the mechanism of the economy: (p. 81f)

(1) The effectiveness of the central administration is to be raised, the tempo, the proportions of development as well as its balancing are to be strengthened.

(2) The independence of the industry and its responsibility is to be raised. Therefore, the industries are to be rearranged through economic accountancy, one covering costs and their own financing.

(3) On all levels of the political economy, economic methods of administration are to be adopted, the system of price formation, of financing and granting of credit to be improved, as well as the developing of effective, costsaving incentives.

(4) The concentration, specialization and cooperation of production is to be adapted to the modern structure of the organization.

(5) The administration of the economy is to be connected as favorably as possible according to the branch and authority principle.

(6) The activity of leadership is a democratizing one, control from below, accountability and publicity are to be strengthened.

We are standing, Comrades, doubtlessly before the most significant transformation of the so-cialistic mechanism of the economy. (p. 82). [The Soviet Union stands first at the beginning of this road. Time and energetic efforts are still required: difficulties and mistakes are not to be excluded.] It is imperative to move towards the goal, step for step in the chosen direction, to supplement the mechanism of the economy on the basis of empirical observation and to improve, and to clear out of the way everything outmoded or which has not proved itself. (p. 83)

Therefore new institutions of direction and leadership will be created. Statistics will be improved. Here, too, it is made clear that Gorbachev thinks in the traditional ways of the planned economy – not, however, about a switch to the market economy – that means, the existing instruments of planning and direction are not to be eliminated, but merely improved. Here already deliberations are announced. The contents, the organization and the methods of labor of finance and credit institutions are to be fundamentally altered. Businesses are no longer to be regulated in a petty manner but stimulated economically.

Prices must become an active instrument of economic and social policy. Before us there stands a planned transformation of the price mechanism as a unified whole in the interest of accomplishing an effective economic system of accountancy and in keeping with the task of raising the real income of the populace and turning it into a fact. A greater flexibility must be given to prices,... (p. 84)

These demands give the impression that it is a question of the price mechanism in the sense of the market economy, but actually they refer to administrative prices fixed politically. In order to work out the distinction between price in the market economy, we will briefly treat here the determination of price under socialism:[7] "Price – in the expressed value of a good in gold which is determined by the socially necessary labor contained in the good. Marx established that value is a relationship between persons (producers of goods) in a tangible veil, therefore a social relationship."[8]

On the basis of this Marxist statement on the value of the social relationship rests the formation of price in socialism on three decisive criteria:[9]

1. Value is the law of prices. It expresses the unity of the production of value and the realization of value which arise from the conditions of development of the forces of production and the production relationship...

2. Price under socialism is a planned one. Its formation and alteration are planned by the socialist state, its effects analyzed and its adherence controlled.

3. All the fundamental political and economic problems of the socialist state clash in price. For that reason, price policy and with it the formation of price, price planning and price control rest firmly in the hands of the state...

With these quotations it is unequivocally confirmed that with the identical terminology price in socialism, i.e., the planned economy, and in the market economy are conceived and expressed with very different contents. A reform of price in the Soviet Union does not thereby lead to a market economic system.

The experts in the ministries are not to browbeat businesses, but limit themselves to the determination of the goals set from above. The enterprise is to be permitted, that is outside of the plan, to dispose of surplus products beyond that planned, or unused raw materials and *Werkstoff*. Here it is plain to us that the planned economy is in no way being surrendered.

Relative to this, Gorbachev remarks: "Comrades! Every transformation of the mechanism of the economy begins, as you know, with the *transformation of consciousness,* with the problem of cliches and practical things which had until now developed, as well as with the clarity of new problems." (p. 89) The question arises, however, whether Gorbachev actually intended a transformation of consciousness or if he did not persist in the old planned economy cliche and wants merely to alter this in a technical sense, make it more flexible. In other words: can he really bring about a structural change with the given theories and institutions of the planned economy? The following demands are also imposed beyond the bounds of this system's international boundaries and efforts at reform:

> ...Yet we have only difficulty in understanding those who wait or act like a hero of Gogol who created all possible sorts of fantastic plans but altered nothing and still did nothing. With the behavior of such collaborators no peace is in sight. We and they are going plainly and simply along different ways. Our ways are all the more different from those who cherish hope that everything would correct itself and return to the old track. This will not happen, Comrades. (p. 90)

Let us note once more that Gorbachev not only technical, but also wants and strives for fundamental, structural changes in the system. Is it realistic to assume that this, at the lower and middle levels, would be understood and carried out by the lower and middle functionaries in a gigantic empire?

The statement of Gorbachev is noteworthy that the *production relationship* and the character of the productive powers must in no way be forces to agree in socialism. Gradually the productive relations have been put in order. They have even developed into a wedge. Therefore, more space is to be given to scientific and technical progress and the human factor is to be placed more vigorously in the center. But the bounds of Gorbachev's propagated reforms are immediately visible, when he says in this connection: "When it is for example necessary and just to apply economic norms in the place of definite, binding indices, this *in no way* means a *renunciation* of the principles of leadership by the plan, but *merely* an *alteration of its methods and techniques*." (p. 91); for the highest criteria of the improvement of leadership as well as the productive relationship under socialism is the strength of socialism. For this reason socialist property remains also the foundation of order in the Soviet society. To be sure, labor had to learn that businesses and unions cause no losses which are covered by the state. And besides: There are still among us *Mitnehmer* who do not consider it a crime to go along with everything in their factory that just "slips through the fingers just as with all other sorts of corrupt elements and grasping individuals who permit the misuse of their position for their own advantage." (p. 93) These are very plain words from Gorbachev. The decisive question however remains, whether a system can be altered, improved by an appeal or whether it would not be necessary to bring forth a different system in which one returns again to private property.

The fundamental transformation of the political economy requires time, on the other hand, an increase in the rate of growth is necessary at once. It is therefore a question of whether the available capacity can be better used than formerly; for machines, plants and equipment do not stand silently by very seldom or only 50 percent of their output is being achieved. This deficient shortage of capacity leads to losses in the billions. The deficiency in discipline in the deliveries of the cooperatives reduces their effectiveness. This is also true of the productivity of labor which in comparison with that of foreign labor is too low.

The *quality of the products* must be improved: An acceleration of scientific and technological progress will not suffice, it must be accompanied by an improvement of quality.

In the past year millions of metres of textiles or else millions of pairs of shoes as well as numerous other consumer goods were sent back to the factories or classed as an inferior sort. The damage is considerable: Raw materials are useless, the work of hundreds of thousands of workers is debased. (p. 98)

For this reason it is necessary to pass a special law on the quality of product. It could be asked here whether the market and competition would effect this quite automatically.

2. The Main Direction of Social Policy

At the center of attention of the Communist Party of the Soviet Union is the concern for the human being; is its social policy. For here the highest aims of socialism are being realized. Here above all the difference from capitalism becomes clear:

Socialism had eliminated the main source of social injustice: The exploitation of man by man, the inequality relative to the means of production. Social justice penetrates all areas of the socialist social relationships. ...There are also extensive social guarantees: assured employment, access to education, culture, medical care, living quarters, concern for older people, for mother and child. (p. 100)

The goal of social policy is "the attainment of a perfect position of well-being and of a free, many-sided development of the members of society." (p. 100). Here one would have liked to know definitely what Gorbachev understands by a "perfect position of well-being" and whether he meant thereby a standard of consumption which had already been reached in Western countries.

In the coming fifteen years, the resources for the *improvement of the standard of living* are to be doubled and the real per capita income is to be raised from 1.6 to 1.8 fold. These plans can only then be realized when the corresponding labor is performed. Therefore "the socialistic transformations have the goal of altering basically the work and the attitude of the worker and peasant masses to work." (p. 102). This means that only good workers should be paid good wages. For equal pay for bad work would contradict the social justice of socialism: "From each according to his capacity, to each according to his need." The *Wage Policy* has to secure a strict dependence of wages on the quality and quantity of the work. Here, there appears to be under consideration a similar assessment in the market economy, to influence individual interest by a wage relative to performance. To be sure in the future, wages and salaries will not be freely supported by the parties to a collective bargaining contract but carried on by the state – the planning authority. This, too, is an example of the fact that it is a question not of a technical but a structural reform.

Contrary to the socialist, that is, communist theory, so criticized Gorbachev, the system of *unearned income* had developed a concept which in the economic order of the market economy is unknown: In this is understood "ne'erdo-wells, embezzlers of socialist property, corrupt men, ...who have taken a way which is essentially foreign to our order which rests on labor." (p. 105) The workers – who engage in honorable employment – demand the suppression of such phenomena.

The *problem of living quarters* requires a solution. Up to the year 2000 each family shall have at its disposal a single dwelling, that is, one's own home. (p. 105). Apart from that, this goal has been reached long ago in the market economy. It is lacking in concrete statements about the size of the dwelling place, the extent to which it is furnished, additional equipment such as lawns and parking lots, shopping facilities, etc. From the indication that the assignment of housing is to proceed in a democratic manner and under constant social control, one can, of course, infer that the present system of allotment by subjective connection is approved. Worthy of notice is also the proposal to alter the rent system, that is, to link this to the size and quality of the house. That could mean that indirectly a ceiling on rent will be envisioned.

This qualitative change in the social sphere is in the field of labor not thinkable without far-reaching alterations. Up to the year 2000, the share of manual labor will be reduced by 15–20 percent and will be replaced by modern, technical methods of production. For this reason, training for an occupation is to be improved and the school and university system reformed.

In the area of *Health Care,* the struggle against drunkenness and alcoholism has been already begun. To this belongs the *protection of the environment* which can be attained by harmony in the mutual relationship between society and nature. In the protection of the environment, the question is raised directly of whether the methods of production adjusted to the fulfillment of the plan (ideology of tons) already had the technical means for air and water content, whether these can be imported for foreign currency, and finally, whether these kinds of measures do not diminish output quantitatively and consequently encroach upon the earlier highly placed goals.

Gorbachev stated: "If we do not succeed in raising to a significantly higher level competition in production, in the economy, in science and in the arts, we will not be able to solve the problems of the acceleration of the socio-economic progress of the country." (p. 110f). Contrary to the assumption in the West, it is a question, however, not of competition in the Western sense of the market economy but of one in the socialist sense.

> Socialist competition [is] the most extensive expression of the creativity of the working masses in the form of the developed socialist society, in which the socialist character of labor reflects itself and is realized. ... Lying close to socialist competition is the fulfillment and the surpassment each day of the economic plans, in each decade and each month according to quantity, kind, quality and costs.[10]

This too is an example of the fact that similar concepts have in no way the same contents.

3. The Democratization of Society

Lenin had already seen in democracy the lively creativity of the worker. Of course *social democracy* is not to be confused with Western democracy, for it is the:

> ...political exercise of power of the working masses of the people led by the working class and its Marxist/Leninist party, which with the foundation of the dictatorship of the proletariat overcame and severed formal civil democracy. ... Social democracy distinguishes itself principally from formal civil democracy in so far as the working class creates and guarantees under the leadership of its Marxist and Leninist Party, by its socialist State for all workers, extensive possibilities practically to realize their common fundamental interests in various political and apolitical forms;...An outstanding sign of socialist democracy consists in its collective form and socially formed forces and orientation.[11]

When Gorbachev therefore speaks on its behalf "to deepen the democracy of the socialist order," (p. 117), it is a question in no way of a transition to Parliamentary democracy in the Western sense.

He expresses his opinion in favor of a stronger *self-governance of labor,* whose most important guarantor is the Party:

It perceived the role of leadership in society and formed at the same time even the highest sort of an organization which is self-governing socially and politically. Whilst the Communist Party of the Soviet Union is developing inner-party democracy and the activity of the Communists, who are active in all constituencies of the political system, rises, it directs the increase of socialist self-government of the people and the reinforced participation of the masses, of each individual in the right direction in the affairs of our land. (p. 118)

Here it is clear that "self-government" in the Soviet sense is not individual self-determination but is a question of an arrangement, a subordination to the collective group which is directed by the Party. Of course the Deputies are accountable to the administration, the collective labor force and the assembly of citizens. For all that there have been established such shortcomings as departmental egoism, provincial patriotism, irresponsibility, bureaucracy and an official attitude of indifference. Therefore only the most worthy should be chosen as Deputies. Significantly, the following demand of Gorbachev, however, sounds hollow:

"In this regard, it would be timely also to undertake these required correctives in our choice of method. Some questions here have accumulated which call for a solution." (p. 121). If one puts this demand in the series of proposals and wishes made so far, one will probably not be able to assume, that it is a question of choice of reform in the Western sense. The constitution of the Soviet Union prefers that discussion of the people and voting be carried out. The dependable channels for the development of direct democracy such as assembly of the citizens, electors' mandate, petitions of labor, the press, radio and television must be better used in order to reach an instant and sensitive reaction to the interests and disposition of the masses.

Sometimes, as soon as there is talk of publicity, one begins to hear challenges, to permit to ruling with greater caution when we speak of our shortcomings and omissions, of the difficulties which in every active job are unavoidable. To this, only one argument can be given, namely, that of Lenin: The Communists are in need of the truth always and in all circumstances. (p. 127).

Those who cannot make the ultimate sacrifice will not rest easily. The endeavors to strengthen the legal order must not be diminished: The legislature must promote even more vigorously the accomplishment of the economic methods of Leitung and the effective control over labor, expenditure and the principles of social justice.

The democratic principles of the administration of justice, the equality of the citizens before the law and the other guarantees which secure the protection of the interests of the State and each citizen must be strictly preserved.

And then Gorbachev continues in the same place that according to the constitution an existing law may be set aside, "that procedure rules according to which a citizen may file in court a complaint against unjust treatment by an official who curtailed his rights." (p. 129). This ambiguous position means two kinds of things: (a) that a Soviet citizen until now had no rights relative to an official, that is cannot act against the latter, and (b) that in the future only a complaint, not a legal action, is to be possible. The agencies of government security "perform too, in strict preservation of Soviet law an extensive job for the unmasking of hostile plots." (p. 129). Can one conclude from this that the State's Security Service until now had not always paid attention to Soviet law?

Before Gorbachev turned towards the Party's strategy of the moment and the modifications of the status of the Party – the presentation of this statement was renounced – he concluded his socio-economic statements with the following words:

It is evident, Comrades, that we, are singling out on this Party day, merely the general framework, the most important outlines for the perfection of our democracy, of the State, of the whole

Soviet political system. The fulfillment of the Party's decisions will doubtless bring with it new forms of phenomena of the people's enterprise, new forms of the social, political creativity of the masses. (p. 130)

II. Will the Reform Movement alter the Structure of the Planned Economy?

The reforms initiated by General Secretary Gorbachev have caused surprise not only in the Soviet Union itself but also in the socialist countries and ultimately in the Western world. On the one side these proposals are saluted and hope is tied thereto that not only is a new era being heralded in the Eastern bloc countries and also in the relationships with the West. On the other hand, it is skeptically expressed that it is merely a question of a tactical maneuver which in no way disturbs the substance of the Communist system.

Another question is whether these proposals for reform can only be reviewed from an economic perspective or whether it is not essential to surround them with a greater, political frame which takes into account even the great problems of the East-West relationship. In this connection, one could also substitute the thesis that Gorbachev arrived at these proposals less of his own accord but was more compelled to it on the basis of the arms race, that is, that he needed a more flexible and more efficient economy in order to keep pace with the Americans in the armaments sector.

1. The Limits of Review of the Proposals for Reform

Not only in the West, but also in the East criteria are sought in order to review these proposals for reform. In the West, therefore, because it is asked whether the Soviet Union and the other Eastern bloc countries are on the way to the Western type of democracy and thereby to reduce the military, political tension; in the East, therefore, because one is hoping for a higher standard of living and more civil liberties.

A complete review of these proposals is for various reasons problematic:
1. Until now only proposals for reform were made. The conversion into concrete measure will require a longer period of time. Not before a few years will one ascertain whether and in what measure these proposals for reform had led to measurable results.

2. The economic and social part of the proposals for reform is not to be separated from the domestic and foreign political components. Particularly, the relationships of the two super powers will influence the conversion of the proposals for reform.If it does not come to concrete disarmament plans and if, moreover, the Americans do not abandon their SDI-Plans, then it is absolutely feasible that the military in the Soviet Union will gain the upper hand relative to the economic plans for reform.

3. Gorbachev's plans for reform shine on the other Eastern bloc countries which can react in very different ways. Should the proposals contain more than technical reforms the possibility exists (or the danger) that a slackness or even a dissolution becomes noticeable in the Eastern bloc. This, however, cannot be in the interests of the Eastern super powers that a curb on these trends is very probable.

These observations make clear that Gorbachev's economic and social proposals for reform cannot only and particularly be reviewed from a theoretical perspective but they necessitate a world-wide, and political-economic, consideration. The theoretical instrument of an economy is not by far sufficient to conceive and review as far as possible the inherent effects in the proposals.

2. Structural or Technical Alterations?

In the endeavor to review these proposals for reform, it seems relevant to ask whether it is a question of structural or technical alterations.

The concept "structure" is used with very different contents:[12] Among these can be understood the internal, qualitative body, that is, the inner order, the relationship of size, the size in itself or the alterations of the conditioning factor of the economy (a change in the system) which arises either in a longer period of time or due to a single revolutionary event. Wagemann[13] has distinguished between *Struktur* and *Konjunktur* (conjuncture, trade cycle): "By structure one understands the permanent and also the economic phenomena which appear just once and by *Konjunktur* the changeable and thereby that which invigorates. Briefly, both concepts glitter in very different colors and significance."[14] Instead of structure or the policy of structure one could also speak of the policy of order.[15] "By the policy of order (qualitative or the policy of structure) is to be understood all properly organized norms which alter the long delayed condition of the framework for creating the economic process and with it the structural (qualitative) relations of the political economy. Frequently the expression *constitution of the economy* is used here for it is a question in these norms of the economic antithesis of the constitution of the State."[16]

By a policy of structure or order, we understand thereby measures which lead *fundamentally* – primarily qualitatively – to changes. Relative to Gorbachev's proposals for reform, one could discuss the socialist, that is, the constitution of the planned economy being replaced by the economic order of the market economy.

These structural reforms are the opposite of technical alterations. Among these we understand the economic and political measures which do not affect the constitution of the economy but are undertaken merely as alterations in the "surface areas" within the given framework of the economic order. One could equate it in the market economy with the *leakage process:* "To the leakage policy belong, on the other hand, all economic and political instruments which in a given order direct themselves to the economic process and thereby alter the quantitative relation (Price, Quantity-Relations). These measures are according to their nature of short or medium duration. A lengthening of the duration of their application happens to be sure."[17]

The question is whether Gorbachev is striving for structural, fundamental, or technical, superficial, alterations with his proposals for reform.

3. Gorbachev's Proposals for Reform do not Lead to the Market Economy

It is noteworthy the intensity with which Gorbachev criticizes the inadequacies of the social system and the planned economy: He refers to the indolence, the stagnation and the conservatism of the system and demands a flexible *Leitungssystem* and a conversion of the economic mechanism, etc.

Relative to that he states: "...of course, the situations are to be created in such a way that it no longer matters if one limits oneself to partial alterations; a radical reform can cause harm." (p. 81). The hint, too, that prices had to be transformed into an active tool of economic and social policy, could indicate a structural alteration.

But this criticism and the proposals for reform which developed out of them should not deceive for no fundamental alteration is envisioned by them, as a criticism of the existing relationships could only mean that these are being surrendered in favor of another structural or economic constitution, that is, that one is switching from the planned economy to the market economy. This would be logical and consistent but is not in keeping with Gorbachev and his proposals for reform. For he says: "When, by way of example, it is necessary and justified to apply economic norms in the place of definite connected plan goals, this means in no way a rejection of the principles of the leadership by the plan, but *merely an alteration of its methods and techniques.*" (p. 91). With regard to property, too, Gorbachev had no structural alteration in mind: "Great matters of fact acquire the problems of socialist property as the foundation of the order of our society." (p. 91). And further: "In the use of social property the role of collective labor must be decisively reinforced." (p. 92)

Both of the most important elements of a socialist planned economy remain in spite of all criticism untouched: The *Plan* is not substituted by the market, and collective property not by private property in the means of production. It is a question, therefore, not of structural reform, which leads to a new (market economy) order of the economy, but only about technical measures which are to be undertaken within the given Communist ideology and of the corrections of superficialities derived from the system, by which economic efficiency is to be improved. That it is merely a question of a technical corrective the rejection of civil ideology attests. "*The bourgeois ideology* is the ideology of the service for capital and monopoly profits, of adventurism and social revenge, the ideology of a society without any future." (p. 171). On the other hand, where the socialist social order is concerned: "We have arranged a world without oppression and exploitation, a society of social uniformity and social security. ... The deep sources of Soviet patriotism rest on our social order, on our humanistic ideology. ... Socialism is a society of a higher morality." (p. 172)

The criticism of the inadequacies of the planned economy and the proposals for reform cannot conceal the fact that it is a question merely of technical and not structural reform.

On the occasion of the visit of the British Prime Minister, Gorbachev had explained at a banquet in honor of Margaret Thatcher: "To assume we gave up our ideals one day, means having lost contact with reality."[18].

4. What Prospects Have the Proposals for Reform in the Soviet Union?

When our presumed thesis comes true that Gorbachev's proposals for reform have as their goal no structural but only technical alterations within the Communist system, the question arises of whether this will be required. Doubts appear to us to mount here.

To the point, Gorbachev remarked: "Every transformation of the mechanism of the economy begins as we know with the *Transformation of Consciousness,* with the task of the intellectual cliche and the practical which until then had developed out of it, as well as clarity about the new tasks." (p. 89). And further stated Gorbachev:

We are enraged quite rightly at all kinds of inadequacies and its actual culprits, people, who have forgotten their duty and are indifferent to social interests; at the bunglers, sluggards, the rapacious and the anonymous calumniator, at the spirit of the civil servant and those who give bribes. (p. 156)

To these two statements – of the demand for an alteration in consciousness, on the one hand, and the description of the modes of conduct, on the other, we remark as follows:

In all societies there are human inadequacies. There are bunglers, sluggards, rapacious individuals, etc. The decisive question, however, is whether society and the economic system of that sort favors or represses such inclinations. While the market economy starts with individual egoism and this is installed as an engine for the whole of society, Marxism starts with the New Man.

According to Röpke[19] there are three social forms of struggle against defects:

1. The ethically negative relationship: One endeavors by power or cunning to procure the means at the cost of the other. (egoism)

2. The ethically positive relationship: It is the altruistic submission, by wich means are used without any return. (altruism)

3. The ethically neutral relationship: By virtue of a confidential reciprocity the goal of one's own increased well-being is striven for with the means of the unknown increase in well-being. The relationship, which has been described as solidarity means, that one's increased well-being follows in some way, which not only harms the others, but yields to them as a by-product no promotion of well-being.[20]

Apart from the fact that these three forms seldom appear in pure form it is to be noted that in the competitive economy where the individual seeks improvement in his own well-being, (income, prestige and power) superiority is permitted by observing definite legal and moral limits. In pursuing these goals, the individual must bring to the market better products of service in order to surpass his competitors. By this act of competition the well-being of the citizenry is *unintentionally* promoted. In the market economies, one has therefore a realistic image of man and his mode of conduct, that is, one proceeds in principle from his subjective, egoistic desires and goals, attempts to avoid deterioration by legal and moral barriers and converts into cash this inclination toward a general increase in well-being.

In Marxism there is a completely different anthropological image of the new man.[21]

The main idea of the transformation and development of man after the abolition of private property and all other alienated causes to the new, socialist or communist man extends through Marxist writings. "This 'other subject' whose needs are satisfied and whose interests coincide with the social common good, knows no longer any greed, envy and egoism."[22] In the class society of capitalism his individualism is determined by the class to which he belongs, that is, the most hideous social traits of capitalism are expressed in a search for profit which despises the human being, in brutality, the joy of aggression, etc. It is completely different under socialism.[23]

In the struggle of the exploited working class against capitalism such modes of conduct as the idea of competition between workers, individualism, egoism, political indifference, which are objectively stipulated in capitalist society, are overcome and there develops the readiness to sacrifice, the collective spirit, solidarity, internationalism, and understanding of the class attitude, constancy, loyalty to principles and similar qualities and modes of conduct of the personality of the class conscious worker.[24]

It is here quite plain that in a socialist, communist economy and society, a new man is to be created. If one compares, however, this expectation about the future man with reality in the Soviet Union – Gorbachev speaks of bunglers, sluggards, rapacious individuals, calumniators – it can be stated that even in a socialist society the "old Adam" is furthermore available and will also be available in the future.[25] In the face of this anthropological actuality there can be legitimate doubts whether Gorbachev's goal of the "transformation of consciousness" can succeed. This doubt will be strengthened still by the following considerations: The socialist and planned economic system exists in the Soviet Union now for more than seventy years. In these two generations definite forms and customs of the hierarchy, bureaucracy and the structural order have developed which might have strengthened even more the fundamental, anthropological streams.

In the face of this analysis, we have great doubt that Gorbachev will succeed in carrying out his reform movement in this gigantic empire, especially since numerous officials, officers, functionaries, etc., have acquired in the course of two generations power, esteem and income which they would lose in the milieu of the planned reforms. Is it realistic to expect that the normal man with all his strengths and weaknesses will be voluntarily ready for this?

These doubts are spread publicly in the circles of Soviet dissidents, even with a slightly different meaning.[26]

In the USA, a document from Moscow arrived which was published in the Russian immigrant newspaper *Problems of Eastern Europe*. Behind the pseudonym, N. Boregow, there is presumed to be the dissident Roy Medwedjew. In this document, the view is advanced that a bitter struggle between reformers and conservatives in the Soviet leadership has broken out.

The *reformers* had no unified concept for they were not united with one another. In this document it enjoined the reformers:

> The view that in our land a gradual reform is taking place is the purest illusion. Since they have at their disposal neither strategy nor a consistent socio-economic plan, the ruling group is forced to live from day to day and, in order to remain in power, to enter every possible political alliance and accept as well doubtful compromises.

The Gorbachev leadership, therefore, resembles a "lesser government." On the other hand, the conservatives unite: The members of the *Breschnewismus* have joined with the *Technokraten*. These are already of the opinion *Perestroika* is already completed with the change of generations and certain alterations in the central system of administration. This neo-conservative group has become a fundamental danger for Gorbachev. In the document it says, in addition:

> The conservatives know what they want. The same cannot be said of the supporters of reconstruction and alteration. The latter have neither strategy nor are they united with one another. [The neo conservative forces] have no doubt that the present course cannot be continued for much longer. They will use the first errors of the reformers to engage in a counter attack.

That there are within a system of government two distinguishable camps – majority party and opposition – or even with a great party two movements (hawks and doves) exist is not exceptional and quite typical of even Western democracy. It is important, however, that within the communist system of the Soviet Union two groups appear to exist both not wanting particularly to alter the principles of Communist ideology and the planned economy. It is rather a technical question of how much or how little a reform movement should or should not be adopted within the given system. It therefore does not appear fitting to speak of the reformers and the neo-conservatives, but of the *Communist Reformers* and the *Orthodox Communists,* for both factions can and will not alter fundamentally, or even abolish, the system accepted by them.

The great latitude given the *Communist Reformers* by Gorbachev will only be of a permanent nature if it succeeds militarily in ending the arms race, economically if by the flexibility of the system it raises its efficiency and thereby the standard of living. It is thoroughly realistic to assume that after 1987 a disarmament agreement between the United States and the Soviet Union will be settled. It is, on the other hand, very improbable that the attempts at greater flexibility will already bear fruit within a reasonable time. On the contrary: in the transformation phase there will be, for example in income, a re-shuffling of areas in which success is achieved. These fluctuations will call into question socia-list traditions leading to a criticism of the course of reform. The stronger the *Communist Reformers* switch over the elements of the market economy into the planned economy and the trend to move over from technical to an alteration of the system, the stronger will be the opposition of the *Orthodox Communists* and will raise the demand for a return to "pure theory." The struggle between the two factions is not decisive, but rather the immanent contradictions in the system.

5. What Effects do the Reform Proposals have on the Satellite Countries?

The statements and reservations made about the Soviet Union are valid in principle also for the East European socialist States, too, that is, similar structures might arise in these political economies, too. In these lands, too, it might not be successful in creating the new (socialist or communist) man. In spite of these similarities, one can deduce from this that the Eastern bloc is in no way monolithic. This means, that in spite of the common factors, socialism and planned economy, *national differences,* are at hand. These differences might be worthy of note relative to Gorbachev's proposals for reform.

In the People's Republic of *Poland,* Gorbachev's proposals have been positively accepted, even with enthusiasm:[27]

Sooner than in the other Eastern bloc countries the new Soviet proposals for reform had been saluted, at the same time with reservations. Gorbachev's criticisms of his own system were saluted – the bunglers, the sluggards, the rapacious and the calumniators – for indirect expression was thereby given to the inadequate economic, social and political inconveniences at hand, not only in Poland but also in the leading Soviet power. The failure of the State and the economy is consequently not a typical Polish problem but also that of the almighty Soviet Union and possibly all Eastern bloc countries. Consequently, Poland finds itself in *good company.*

This positive review of the criticisms of Gorbachev on the actual events and his positive acceptance of the proposals for reform in Poland cannot however deceive us about the reservations. The Poles feel they belong to Europe and the West. They have since the repeated divisions of countries not only reservations about Germany, but also about Russia, regardless of whether the Czar or the Communists ruled. The enthusiastic welcome of Gorbachev's plan by the Vice President of the Polish Parliament, Miecyslaw Rakowski, cannot delude[28] us either about these reservations. In front of the press club in Bonn, he explained: "We support his (Gorbachev's) concept with all our hearts. They are close to us and correspond to our concepts. I (Rakowski) am almost enthusiastic by this development." Whether the expected inner political relief relative to foreign politics outweighs fears is in the short run not possible to review.

The welcoming of the movement for reform is one thing, the successful implementation of economic reform another:[29]

The Polish party newspaper *Trybuna ludu* writes that the population is sorry about the protracted discussion. The working people want to see action. The government's newspaper *Rzeczpospolita* has made the people familiar with 174 proposals for "the construction of a modern economic system" – as Minister President Messner defined it in 120 typewritten pages. These arguments the Poles should also read when they instead of discussion want to see action, "for what is being spread among them here are overturned plans besides which Gorbachev's 'reconstruction' appears as pure cosmetics." (Dietrich). If the 174 theses were to be realized at the second stage of the economic reform, then Poland's socialistic economy would be scarcely recognizable in three years. There would be free entry into the market, a free price mechanism, State factories which are geared toward profit making and not toward bureaucracy, industrial factories with private capital participating, unemployment, prosperity, competition, managers with fantastic salaries, and a planning bureaucracy which no longer knew the purpose for which it was there.

Stefan Dietrich asks: "Can it be believed that it would come so far? All experience teaches the opposite. No one counts any more how often the government had established reforms which came to naught."

The economic newspaper *Zycie Grospodarcze* scared the Poles shortly before the turn of the year with the warning that the economy found itself on a steep road. Poland was becoming unhesitatingly one of the Third World countries if the demands for the economic reforms announced in 1982 were not finally realized. The view that an economy with a market and with enterprise – that makes profit or can suffer losses – cannot function has been around for a long time. Particularly forty years of socialist economic methods have proven that even the richest land can be brought down to beggardom. "However, the *political will* alone was *not* on hand at the decisive spot to see the consequences. Whoever has the power wants chiefly to keep it." (Dietrich). This is, as we repeatedly indicated already, the decisive point: It does not depend on technical (cosmetic) correctives but on the success of an altered structural system. Is this, however, at all possible in a socialist system, be it so, then it begs itself the question. Can one expect this in a realistic manner?

The ideas of reform in Poland contain chiefly material incentives: Who works well shall also earn well. That would be a powerful step forward, for all earn equally bad in state factories, regardless of how they work. A normal average wage suffices to just cover fundamental needs at the lowest level.[30] "Unbelievable forces of production are dissipated by slovenliness, corruption, standing in queues, common theft and nepotism." (Dietrich)

Minister President Messner had decided on the withdrawal of the State from areas which formerly had been reserved for it alone.

> Less government sounds good. But where are the independent institutions which in the market economy set in motion the free play of the forces of production? Where are free trade unions and associations with common interests, independent parties and the press? A free economy can only thrive when the individual there is able to move freely. (Dietrich)

These demands, which in the West are self-evident constituents of democracy and the market economy would lead to the necessary structural change in the system. Is it however, realistic to assume that this in a reasonable period of time will be the case in a socialist country, not only in Poland?

On the other hand, *Czechoslovakia* reacted essentially more reservedly and cautiously.[31]

In 1968, Dubcek had already undertaken the task of reforming the Communist system and giving it a human visage. This attempt was abruptly interrupted by the entry of troops from the Warsaw Pact – *der Bruderparteien.* Dubcek was removed and exiled to the country. After the fall of Dubcek the ideas of reform of the Husak regime were immediately, uncompromisingly suppressed. At this time, Gorbachev's proposals drew attention to the *Spring of Prague* so that the same functionaries in Prague who were called upon by the Kremlin to imitate that which they almost twenty years ago suppressed. "The grave-diggers of a reform offer themselves as midwives of a new society." (Horsky)

Within the administration of Prague two camps have apparently formed, on the one hand, the pragmatists around Minister President Lubomir Strougal, and on the other, the orthodox dogmatists around the Secretary of the Central Committee, Vasil Bilák. This contrast has led to a stalemate which is the expression of a benumbed personal structure, for the trimming of the administrators who were identified as being against the reforms of 1968 are now to be convinced under the leadership of the Soviet Union of the necessity of the reforms. For this reason, the 74-year old State and Party Chief, Gustav Husák, uses very careful tactics. At a Central Committee Assembly which lasted two days, he had merely spoken of "necessary economic and political mechanisms, or, if you wish, reforms." ... "On closer examination, it becomes indeed clear that Husák's announcements contain nothing which the Party compelled previously to some kind of practical alterations." (Horsky)

If Prague should "wheel around" from Gorbachev's proposals for reform then certain individuals might unavoidably suffer the consequences. It is, however, questionable whether the ruling class would volunteer to do this.

Gorbachev's visit to Prague – apparently for reasons of health – was cancelled. During his visit, he had made the endeavor to speak not only with the Party leadership about the necessity of the reforms sought, but also to make direct contact with the population which applauded him. In his after dinner talk, Husák aligned himself wholly and entirely on the side of Gorbachev. This concurrence was of such an unrestricted sort that many people questioned the authenticity of its contents. To be sure, some members of the administration of Prague look doubtfully in the direction of Moscow and ask themselves whether Gorbachev will succeed in this,[32] for "At one time the tanks of the Kremlin mounted their guns at the *Prager Frühling.* The political impetus and ideas today come out of the same Kremlin which appear to renew the almost forgotten 'Socialism with the human countenance'." (Horsky)

During his visit in Czechoslovakia, Gorbachev had aroused hope merely by his contacts with the population for which he could not possibly even pay a fee. Above all, the contents of the concept "democracy" were interpreted in various ways. In this connection he indicated, of course, that no Communist Party has a claim to monopoly, but, nevertheless, the Soviet Union will not withdraw its troops from the CSSR. Even if the contingent of Soviet troops should be reduced, the arm of power will still be retained.

Of course one can count on Gorbachev's desire for a change in the top leadership in Prague,[33] that is that a "younger guard" takes the place of the "old gentlemen". The "younger guard" is of course ideological secure but as modern managers have to accomplish economic and technological progress in order to raise the efficiency of the system:

> The great misunderstanding to which many Czechs yield lies in the fact that the man from Moscow regards the "democratization" not as his own goal but as a *means to improved performance.* Perhaps he will contribute thereby to a new and false interpretation with dire consequences between Moscow and the Eastern Europeans.[34]

The situation in *Hungary* is comparable to that in Czechoslovakia, and at the same time incomparable. In Hungary, an economic reform is already underway which, especially in Budapest, offers an almost Western supply of goods, on the one hand, and on the other, has already economic difficulties, for the balance of trade deficit for 1986 is estimated at more than one million dollars and the debts to the West amount just now to fourteen billion dollars.[35] The reproach can be made that the policy of reform has not succeeded.

> In converting in such a way the economic order, social life and especially the attitude in the country so that Hungary could protect itself today sufficiently quickly and drastically against the adversities of the international economic downturn. This, however, is not the result of reform but the consequences of too little reform, the consequences of the *political and ideological resistance,* of leaders who wear blinkers or pursue the interests of the officials – in the final analysis the consequence of socialism. The policy of reform cannot help the country any more because its boundaries are fixed. These boundaries the Russian tanks occupied in the year 1956 and they were called in the era of Brezhnev clearly to mind. (Meier)

The example of Hungary makes it clear that political and ideological limits are set to economic reforms for it is not a question of a change in structure in the system, but of a technical change.

In spite of these difficulties, Gorbachev's course of reform might be sympathetically received.

The behavior of the German Democratic Republic relative to Gorbachev's course of reform is reserved and cautious. Kurt Hager, member of the *SED-Politbüro* [Sozialistische Einheitspartei Deutschlands. This is the union of Social Democrats and Communists in East Germany.] – since 1955 he was Secretary of the Central Committee and was considered the SED *chief of ideology* – had expressed himself in an interview with a Hamburg illustrated magazine on the desired reforms of Gorbachev in the Soviet Union. In this interview, the various positions on foreign, economic and social policy have become clear.[36]

In *foreign policy* – especially in disarmament and the limits to armaments – Honecker supports the course without reservation. Honecker can claim even for himself that he is in favor of further political talks with the West on the location of American medium range missiles in Western Europe. Since then, Gorbachev has moved on to the same platform in foreign policy. Hager remarked in addition: "Whatever concerns foreign policy, especially the security of peace, we support completely the contents of the peace program of socialism spread by Mikhail Gorbachev..."

With regard to Soviet efforts to renew the economy, the SED can refer to its own economic reform: In the German Democratic Republic combinations have been formed and the competence of the combinations' performances have been shifted, that is, down. In many Soviet publications, the economy of the German Democratic Republic is praised, something which in the German Democratic Republic is .carefully noted. What cannot be overlooked is that the second German state in spite of an unfavorable passage out – no basis for raw materials, reparations, dismantlement, flight of the active population from the building of the wall – has risen to the tenth leading industrial nation of the world. Even if a gap in prosperity is put forward between West and East Germany, the German Democratic Republic has still the highest standard of living in the Eastern bloc.

Gorbachev's ideas on society's policy is more important than these comments on economic reform:

To Gorbachev's proposals, Kurt Hager gave the almost "classical" commentary. "Would you, when your neighbor papers the walls anew in his home, feel an obligation to yourself to paper the walls anew in your home, too?" He indicated the SED had already adopted and drawn from the rich treasure of experience of the Communist Party of the Soviet Union, the teachings of Lenin, especially the theory of the socialist revolution, of socialist structure and the theory of the Party. Says Hager: "This means however that we do not, in the past either, imitate what happens in the Soviet Union." It is very plain here that the German Democratic Republic relative to Gorbachev's proposed movement for reform is staying at a distance. This distance will be lengthened even more as Hager quotes from the following sentence from the *Appeal* of the Communist Party (KPD) of June 11, 1945. "We are of the opinion that the way along which the Soviet system is forcing Germany is false for this way corresponds not to the present conditions of development in Germany."[37] This reference to an *Appeal* of 1945 is surprising for these demands for one's *own way* were forgotten in the ensuing years. Is a superiority of the economy of the German Democratic Republic over that of the Soviet Union being demonstrated with the hint to the East German special way of socialism? Are doubts about Gorbachev's course of reform evident here? For: "If the highest *Kulturchef* of the German Democratic Republic compares Gorbachev with a paper hanger, he vouches for his own lack of seriousness and hypocrisy. Or he expresses at least the hope that this *Perestroika* is not a superficial maneuver meant especially to hoodwink the West."[38]

Gorbachev has as his goal not only a transformation of the economy but also one of society, too. Of course, one cannot speak of such a thing in the German Democratic Republic for openness and critical thinking are not promoted there, the privacy of the party and its dogma continue to hold good.

To the proposal of Gorbachev to choose factory directors in the future, Hager replied: "That is not a problem for us to discuss." For the SED, it is decisive that a labor leader stands at the head of a factory possibly for years, one who possesses a corresponding qualification and is in the position to organize production with greater effectiveness, quality and profit. During the SED reforms which the system does not want to touch, and which still wants to exclude the area of the economy, it revealed itself in opposition to what Gorbachev called the "democratization" of society. "Today in accordance with the principle work together, plan together, govern together, every third citizen of the German Democratic Republic is included in an honorable official capacity in the leadership of the State and society," observed Hager and implied that there was in the German Democratic Republic *no need for democratization.* (Winters)

Hager describes their own socialist way as follows:

Of course, all socialist countries learn from each other. They have after all fundamental common ties such as the world view of Marxism-Leninism, and the common goal, socialism and communism. But every socialist country has also a definite kind of economic and social development, historical and cultural traditions, geographical and other conditioning factors which have to be considered.

Is the way to socialism claimed by the German Democratic Republic only a temporary phenomenon or the onset of a democratization within the Eastern bloc countries? If one draws near to the constitution[39] of the German Democratic Republic and further to the GDR constitutional law[40] one arrives at the conclusion that it cannot be a question of a democratization in the Western sense: Article 1, paragraph 1, of the GDR Constitution already states: The German Democratic Republic is a socialist state of workers and peasants...." In Article (1) it is stated: "the political economy of the German Democratic Republic rests on *socialist property* in the means of production...." And Paragraph 3 reveals this decision: "In the German Democratic Republic the principle of *Leadership and Planning* of the political economy is valid as well as of all other socialist areas. The political economy of the German Democratic Republic is a *socially planned economy*..." According to Article 12 (1) private property is forbidden in mineral wealth, mines, power-stations, dams, industrial enterprises, banks, insurance companies, public goods, roads and highways, railroads, shipping, airways, mail, telephone and telegraph installations, etc. An alteration of the system consequently would also have to have above all an alteration in the constitution. According to Article 63 (2) of the Constitution of the GDR an alteration of the constitution requires a majority of at least two-thirds of the chosen representatives.

In the official textbook of the constitutional law of the German Democratic Republic it is stated:[41] "The constitution of the GDR is according to its kind socialistic. ... It has the same characteristics which first of all described the Soviet constitution and which also determines the constitution of the other lands in the socialist community of states." It is, thereby, made plain that the determination of the constitution of the GDR cannot be considered in isolation, it is rather the constituent of all socialist countries.

Socialist property relationships are a decisive ingredient of socialist production relationships:[42]

> The economic basis of socialist society's order and the order of the State are socialist property in the means of production, the socialist production relations in city and in the country, the socialist economic system, that is, the political economy as a united mechanism organized according to the democratic central authority and the political leadership and planning of the economy (planned economy).

Since 1974, the total output of industrial goods has been produced in public works. The attacks of the bourgeois ideologists, especially the modern revisionists, are directed against these facts. Thus, O. Šik and others demand the introduction of a "socialist market economy," the elimination of the uniformly applicable state planning and the break-up of public property into group property. These are the demands for the renunciation of the merits of socialism. They amount to a disintegration of the socialist character of the production relationship and direct themselves to the re-introduction of spontaneous, anarchistic, capitalistic elements into society.[43]

In the light of these determinations of the constitution is it to be expected that the GDR or other socialist states, too, reach beyond a technical reform to an alteration in the system? Even if particular supporters of reform wanted this (which is to be doubted), could they abolish socialist property and the planned economy?

6. Are The Eastern Bloc Countries Insecure?

The reforms initiated by Gorbachev – about whose outcome one can give very different prognoses – must really have been positively accepted in the Eastern bloc countries, for they put democracy in perspective, which could possibly be limited not only to the internal relationships in the Soviet Union. If one overlooks the reactions, one can state – it simplifies it – the following cluster is at hand:

(1) Czechoslovakia and the GDR announce reservations relative to the course of reform, Prague because already under Dubcek a reform was crushed by the use of force, the GDR because it felt itself economically superior and wanted to go its own way.

(2) Poland and Hungary salute the proposals for reform: Poland hopes for flexibility and with it a reassurance in domestic politics. In Hungary is to be found a confirmation of its own successful ways.

However, the insecurity in the Eastern bloc countries is unmistakable:[44] Thoughtful East Europeans after an analysis of the power structure in the Kremlin come to the conclusion that Gorbachev has to take into consideration, now as before, the opposition of the army to his plans for reform. Since, however, the army is dominant not only in the Soviet Union itself but also in the satellite states the course of reform has not yet been decided. This could also be the reason why Gorbachev again and again makes repeated proposals for disarmament and control of armaments. He must apparently show results in this area in order to appease the military. By such a settlement, his prestige would not only rise within the Soviet Union and abroad, but he would create for the "military front" the required calm in order to be able to continue undisturbed his course of reform in the area of the economy and society.

Independently of this element of insecurity, the East Europeans are much too skeptical from their own experience to be able "to believe in a golden age in the Soviet Union, one whose onset has suddenly been ordained from above." (Ströhm)

Even the supporters of the course of reform would not want to penetrate the whirlpool of uncontrolled Soviet eruptions:

> For the Communist reformers in Eastern Europe could press on with their economic and political course until now in the certainty that a political, accountable Soviet Union was in the background, of course, often inconvenient and threatening – that presented a guarantee for the preservation of the system, however, during possible breakdowns. If, however, the Soviet Union itself, stagnating until now, begins to experiment and to call into question the old tables of law – then the "Little East" of the countries on the perimeter will fall into the undertow of the uncontrollable development of the "Big East", that is, of "Big Brother". (Ströhm)

This insecurity is brought forth by at least two more elements: The shattering of previous reforms and the rule of the old in the Eastern bloc: In the early twenties, Lenin had already begun the experiment with a new economic policy (NEP) and fought among others against the bureaucrats and bureaucracy. The bureaucracy is however, not an independent part, but a constituent of the whole system, that is, the consequences of the nationalization of the factors of production, banking and insurance, as well as the collectivization of agriculture. This socialist and planned economic system had created a system of central planning and central administration. From the socialist, that is, Communist ideology, arose the central system of planning and direction and from this finally the almighty bureaucracy. To try to shake up or abolish this bureaucracy assumes in advance that the system can be not only technically but also structurally altered, or abolished. This is, however, neither the goal of Gorbachev, nor would it be realistic. For that reason, the NEP experiment was also shattered, even that of Nikita Kruschev introduced during the *period of thaw* after the death of Stalin.[45] He, too, tried to break the omnipotence of the Party machine and to decentralize the economy, that is, regional economic advisers should be substituted for central ministers, the division of all Party Committees into urban and rural should serve as a pretext for a gigantic cleansing of the Party machine. However, for the first time in Soviet history, the machine mutinied and led by Brezhnev eliminated Kruschev. The reforms until now have been shattered. Why should those of Gorbachev at present succeed?

A further reason exists for insecurity in that until now not only in the Eastern bloc countries but also in the Soviet Union the "old gentlemen" ruled. In the Soviet Union the rule of the old has been dissolved. In the GDR, Czechoslovakia, Hungary and Bulgaria the "Seniors," who on the average are twenty years older are still at the helm. From this difference in age alone arises psychological problems. The "old gentlemen" in the Eastern bloc countries live according to tradition, and are ideological. However, they are also intellectually and psychologically open in a very limited way to a new course, particularly one which is laden with risks. At present, Gorbachev faces them. He is younger and embodies the type of manager and doer who uses and controls the mass media and who also makes an impression in the West. Comparisons with this problem can be made: Adenauer made no contact with the young Kennedy, for between the two there was a gap of a generation, but did with de Gaulle, who belonged to the same generation. Since politics are carried out in no way in a rational place free from air, this aspect of productive power should not be underestimated.

The insecurities to be described in the Eastern bloc countries have various causes and point to diverse depths. They are, however, there.

III. Attempt at an Evaluation

In the discussion of reform initiated by Gorbachev two expressions are used which beyond the literal significance are at the same time important with regard to content: *Perestroika* and *Glasnost*. *Perestroika* means reconstruction, transformation, and *Glasnost* means frankness, openness. With both expressions, it is indicated literally that it is not a question of a new construction of the Soviet economy and society, but merely of a reconstruction of the existing system. A reconstruction can occur superficially and signify merely a cosmetic operation. It can also contain, however, a far-reaching reformation so that one could speak not only of a technical alteration, but of a structural change. The intensity of the reconstruction, that is, the reformation, could not be recognizable at the present point in time not even in the Soviet Union much less in foreign lands in the West. The expression *Glasnost* also shows the possible limits of the course of reform: It is not a question of freedom (of the press) and democracy in the Western sense, but of openness. Do we mean by openness that which comes from above, or, alternately, that which comes up from below? And who determines the degree of openness? The substitute leader of the department in the Central Committee of Moscow, Nikolai Schischlin, has determined the limits of the course of reform as follows in an interview with the trade union newspaper in Budapest, *Nepszava*.[46] "Political life in the Soviet Union knows no pluralism in the bourgeois sense." However, "a good relationship with the West would be promoted by the transformation *(Perestroika)*." With that the content and the limits of *Perestroika* and *Glasnost* are appropriately marked.

In the face of these "literal" boundaries is it legitimate to raise the question of whether it is a matter at all of reforms or merely technical correctives: If one understands by the expression *reformer*, for example, Martin Luther, one understands him who alters completely an existing order with a new idea and thereby creates a new structure, then Gorbachev is certainly no reformer, for he, furthermore, clings to the principles of the Communist Party of the Soviet Union, that is, that Communism and the planned economy remain in the future the sustaining elements of the Soviet Union and the Eastern bloc countries. It is rather a question of an attempt at "renovation" within a given ideological and political system in order to raise economic efficiency.

The expectations linked to the concepts *Perestroika* and *Glasnost* could be very different in the East and the West:

(1) In the Soviet Union and in the Eastern bloc countries, expectations between hope and fear might waver: especially the young generation, but the intellectuals, too – the scientists, the artists, the journalists – are hoping for more freedom in the Western sense; the modern generation of managers want more latitude for themselves in order to be able to economize more efficiently. The individuals with technical titles [die Nomenklatura] – the functionaries and the holders of power – fear their influence will disappear, their income possibly fall. They will support the course of reform only to the extent that it does not endanger their own position. If this is the case, then the Nomenklatura will appeal to the principles of Marxism/Leninism and stop the course of reform. The Eastern bloc countries, especially the GDR and the CSSR, will join this movement when the old rulers resign and have been replaced by a younger, naturally, ideologically secure, but more pragmatically oriented generation.

(2) In Western Europe expectations might be very high for behind the hopes for a liberalization and democratization – in the Western sense to be sure – lie the wish that democratic principles will also penetrate the socialist world. With the liberation from the shackles of the planned economy an economic revival is anticipated which in the Western nations, too, as in the case of China – brings some good. From a political point of view an easing of tension is anticipated so that the arms race and the threat from both sides can be ended. Contrary to these optimists, critics and skeptics indicate that the former attempts at reform of Lenin (NEP) and Kruschev, of course, aroused great expectations at the beginning but were shattered by the resistance of the Nomenklatura. This reform does not deserve the name of reform. It is merely the attempt to win the West's support in the area of politics and economics with expensive propaganda in order to get breathing space for the ideological altercation.

If this analysis – which in reality is much more complex and complicated should prove by chance to be true, then there exists no reason to greet Gorbachev's course of reform as something euphoric. In the past, similar beginnings have already been overestimated and saluted optimistically in the Western world.[47]

Previously in the 1930s renowned Western intellectuals have praised Stalin's "democratization" and saluted especially the constitution of 1936. Gorbachev's spectacular telephone conversation with Sacharow over the abrogation of the latter's exile already had a predecessor, too, for Stalin had in the same way telephoned the authors, Bulgakow and Pasternak. Kruschev had also put "democracy" essentially in perspective on the twenty second Party Day. The result is known.

On the twenty-seventh Party Day in 1986 at the latest, the extent became clear. Gorbachev strove for a regeneration of Leninism as he, himself, wanted to be regarded also as a Founding Father of the Soviet Union. At the same time, he engaged in rituals as they had been practised with the advent of the First Writers Congress in 1934 in the UDSSR of Stalin, but also in Western capitals. The recently formed Peace Forum in Moscow has set its sights, too, on the social groups which sustain the system; banking, combines, trade unions, churches, political parties and influential professional associations. (Gerstenmaier)

This skepticism toward the reforms of Gorbachev is also shared by Soviet emigrants. The former, high-ranking functionary of the Party in Moscow, Mikhail Voslensky[48] has described this as the *new class* in his book *Nomenklatura* which administers the giant empire. These administrators have carefully camouflaged themselves. The new class continues in its disguise as members of the feudal barons and of the capitalists:

They deny their own existence. In the realm of theory Stalin's model of the structure of Soviet society is used for this purpose. In practice, the class of "administrators" makes use of every pretence in order to pass off as part of a normal – in actual socialism of course pathologically puffed up – administrative machine, as ordinary employees as they are to be found in all countries in the world. The *Nomenklatura* is that "intelligence force" which "concerns itself professionally with the leadership" and in a "certain respect finds itself in a special position opposite those who are entrusted with the performance of the work. To it "belongs a special place in the social organization of work in socialism." Admitted into the *Nomenklatura* are "persons who in the name of society ... perform the function of organization in production and all other spheres of social life." ... The ruling class of Soviet society, the "new class" is the *Nomenklatura*. It knows this and surrounds itself with the veil of secrecy. Declarations about positions in the *Nomenklatura* are most secret. The registers of the *Nomenklatura* are to be classed with documents at the higher level of secrecy.[49]

On account of this secrecy, it is impossible to quote even an approximate number. On the basis of the censuses of 1959 and 1970, Voslensky has undertaken an assessment.[50] There are in existence two levels of *Nomenklatura*.

(1) First level of Nomenklatura: The leaders of the agencies of the party, society and the state at the federal level, unions and self-governing republic, regions, areas, districts and large cities with more than half a million inhabitants.

(2) Second level of Nomenklatura: The leaders of the same agencies at the level of the Rayons (that is one of the lowest areas of administration) and towns with less than a half million inhabitants.

With reference to the size of the *Nomenklatura* at both levels, Voslensky had made the following assertion:[51]

(1) *First Level:*

1959	77,063 members
1970	76,847 members
reduction	*216 members*

These figures are on the one hand to be reduced since not all leaders of subordinated departments of the national administration, of the associations and of social organizations belong to the *Nomenklatura;* on the other hand, it must be raised by the *Nomenklaturisten* [Members of the *Nomenklatura*] of the Party machine, the state security agency, the diplomatic services and all the military forces. The number of the *Nomenklaturisten* amounts to the great size of 100,000 persons.

(2) *Second Level:*

1959	152,628 members
1970	145,248 members
reduction	*6,370 members*

With reference to the *Nomenklaturisten* on the second level corrections above and below are required. The final total Voslensky estimates at 150,000 persons.

Thus, the political control of the *Nomenklatura* in the Soviet Union is exercised by a group of approximately 250,000 persons – by one thousandth of the population of the country. This group which cannot be chosen nor removed, determines fate and gives it political directives.[52]

The numerical strength of the *Nomenklatura* is still not answered by the preceding statistical analysis: Deputies in the key positions of the economy, in scientific institutions and in educational affairs, do not belong to the core of the ruling class, but they exercise in their actual areas the classpower of the *Nomenklatura*. To the group of leaders of industry and agriculture belong in 1959   283,346 and in 1970   300,843 persons. In research, in the university and in high school approximately 150,000 *Nomenklaturisten* are occupied. It is a question, consequently, altogether of 450,000 to 500,000 persons in this area.

The answer to the question of how many persons belong to the *Nomenklatura* reads: "The number of *Nomenklaturisten* in the UDSSR moves in the order of magnitude of three quarters of a million."[53] If it is calculated here – on the statistical basis of a 4 person household – in addition to family relatives, the complete total amounts to 3 million persons. Including family relatives, the *new class* amounts to less than 1.5 percent of the population of the Soviet Union.

Not only are these figures important, but more important still is who in the Soviet Union actually rules: The General Secretary of the Central Committee or the *Nomenklatura*?

According to Voslensky[54], the General Secretary does not rule the land. It is the Nomenklatura which rules:

> ...and the politics of the Central Committee of the Communist Party of the Soviet Union is not the politics of the General Secretary, but of this class. The Fathers of the *Nomenklatura*, Lenin and Stalin, determined the direction and the important guidelines of the government of the *Nomenklatura* in keeping with their wishes. This is the reason in no small measure why Lenin and Stalin are regarded as such autocratic rulers. ... On the other hand, Kruschev and Brezhnev have always been just highly placed executors of the will of the *Nomenklatura*. The General Secretary of the Central Committee is the highest of all *Nomenklaturists*, consequently, he is also the most powerful man in the society of actual socialism.[55]

Without doubt, the power of the General Secretary is – especially then when he has thrust his own proteges into the *Politbüro* and the Secretariat – great but in no way the only power. To the degree that the General Secretary succeeds in bringing his vassals to the top of the *Nomenklatura* his strength grows for the *Politbüro* and the Secretariat are reduced to assistants of the General Secretary. Quite openly, in his first phase as General Secretary, Gorbachev had surrounded himself not only with new people but also with those who were devoted to him. Since there is no shortage in the Kremlin of power struggles, it was a question not of the means of the Parliamentary art of speech as in the Parliaments of the West, "but by year-long ambushes and the most refined intrigue which a politician of the West would probably be unable to understand."[56] The question arises whether and to what extent in the middle and longer view, Gorbachev can accomplish his *new course.*

For this reason, the third attempt of Gorbachev will also (after Lenin and Kruschev) be skeptically reviewed. Soviet emigrants presume that this will make no headway and be demolished:

> Doubtless, Gorbachev is seriously determined to alter certain things in the Soviet Union, especially to bring forward the urgent, necessary improvement in the efficiency of the economy. Every transformation, however, must encroach upon the privileges of the *Nomenklatura* and in the bitter resistance of the functionary class fearful for its power and advantages Gorbachev will also finally be wrecked. To carry out reforms without at the same time altering fundamentally the structure of the Soviet system resembles the attempt to square the circle. (Neue Zürcher Zeitung).

We agree with this diagnosis.

This skepticism towards Gorbachev's course of reform is also from that time shared by the German Ambassador, Jörg Kastl.[57] In this instance only critical observations regarding the economic portion of the reforms are of interest, the carrying out of the disarmament is to be disregarded.

Kastl is surprised by the enthusiasm with which our politicians of all shades saluted Gorbachev's initiatives. Of course, had the *Politbüro* – after the death of Tschernenko – decided for the troublesome Gorbachev it would thereby have decided:

...for the transformation in order to keep step with the forces already engaged in competition with the innovating industrial states and the Chinese reformers. The members of the *Politbüro* could be of different opinions on how far and how quickly *Perestroika* should proceed, but they are like Gorbachev, Lenin's faithful pupil. ... We do not have therefore to worry ourselves about the political survival of the doughty General Secretary. On that matter there exists only little danger that he be hauled in front of an orthodox Lenin sort of inquisition on account of a destructive heresy. Should he be considered by us as a dove, his closest advisers express themselves most "hawklike," when it is a matter of the general approach relative to the international class foe. (Kastl)

This statement of the former German Ambassador in Moscow from direct experience of Soviet leadership at the top comes with special meaning.

Like Lenin, Gorbachev possesses also an inexorable glance for the weaknesses of the Soviet State, but his *Perestroika* is so far more timorous than Lenin's New Economic Policy in the year 1921. The *reform from above* is still without any sure conception, the slogans are not new:

Discipline, acceleration of technical and scientific progress, higher productivity! Once again they are to become more sober, honorable, reasonable, better and – naturally – to work more. The people are meanwhile compelled further to live in neglected, musty community houses, stand in queues, demoralized in dirty outpatients' department of the hospitals where physicians and doctors are lacking, or suffer the distress of old age. (Kastl).

If the Communists in the Kremlin would jump over their own shadows and loosen the shackles of the planned economy then the Russian peasants as well as the workers – without slogans – would bring forth the performance required by Gorbachev. To be sure, the institution of property has to be at least relaxed. In a word: an alteration in the system has to ensue.

In our opinion, however, Gorbachev cannot and will not carry out a structural reform or a reform of the system: He *cannot* undertake it, because the system – the *Nomenklatura* – is against it, and he would be expelled as an *Abweichler* [deviant], one who deviated from the system, if he broke the unwritten laws of the system. He *does not want* to do this because he is ideologically and, on account of his origins, a part of the ideological (Communist) system. It remains to be seen what free space in a technical sense he will conquer in the system.

Even if the course of reform is curtailed, the residue of more openness will remain as the residue remained after Kruschev's complaints against Stalin, since mass destruction is no longer the rule. It is, consequently, not a question of reform, which would alter the system structurally, but probably a small step, with others being able to follow so that in the end – in the next century – an alteration of the system could result from the sum of such individual steps. Whether it is a question of a process with cyclical movements – in intervals of 32 years: 1921 Lenin; 1953 Kruschev; 1985 Gorbachev – could be uncertain. If, however, every new generation of leadership undertakes an attempt at reform, then the quantity and quality will be dialectically overturned. In this, there is in the long run a certain optimism which, however, gives no reason for Gorbachev's course of reform.

Notes

[1] Mikhail Gorbachev, *Aufbruch ins Jahr 2000 – Der sowjetische Abrüstungsplan, die innere Reform der Sowjetunion und Westeuropas,* Kleine Bibliothek 397, Cologne, 1986. (Translation by the APN Moscow).

[2] *Ibid.,* pp. 13–29.

[3] *Ibid.,* p. 30ff.

[4] *Ibid.,* pp. 36–60.

[5] *Ibid.,* p. 60, emphasis supplied

[6] *Ibid.,* pp. 61–116.

[7] Note under the heading of *Prices* in *Lexikon der Wirtschafts-Preise,* 3 Aufl., Ost-Berlin, 1979, pp. 165–167.

[8] *Ibid.,* p. 165.

[9] *Ibid.,* p. 165f, emphasis in the original

[10] See under the heading: *„Wettbewerb, sozialistischer" Ökonomisches Lexikon,* 3 Aufl, Ost-Berlin, 1980, Bd.III, pp. 635–636, citation is from p. 635.

[11] Note the heading: *„Sozialistische Demokratie",* Wörterbuch zum sozialistischen Staat, Ost-Berlin, 1974, pp. 287–289, quotation is from p. 287f.

[12] Note *„Strukturwandlungen in einer wachsenden Wirtschaft",* Schriften des Vereins für Socialpolitik, N.F., BD. 30/I and II, herausgegeben von F. Neumark, Berlin, 1964.

[13] Wagemann, Ernst, *Wirtschaftspolitische Strategie,* 2 Aufl., Hamburg, 1943.

[14] *Ibid.,* p. 62f.

[15] Tuchtfeldt. Egon: *„Das Instrumentarium der Wirtschaftspolitik – Ein Beitrag zu einer Systematik",* reprinted in *Grundlagen der Wirtschaftspolitik,* herausgegeben by G. Gäfgen, Cologne-Berlin, 1966, pp. 260–272.

[16] *Ibid.,* p. 264.

[17] *Ibid.,* p. 264.

[18] See the Report: *„Gorbatschow weist Kritik zurück",* Neue Zürcher Zeitung, March 31, 1987.

[19] Röpke, Wilhelm, *Die Lehre von der Wirtschaft,* 9 Aufl, Erlenbach-Zürich and Stuttgart, 1961, p. 41f.

[20] Ibid., p. 41f.

[21] Note from the extensive literature of Baumeister, Reiner, *„Die Konzeption der Zukunftsgesellschaft bei Karl Marx, Friedrich Engels und neueren westeuropäischen Marxisten – eine ordnungspolitische Analyse",* Institut für Wirtschaftspolitik der Universität Köln, Bd. 34, Cologne, 1976.

22 *Ibid.*, p. 157.

23 Note the heading: „*Persönlichkeit*", *Wörterbuch der marxistisch-leninistischen Soziologie*, herausgegeben von einem Autorenkollektiv Ost-Berlin, 1977, pp. 476–481.

24 *Ibid.*, p. 478.

25 It is in no way here denied that the education of man as a member of a community is fruitless. However, an education – exceptions apart – cannot prevent the development of the ego.

26 See in this regard, Ströhm, Carl Gustav, „*Rennen gegen die Uhr in Moskau?*" – *Dissidenten-Dokument zweifelt an Gorbatschow-Erfolg, Medwedjew als Autor vermutet*, Die Welt, April 23, 1987.

27 In this regard see the Report of Ströhm, Carl Gustav; „*Warum Jaruzelski so eilfertig ja sagte*", Die Welt, March 27, 1987.

28 See the Report: „*Rakoswki ist vom Kurs Moskaus ,fast begeistert'*", Die Welt, February 18, 1987.

29 See Dietrich, Stefan, „*Jetzt oder nie in Polen – Abermals Vorschläge zum Aufbau eines ,modernen Wirtschaftssystems'*", Frankfurter Alltemeine Zeitung, April 22, 1987.

30 See in this regard Baumgarten, Gert, „*Den bunten Strauß kann sich keiner leisten – die Polen müssen wieder Preiserhöhungen verkraften*", Hannoversche Allgemeine Zeitung, April 22, 1987

31 Horskÿ, Vladimir, „*In Prag kam ein Stein ins rollen - Gustav Husáks Lippenbekenntnisse vor Michael Gorbatschows Besuch*". Die Zeit, March 27, 1987.

32 See the Report: „*Gorbatschow wirbt in Prag für seinen Kurs ,der Umgestaltung und Demokratisierung'*" Die Welt, April 11, 1987.

33 Ströhm, Carl Gustav, „*Nach Prag im Frühling*", Die Welt, April 6, 1987.

34 Ströhm, Carl Gustav, „*Der Prager Auftritt*", Die Welt, April 13, 1987.

35 Meier, Viktor, „*Nicht zuviel Reform, sondern eher zu wenig – Widersprüche in Ungarns Wirtschaft und Gesellschaft*", Frankfurter Allgemeine Zeitung, February 25, 1987.

36 Winters, Peter Jochen, „*Wenn der Nachbar neu tapeziert – Wie sich die DDR-Führung zu Gorbatschows Reformbestrebungen stellt*", Frankfurter Allgemeine Zeitung, April 11, 1987.

37 Of course, Hager did not quote the following sentence from the Communist Party Appeal of June 11, 1945; "We are rather of the opinion that the present decisive interests of the German people in the present situation prescribe a different way, specifically the way of the formation of an anti-fascist, democratic regime, of a Parliamentary-democratic Republic with all democratic rights and liberties for the people."

38 Zehm, Günter, „*Das Risiko Tradition*", Die Welt, April 10, 1947.

39 Note „*Die neue Verfassung der DDR*", with an introductory commentary by Dietrich Müller-Römer, Cologne, 1974. (The constitution of the GDR dates from April 6, 1968. It was supplemented and altered by legislation on October 1974.)

40 Autorenkollektive. *Staatsrecht der DDR – Lehrbuch*, Ost-Berlin, 1977.

41 *Ibid.*, p. 38.

42 *Ibid.*, p. 216, emphasis in the original

43 *Ibid.*, p. 128.

44 See Ströhm, Carl Gustav, „*Scheu der gebrannten Kinder*", Die Welt, March 2, 1987.

45 Struminski, Julius, „*Die Bürokratie ist das Rückgrat des Systems – Michail Gorbatschows Reformsätze auf den Trümmern gescheiterter Experimente*", Handelsblatt, February 27, 1987.

46 Citation from Ströhm, Carl G., „*Mit Privatinitiative geht vieles besser*", Die Welt, April 7, 1987.

47 Note Gerstenmaier, Cornelia, „*Versuch der Frischzellenkur für die letzte Kolonialmacht der Welt – Die UDSSR zwei Jahre nach Gorbatschows Machtantritt*", Die Welt, March 14, 1977.

168

[48] Voslensky, Michail, *Nomenklatura – die herrschende Klasse der Sowjetunion*, Moewig-Sachbuch (Taschenbuchausgabe), 3. Aufl., München, O.H. (erste Ausgabe, 1980).

[49] *Ibid.*, p. 170f.

[50] *Ibid.*, pp. 197–202.

[51] *Ibid.*, p. 200f.

[52] *Ibid.* p. 201.

[53] *Ibid.*, p. 202.

[54] *Ibid.*, p. 394.

[55] *Ibid.*, p. 394

[56] See in this regard: „*Skeptische Einschätzung von Gorbatschows Reformchancen – Stellungnahme von sowjetischen Emigranten*", *Neue Zürcher Zeitung*, March 31, 1987. – GG., „*Reformpolitik nicht überschätzen: Russische Exilanten warnen den Westen. Widerstand der Nomenklatura gegen Gorbatschow vorausgesagt*", *Frankfurter Allgemeine Zeitung*, March 31, 1987.

[57] Kastl, Jörg, „*Ein Schritt zurück, um zwei Schritte voran tun zu können - Gorbatschows Perestroika und die Bundesrepublik Deutschland*", *Frankfurter Allgemeine Zeitung*, April 25, 1987.

This manuscript was translated from the German by Professor John C. O'Brien, Fresno, California, USA.

4.

Creating the Structures for an Efficient Economy

Industrialization in a Resources-poor and Labor-rich Developing Country: The Experience in Taiwan

by Rong-I Wu

I. Introduction

Most developing countries regard industrialization as a central objective of their economic policies. Therefore, what kind of policies can be used as the main instruments to achieve rapid industrialization consequently became the central issue of studies by the development economists. Among various policies, import-substitution (IS) and export expansion (EE) attract the most attention. Actually, industrialization via import substitution has been considered as the typical policy measure in most developing countries in the early stage of industrialization (Little et al, 1970, p.1; Ballance et al, 1982, p.39). However, the disappointing result of import substitution policy and the rapid industrialization in several developing countries which undertook export oriented policy made the arguments favoured a shift towards export promotion policies, particularly, since the 1960s. Therefore, debates on the strategies of industrialization are still going which concentrate usually on the choice between import substitution and export expansion. However, these two policies are not necessarily exclusive. This paper tends to argue the strategy that import substitution and export expansion can be executed concurrently. The experience of industrialization in Taiwan, during the last three decades may provide a vivid example. This paper also provides an interesting case study on the pattern of industrialization in a resources-poor and labor-rich developing country.

The paper is organized as follows: after the introduction, in Section II, the argument about the concurrent IS and EE is stated. The industrial development in Taiwan, for the past three decades is analyzed in Section III. The important measures about IS and EE are reviewed respectively in Section IV and V. Comparative advantage in labor-intensive industrial technology is presented in Section VI. The paper ends with a brief section of prospects for future development in Taiwan, Republic of China.

II. Import Substitution versus Export Promotion

Whether industrialization via import substitution or export promotion becomes a very popular issue both from theoretical and empirical point of view, is particularly interesting for the policy makers of the developing countries. They are eager to know which one is superior in order that they can adopt it to achieve rapid industrialization. Although the theoretical analysis has not yet reached any conclusion, the empirical evidence about the superiority of export-promotion strategy is various.

For example, professor Anne Krueger (1981) indicated:

"By the early 1970s, it was apparent to all observers that the rates of growth achieved by the export-promotion or outer-oriented developing countries were vastly superior to those achieved by countries adhering to restrictive trade policies, and encouraging the growth of their industrial sectors through import substitution. Numerous studies, including those of the O.E.C.D. analyzed in Little, Scitovsky and Scott (1970), and those of the National Bureau of Economic Research, synthesized in Bhagwati (1978) and in Krueger (1978), all attested to the many difficulties inherent in import-substitution strategies, and the better performance associated with export promotion." (p.3)

However, the above observations still base on the assumption that an individual developing country undertakes either import-substitution strategies or export promotion strategies. Then it is meaningful to undertake comparative studies on the performance of economic growth and industrialization under different strategies. In fact, if we define an export-promotion policy as anything which gives greater incentive to produce an item to be exported than would occur under a free trade situation, while an import-substitution inducement would be one providing greater incentives to produce rather than import the item than would exist in a free trade situation, both sorts of policies could coexist (Krueger, 1981). In practice, there are always some "export-promotion" measures within import-substitution regimes and some import-substitution activities within export-oriented regimes. Thus, it is not easy to distinguish whether certain measures belong to import-substitution or export-promotion strategies.

From the experience of developing countries, the actual policy decision of their governments typically represent unplanned and often ad hoc responses to emerging and unforeseen economic crises. Within the broad framework of development objectives, diverse economic policies tend to have less internal consistency and economic rationality. Although we can easily group the existing measures into import substitution or export promotion, it is uncertain whether governments had clear mind of the strategies when they made decision.

When the governments are considering the strategies of industrialization, usually they are not in a position to make free choice between one of the two. Normally, it have already existed many economic measures. Any drastic change of the measures is very difficult, if not impossible which often meets strong opposition from various administration and interest groups. The possibility of a successful change depends on how strong and efficient the government is. Unfortunately, many observers argue that the lack of managerial and administrative capability is the simple scarcest resource in the developing countries, especially, in the early stage of development. (Todaro, 1981, p.482–3). Thus it might be useful and interesting to undertake a case study to examine the real process of policy decision making.

III. Industrial Development in Taiwan

During the last three and more decades, Taiwan has experienced one of the fastest economic growth in the world, with real GNP increasing annually by 8.6 per cent from 1952 to 1985. Though many factors contributed to such high economic growth, rapid industrialization is one of the most important. This can be shown from the very high industrial growth rate during the period under study. Industrial output grew 11.9 per cent annually in 1962–85 while the agricultural and service sector expanded only 2.4 per cent and 8.8 per cent per annum during the corresponding period. Consequently, the share of the industrial sector in gross domestic product rose significantly, from 23.9 per cent in 1951 to 52.0 per cent in 1979, the highest record in the period under study and then declined slowly. However, it is still as high as 50.1 per cent in 1985. The sustained high growth rate of the industrial sector in 1962–80, which amounted to 13.6 per cent per year, can be considered as the most salient characteristic in the economic development of Taiwan during the post war period. Since the share of the service sector in GDP maintained around 40 per cent – 44 per cent, the drastic decline in the importance of agriculture became another impressive characteristic corresponding to the increasing share of industry during the period of speedy economic transition. This implies that the industrial sector grew much faster than average GDP, and was the most important sector contributing to rapid economic growth. If the share of the industrial sector in Gross Domestic Product can be used as a rough indicator of industrialization, then Taiwan, has become an industrial country since the industrial share in GDP for the first time exceeded 50 per cent in 1978.

Table 1

Gross Domestic Product by Industry of Origin					
Period	Total	Agriculture	Industry	Manuf.	Service
Structure (%)					
1951	100.0	32.4	23.9	17.3	43.7
1961	100.0	27.6	29.5	21.8	42.9
1971	100.0	13.1	43.5	35.9	43.4
1979	100.0	8.7	52.0	42.4	39.3
1981	100.0	7.4	50.2	40.2	42.4
1985	100.0	5.9	50.1	40.9	44.0
Growth Rate (%)					
1962–70	9.9	4.1	14.8	16.4	9.4
1971–80	9.7	1.7	12.5	12.7	9.0
1981–85	6.0	4.8	5.8	6.6	7.2
1962–85	8.7	2.4	11.9	12.7	8.8

Sources: *Statistical Abstract of National Income in Taiwan Area, R.O.C. (1951–1985),* Directorate-General of Budget, Accounting and Statistics, Executive Yuan, December 1985.

IV. Policies for Import Substitution

Industrialization via import substitution in underdeveloped countries is so popular that we can see it from a vivid description in the summary of a study undertaken by Little, Scitovsky and Scott (1970) as follows:

"In this century, and especially since the second world war, industrialization in developing countries has typically meant import substitution. Industries have been set up to produce goods that were previously imported, and these goods have mainly been sold in the home market. Governments have ensured the profitability of these industries by protecting them against competing imports through tariffs and controls." (p.1)

From the above statement, although you can see it from the viewpoint that governments in the developing world intend to promote industrialization via import substitution, you can also interpret this policy from the constraints in developing countries. In other words, developing countries encounter two difficult problems: first, industrial technology is less developed as compared with industrial countries, therefore, their products are not competitive enough in international as well as local markets. Thus, their products can not be exported. In addition, if government does not adopt tariffs or non-tariffs barrier to protect local industries from the competition of foreign products, domestic products can not stand against the competition from import goods. Second, since developing countries, except those which can produce raw materials for export, can not export industrial products to earn foreign exchange, most developing countries have problems of foreign exchange shortage. This is even worse when we consider that industrialization requires to import machinery and intermediate products from industrial countries which need a larger amount of foreign currency. Therefore, the most simple way to solve the dilemma is to promote local investment in production of consumer goods, which can satisfy the domestic need of consumption, decrease the demand of foreign exchange and most important-ly, encourage the development of domestic industry. Another important reason why governments of developing countries favored import substitution policies is the consideration of tax revenue. Most developing countries face the shortage of government revenue. Tariffs is probably the most easy tax to collect, considering the low administrative competence in the developing world. This is the reason why tariff revenue usually accounted for quite a large share of total government tax revenue in many developing countries.

The above analysis seems to suggest that import tariffs and import restrictions are the popular and convenient measures to promote import substitution policy. Judging from the experience in Taiwan, we can find that these two measures are effective measures to stimulate import substitution.

Import controls

Import controls, including quantitative and non-quantitative restrictions, are highly effective in protecting domestic industry. In the extreme, a government can restrict the import of specific products to create a vacuum in the domestic market. It is very profitable for the investment in the production of these products and, under such conditions, local industry will grow rapidly.

It is not easy to find an indicator to measure the degree of import controls. According to the data available, the number of imported industrial products grouped by degree of control can be used as the approximate indicator as shown in table 2. The number of imported commodities listed in the prohibited category and its share to the total is very small and decreasing. This category includes mainly arms, liquors, drugs, etc. and those commodities only government can import. This category became negligible after 1972.

Actually, the share in the category "controlled" can roughly represent the degree of import controls. Commodities placed under this classification are those for which import licenses are granted only if comparable products are not produced, or can not be supplied domestically. In other words, products classified under the category of "controlled" implies government policy to encourage import substitution in these products. Products placed under category of "permissible" can be changed to the category "controlled" if any domestic industries can produce it and apply for the change, subject to the following three criteria:

1). quality equals to international standard or national product standard

2). domestic production cost can not exceed 25 per cent of the import price (CIF) for the same product.

3). foreign exchange requirement can not exceed 70 per cent of domestic product cost.

Table 2

Evolution of Import Control of Industrial Products 1953–1986									
	Permissible		Controlled		Prohibited		Other		Total	
Year	No.	%	No.	%	No.	%	No.	%	No.	%
1953	280	55.2	185	36.5	28	5.5	14	2.8	507	100.0
1956	252	48.1	241	46.0	25	4.8	6	1.1	524	100.0
1960	506	53.7	381	40.5	33	3.5	22	2.3	942	100.0
1966	493	52.3	395	41.9	36	3.8	18	1.9	942	100.0
1968 Dec.	5,451	57.9	3,770	40.1	191	2.3	–	–	9,412	100.0
1970 July	5,612	57.1	4,030	41.0	190	1.9	–	–	9,832	100.0
1972 July	10,860	82.1	2,365	17.9	5	0.0	–	–	13,236	100.0
1974 Feb.	12,645	97.7	293	2.3	4	0.0	–	–	12,942	100.0
1975 Jan.	12,688	97.5	318	2.4	4	0.0	–	–	13,010	100.0
1976 June	12,846	97.2	362	2.7	13	0.1	–	–	13,211	100.0
1978 July	15,773	97.6	375	2.3	17	0.1	–	–	16,165	100.0
1979 Dec.	15,836	97.6	380	2.3	17	0.1	–	–	16,233	100.0
1980 Dec.	15,818	97.4	410	2.5	21	0.1	–	–	16,249	100.0
1981 Dec.	25,681	96.8	833	3.1	17	0.1	–	–	26,531	100.0
1982 Dec.	25,657	96.5	904	3.4	17	0.1	–	–	26,566	100.0
1983 Dec.	25,664	96.5	921	3.5	17	0.1	–	–	26,602	100.0
1984 June	25,847	97.2	749	2.8	14	0.1	–	–	26,610	100.0
1984 Dec.	25,972	97.1	744	2.8	14	0.1	–	–	26,750	100.0
1985 May	26,067	97.4	670	2.5	14	0.1	–	–	26,751	100.0
1986 Juni	26,073	97.4	681	2.5	9	0.03	–	–	26,763	100.0

Source: For 1953 – June 1984, see S. C. Tsiang et al, "Developments Toward Trade Liberalization in Taiwan, ROC." *Conference on U.S.–Taiwan Economic Relations,* March 27–28, 1985, Taipei; for Dec. 1984 – June 1986, Board of Trade, Ministry of Economic Affairs.

Note: "Controlled" means that import licenses are given only if comparable goods are not produced, or can't be supplied, domestically; "Permissible" means that import licenses are, in general, automatically granted although there may be restrictions on particular sources of origin and other conditions.

Because of the change in the method of commodity classification, the trend in the share of the categories is a better indicator. As can be seen in *Table 2,* the share of commodities in the "controlled" category accounted for more than 40 per cent before July 1972. In other words, more than 40 per cent of the commodities could not be imported before 1972. The share dropped significantly after February 1974. The main conclusions these figures suggest are as follows: (i) strict import controls remained in effect before July 1972, and only since then have they been gradually reduced; (ii) more than 40 per cent commodities were completely excluded from the foreign competition before July 1972.

The share of commodities placed under "permissible" was 57 per cent before 1972. It increased rapidly and reached more than 97 per cent since 1974. In other words, tariffs became the main instrument of protection instead of import control after 1974. Although this implies the gradual trade liberalization, those commodities permitted to import do not mean that they can be imported without tariffs. On the contrary, commodities can only be imported after paying high tariffs which is the topic to be investigated in the next section.

Tariffs

As we have mentioned earlier, import tariffs can play two important purposes. First, it can be used as a protection measure against the foreign competition. Any import tax will increase the cost of imported commodities and thus worsen the competitiveness of foreign goods in the domestic market. Therefore, import tariffs can encourage the investment in the production for the domestic market. Second, import customs are the simple and important tax revenue in the developing world. The experience in Taiwan has shown that import customs are a very important measure for industrial protection as well as government revenue during the period under study.

Although the tariff schedule has been revised several times, there is no significant decline in the average tariff rates until 1980 as shown in table 3. Average tariff rate was as high as 55.7 per cent in 1974, dropped to 49.1 per cent in 1976 and 39.1 per cent in 1979. A significant tariff reduction only started after 1980. A new double tariff rate system was put into effect this year. The favorable tariff rate was 31.2 per cent in 1980 which applied to goods imported from countries or areas that had reciprocal treatment with Taiwan. It dropped continuously and amounted to 20.6 per cent in 1987. These statistics clearly indicate the adoption of a high tariffs policy in Taiwan during the period under study.

Another indicator about the degree of protection can be measured by the ratio of customs revenues to total value of imports (see table 4). This ratio stood at a level of more than 20 per cent in 1952–58 except 1956. Then it showed a trend of gradual decline but maintained at a level of higher than 12 per cent until 1980. This indicates again the heavy burden of customs duties of import products which implies high protection for domestic industry against foreign competitors.

The important contribution of customs revenues to overall government tax revenues in Taiwan can be shown from the data in *Table 4*. Although the ratios of customs revenues to government revenues fluctuated year by year, it was maintained around 12–16 per cent during the whole period except 1974–79 which amounted to 20 per cent and over. This suggests that customs revenues have contributed an important part of government revenues.[1] This explains the reason why tariff rates can not decline quickly.

In short, the above two measures provided an effective protection for domestic industry and represented a typical regime of import substitution. These measures show that Taiwan was maintaining strict import controls and high tariffs before 1980. Therefore, domestic industry enjoyed a favorable climate of investment which provided a profitable condition of rapid industrialization. However, continuing industrial development and persistently huge trade surplus since the 1970s reveal the conditions of a turning point for another stage of policy, i.e. trade liberalization.

V. Policies for Export Expansion

When the persistence of balance of payment difficulties was prevailing in a developing country, adopting a strict import control in order to save foreign exchange is quite natural. However, government can undertake more positive measures to ameliorate the

Table 3

Average Tariff Rate (Unit: %)			
Year	column 1 *)	Tariff rates	column 2 **)
1974		55.7	
1975		52.7	
1976		49.1	
1977		46.2	
1978		43.6	
1979		39.1	
1980	36.0		31.2
1981	36.0		31.2
1982	36.0		31.0
1983	36.0		31.0
1984	36.0		30.8
1985	32.8		26.5
1986	31.8		22.8
1987	25.8		20.1

Source: Ministry of Finance.

Note: Tariff rates are calculated by simple arithmemtic average.

*)   Tariff rate in the first column applies to goods imported from countries or areas in general.

**)   Tariff rate in the second column applies to goods imported from countries or areas that have reciprocal treatment with ROC.

problem of foreign exchange shortage. Incentives for export promotion to earn more foreign exchange consequently becomes a favorite policy. Since Taiwan has met serious deficit of balance-of-payment during the period before 1976, export promotion has always been an important economic policy in order to improve the balance-of-payment situation.

Among many measures the government has taken during the period under study to promote exports are import exchange entitlements, rebates of taxes and duties, low-interest export loans, the establishment of export processing zones, and subsidies. Here we will concentrate only on tax and tariff rebates, low-interest export loans and export processing zones, which can be considered as the three most important export promotion measures from the experience of Taiwan.

Tariff and Tax Rebates

The system of tariff rebates was first implemented in Taiwan in 1951 to facilitate the importation of a particular kind of fiber from Japan used in making straw hats for reexport to the same country. The following year, the system was extended to cover the import of hemp-piece goods to make embroidery pieces, and other kinds of fibers to make hat

Table 4

Ratio of Tariff Revenues to Imports and Government Revenues			
(Unit: NT$Million, %)			
Customs Revenues	Imports	(3) = (1) / (2) (%)	Customs Revenues as % of Go-vernment Revenues
Year (1)	(2)	(3)	(%)
1952	574	2,533	22.7	15.8
1953	581	2,754	21.1	15.0
1954	704	3,304	21.3	14.6
1955	752	3,146	23.9	12.5
1956	825	4,800	17.2	11.7
1957	1,120	5,259	21.3	13.6
1958	1,509	5,605	26.9	15.1
1959	1,502	8,420	17.8	13.1
1960	1,549	10,797	14.3	11.9
1961	1,886	12,894	14.6	13.0
1962	1,990	12,174	16.3	12.9
1963	2.340	14,483	16.2	13.4
1964	2,801	17,162	16.3	13.2
1965	3,787	22,296	17.0	15.6
1966	3,964	24,957	15.9	13.9
1967	4,949	32,314	15.3	14.8
1968	6,486	36,222	17.9	16.2
1969	7,297	48,629	15.0	15.2
1970	8,077	61,110	13.2	14.9
1971	9,858	73,942	13.3	15.9
1972	14,445	100,791	14.3	18.5
1973	21,132	145,079	14.6	20.6
1974	32,533	265,395	12.2	26.0
1975	30,659	226,460	13.5	20.4
1976	36,377	289,139	12.6	20.2
1977	41,909	323,839	12.9	19.6
1978	54,949	408,378	13.5	21.1
1979	67,194	532,928	12.6	20.5
1980	70,348	711,433	9.9	17.5
1981	71,208	778,633	9.1	15.3
1982	65,310	736,084	8.9	13.1
1983	76,508	813,904	9.4	14.9
1984	84,078	870,861	9.7	15.3
1985	74,908	801,847	9.3	12.2

Sources: *Yearbook of Financial Statistics of the Republic of China,* 1976, 1985. Department of Statistics, Ministry of Finance.

Note: Customs Revenues include customs duties and harbor construction dues.

bodies – all of which were destined for export. In all three cases, the system regulated handicraft-making industries in which mainly imported raw materials were processed and finished goods were for the most part exported. This system was extended in July 1954 to cover all export goods. Initially, customs duties were the only tariff refundable. However, since manufactured goods were subject to commodity taxes and other duties, the scope of tax rebates was later extended to include the commodity tax and defense surtax (1955), habor dues (1958), salt tax (1960) and slaughter tax (1964). Among the types of tariffs and taxes rebates, customs duties accounted for the biggest share. Next came the commodity taxes.

The amount of tariffs and taxes rebated increased very fast as the coverage of tax rebates enlarged and exports grew rapidly. Taxes rebated increased from NT$21 million in 1955 to NT$19,985 million in 1975. It reached a peak of NT$36,241 million in 1980 and started to decline slowly (see Table 5).

Another indicator is total taxes refunds as a percentage of total tax revenues. This was only 1.2 per cent in 1955 and rose to 13.1 per cent in 1961. The share reached as high as 61.8 per cent in 1972, the highest record, and began to decrease afterwards (see Table 5). These data suggest how important the rebate system is to the incentive of export and thus competitiveness of Taiwan products. Undoubtedly, exports are difficult to compete with foreign products if they should bear such a high tax burden without refunds.

Low-interest Export Loans

The Bank of Taiwan initiated a low-interest export loan program in July 1957, under which short-term loans were extended to finance the materials and work-in-progress of exporters. Designed as part of the government's export-promotion measures, these short-term loans were offered at 6 per cent per annum for those payable in foreign currency and at 11.88 per cent annually for those payable in local currency in July 1957. These rates were substantially lower than the 19.8 per cent (secured) and 22.32 per cent (unsecured) loans then available to private sector enterprises for general business purposes. The favorable margin for exporters really provided an "export subsidy" and thus an effective measure to encourage exports.

The amounts of export loans increased rapidly as shown in Table 6 and started declining only after 1981. Although export loans accounted for only 2–6 per cent in total loans and discounts of domestic banks, the ratios of export loans as percentage of exports reached 20–60 per cent in 1971–1985. Though the favorable margin of export loans was narrowing gradually, the program came to meet the short-term fund needs of the export manufacturing – from raw materials procurement to finished-goods delivery. This undoubtedly provided a great help to the financial facilities of export firms.

Table 5

Tax Refunds on Exports, 1955 – 1985 (Unit: NT$Million, %)

Year	Total				Customs Duties			Defense Surtax Duties on Customs			Commodity Tax			Salt Tax			Harbour Construction Dues			Flood Rehabilitation Surtax FY 1960		
	1	2	3	4	1	2	3	1	2	3	1	2	3	1	2	3	1	2	3	1	2	3
1955–1985	393,818	1,258,809	31.3		255,895	636,045	40.2	3,826	12,157	31.5	91,410	476,409	19.2	162	3,512	10.2	42,304	129,856	32.6	20	801	2.5
1955	21	1,787	1.2	—	17	741	2.3	3	355	0.7	1	477	0.2	—	110	—	—	—	—			
1956	42	2,034	2.1	1.1	35	837	4.2	5	372	1.4	2	583	0.3	—	116	—	—	104	—			
1957	60	2,600	2.3	1.4	35	1,180	2.9	5	468	1.2	20	674	3.0	—	123	—	—	127	—			
1958	119	2,670	4.5	1.6	86	1,305	6.6	11	239	4.5	22	802	2.8	—	123	—	—	155	0.4			
1959	308	3,649	8.5	4.7	183	1,354	13.5	36	264	13.5	76	895	8.5	—	137	—	14	198	7.1			
1960	424	3,251	13.1	6.5	222	1,532	14.5	43	290	14.7	133	1,066	12.5	—	146	—	26	216	12.2	0	801	—
1961	705	3,366	20.9	5.4	332	1,641	20.3	66	322	20.6	248	1,018	24.3	—	147	—	54	237	22.8	0		
1962	736	4,090	18.0	6.4	405	1,871	21.6	78	370	21.2	188	1,452	13.0	—	138	—	60	260	22.8	17		
1963	1,468	4,955	29.6	8.7	871	2,245	38.8	159	449	35.3	322	1,789	18.0	4	153	2.7	109	319	34.0			
1964	1,661	6,125	27.1	8.5	898	2,897	31.0	178	580	30.8	440	2,074	21.2	7	156	4.3	118	418	28.3	0		
1965	1,966	7,160	27.5	9.0	1,116	3,426	32.6	223	684	32.5	480	2,390	20.1	7	150	4.6	136	510	26.7			
1966	2,659	8,129	32.7	9.3	1,501	3,706	40.5	300	740	40.6	645	2,936	22.0	11	175	6.5	199	571	34.9	0		
1967	3,328	10,341	32.2	8.7	1,847	4,714	39.2	370	941	39.3	842	3,634	23.0	13	171	7.8	251	861	29.2			
1968	3,933	14,297	27.3	8.1	2,125	5,838	36.4	428	1,567	27.3	1,058	5,637	18.7	14	176	7.9	306	1,159	26.4			
1969	6,041	16,300	37.1	10.0	3,297	6,696	49.2	669	1,895	35.3	1,577	6,272	25.1	18	188	9.7	480	1,249	38.4			
1970	9,998	17,582	56.9	9.8	5,474	7,078	77.3	1,254	1,981	63.3	2,401	6,999	34.3	17	176	9.6	844	1,348	62.6			
1971	13,124	21,239	61.8	8.3	8,853	10,287	86.1		640		3,070	8,235	37.3	26	178	14.4	1,174	1,899	65.4			
1972	16,309	28,417	57.4	7.9	10,380	14,363	72.3				4,291	11,419	37.6	27	180	15.2	1,605	2,454	30.5			
1973	17,668	44,627	39.6	9.1	11,514	24,904	46.2				4,403	12,879	31.7	41	224	18.1	1,713	5,619	39.5			
1974	19,985	42,361	47.2	9.3	12,838	23,527	54.6				5,291	14,018	37.7	33	194	16.9	1,827	4,621	31.1			
1975	20,603	52,445	39.3	9.5	12,270	29,078	42.2				6,553	17,565	37.3	27	189	14.4	2,649	5,613	45.3			
1976	28,948	57,604	50.3	7.0	18,318	32,023	57.2				7,940	19,533	40.6	36	191	18.7	2,334	5,851	29.4			
1977	27,181	71,935	37.8	7.8	16,194	40,027	40.5				8,623	23,967	36.0				2,929	7,942	29.4			
1978	36,057	96,310	37.4	5.5	21,597	53,597	40.3				11,330	32,761	35.2				4,164	9,952	36.5			
1979	36,241	110,089	32.9	5.1	23,667	57,003	41.5				8,410	41,678	20.2				3,895	13,216	29.5			
1980	29,356	120,199	24.4	4.0	22,640	57,781	39.2				2,821	43,202	5.7				3,650	12,658	28.8			
1981	28,305	117,176	24.2	3.3	21,706	56,323	38.5				2,949	48,195	6.1				3,681	12,089	30.5			
1982	24,640	115,830	21.3	2.6	16,745	55,570	30.1				4,213	48,170	8.7				3,694	14,523	30.9			
1983	28,920	136,616	21.2	2.6	18,863	67,622	27.9				5,563	54,471	10.2				3,846	14,078	27.3			
1984	33,012	135,524	24.4	2.5	21,869	66,873	32.7				7,296	54,573	13.4									

Column: 1 = Tax Refunds; 2 = Tax Revenues; 3 = Percentage of Tax Refunds to Tax Revenues; 4 = Tax Refunds as % of Exports

Source: Yearbook of Financial Statistics of the Republic of China, 1985.
Note: Harbor Dues has changed into Harbor Construction Dues since October 1981.

Table 6

Export Loans in 1971–85 (Unit: NT$billion, %)				
Loans and Discounts of all Domestic Banks	Export	Export Loans Amounts	= (3) / (1)	= (3) / (2)
(1)	(2)	(3)	(4)	(5)
1971	90.5	8.9	5.2	5.7	58.6
1972	104.6	12.7	6.5	6.3	51.7
1973	151.5	16.5	8.7	5.8	53.1
1974	214.8	19.2	7.5	3.5	39.0
1975	284.5	22.4	8.0	2.8	35.7
1976	317.7	33.7	8.9	2.8	26.3
1977	375.9	38.9	11.1	3.0	28.6
1978	470.2	45.3	24.8	5.3	54.8
1979	544.7	53.2	24.0	4.4	45.0
1980	693.6	67.0	33.5	4.8	50.1
1981	760.4	72.0	38.7	5.1	53.7
1982	903.6	82.8	36.0	4.0	43.5
1983	1,033.2	92.3	30.5	3.0	33.1
1984	1,146.1	92.6	23.4	2.0	25.3
1985	1,221.4	103.7	22.2	1.8	21.4

Sources: a. *Monthly Statistics of Exports and Imports, The Republic of China,* various issues.
b. *The Republic of China/Taiwan Financial Statistics Monthly,* various issues.

Export Processing Zones

The purpose of an export processing zone is mainly to attract foreign and local investment to the zones for export manufacturing by providing necessary public utilities, simplifying red tape and offering tax exemptions. The first export processing zone was established in 1967 and two others in 1972. The immediate objectives were employment creation and foreign exchange earning. Annual exports from the zones expanded rapidly, from US$109 million in 1970, to US$1,424 million in 1980 and US$2,036 million in 1984, accounting for 7.3 per cent in total exports in 1970 and in 6.7 per cent in 1984. Employment in the zones was only 5 thousands in 1967, rose to 70 thousands in 1972–73, accounting for about 5 per cent in total manufacturing employment. In particular, deducting imports of machinery, raw materials and intermediate products from exports, net export surplus of the export processing zones increased continually and rapidly from US$8 million in 1969 to US$964 million in 1984. This has made an important contribution to the foreign exchange earning, especially, in the period of balance-of-payment difficulties.

VI. Comparative Advantage in Labor-intensive Industrial Technology

The above analysis suggests that government measures to simultaneously promote import substitution and export promotion since the 1950s were the most significant policies of industrialization in Taiwan. Such simultaneous policies enabled Taiwan's industry to overcome weakness from import substitution such as limit of domestic market, insufficiency of competition, etc. and benefit the potential comparative advantage of the factor endowment of the economy. In many instances, the protection policy of import substitution resulted in higher prices, inferior quality of domestic products, and excess capacity of import-competing industries. However, export promotion policy would encourage local producers to sell their products in the international market where the price and quality of their products are the crucial factors of their competitiveness. The tax rebates of export commodities will offset the disincentives created for exporting in the import substitution regime. In other words, tax and tariff rebates permit exporters to have free and ready access to international markets for their raw materials, intermediate goods, and spare parts. Since labor is abundant and natural resources are poor in Taiwan, labor-intensive products have naturally an important comparative edge in the international market.

There are several conditions about the labor market and government incentives in Taiwan, which are decisive to develop labor-intensive industries.

First, population growth was very fast during the period under study. Average population growth rate was as high as 3.6 per cent in 1952–60 and 3.12 per cent in 1961–70. This is very high by any standard. It still stood at 1.85 per cent in 1971–80. Therefore, labor supply was very abundant.

Second, institutional factors such as labor unions and minimum wage law are not favorable to the wage negotiations of labor. Official minimum wage rate is usually lower than actual prevailing minimum wage.[2] Thus, minimum wage requirement would not lead to push wage increase. Furthermore, Martial Law prohibits strike, thus labor unions have no power of bargaining on wage issue. Consequently, wage rates are mainly determined by supply and demand in the labor market.[3] In a competitive environment where the supply of labor is abundant, wage rate would increase only slowly, especially those for unskilled labor.

Third, government incentives to promote investment as well as export are roughly non-discriminative to all manufacturing. For example: The Statute for Encouragement of Investment was first promulgated in 1960 to provide the following two important tax exemptions and deductions:

I) Income tax holiday: The strongest incentive was "five-year tax holiday" set forth in Article 5 of the Statute whereby a productive enterprise conforming to the Statute's criteria was exempted from income tax for a period of five consecutive years. The criteria was very broad, thus almost all enterprises can enjoy this tax holiday.

II) Business income tax: The maximum rate of income tax would not exceed 18 per cent of its total annual income,[4] which was much less than ordinary enterprises should pay.

The most salient feature is probably the incentives to encourage exports. Actually, all exports can enjoy the benefits of tax and tariff rebates. This has developed the influential "export-as-first-priority" policy in Taiwan during the period under study. Therefore, all exports can profit the incentives and thus become an effective stimulant for export manufacturing.

Investment in the export processing zones was a typical example where products were much more labor-intensive than those outside the zones. In 1972, average employment per enterprise in Kaohsiung export processing zone was 312 persons relative to 28 persons in the average size of employment in manufacturing. Average amount of investment per person in Kaohsiung EPZ was US$825, which was much lower than average manufacturing, i.e. US$4950 (see Table 7). The above data indicate that enterprises in the three export processing zones are much more labor-intensive than average manufacturing. Since necessary public utilities are provided, red tapes were simplified, tax exemptions were offered (including tariff, commodity tax, business tax, five years income tax holiday, ets.), labor market was abundant and competitive, we can assure that investment in labor-intensive industries in the zones would represent comparative advantage of the economy.

Table 7

Wage Structure and Employment in Export Processing Zones and Manufacturing			
	Kaohsiung EPZ	Taichung EPZ	Nantze EPZ	Manufacturing (1971)
Average monthly wage rates (US$)	31.52	24.58	26.35	43.75
Total employment (persons)	48,677	3,763	5,164	1,023,000
Average employment per enterprise (persons)	312	314	272	28
Average amount of investment per employee (US$)	825	1,375	1,275	4,950
Year of establishment	1967	1971	1971	—

Source: Wu (1985B)

Note: EPZ means Export Processing Zone, data for Oct. 1972, Manufacturing is census data of 1971.

Since labor can move freely and choose employment inside or outside the zones, we can assume that the labor market is competitive. In addition, investment in the production for export outside the zones can also enjoy almost all the tax incentives. We can conclude that the same labor-intensive technology would prevail outside the export processing zones. The higher average wage level outside the zones may be attributed to the differential labor structure in skill from state-owned enterprises. Wage rates in the state-owned enterprises were more than double as compared with private enterprise in 1971.[5] Thus the wage differential between employment inside and outside the zones could be attributed to the high proportion of female and unskilled labor in the zones relative to firms located outside the zones.[6]

In other words, it seems clear that investment in these export processing zones largely took advantage of the abundant and inexpensive supply of labor. These workers were mostly unskilled but hard-working hired from a pool of surplus labor force. Therefore, their wage rate which was only modest increase may represent the supply price for unskilled labor. Consequently, labor-intensive industries became highly competitive in the international market and crucial in explaining the rapid industrialization in the period under study.

VII. Prospects for Future Development

Real wages have been increasing significantly, especially since the first oil crisis in 1972. Actually, growth rates in labor productivity was for the first time exceeded by real wage rates after 1973 (see *Table 8*). Therefore, the advantages of low wages in Taiwan are gradually disappearing. More specifically, many low wage underdeveloped countries have adopted various export promotion measures in order to improve the competitiveness of their products in the international market. For labor intensive products, international competitiveness is determined mainly by the level of wage rates rather than by technology. Therefore, some Taiwan products have been losing their competitiveness. How to shift Taiwan export products from traditional labor-intensive to technology-intensive products has become the major concern of recent policy measures. In fact, the structure of export products has been changing drastically (see *Table 9*). The share of textile products increased rapidly from 0.8 per cent in 1952–53, to 30.6 per cent in 1971–72. It dropped to 21.6 per cent in 1981–82 and again to 19.8 per cent in 1984–85. On the contrary, the share of electrical machinery and apparatus

Table 8

Selected Indicators of Changes of Wage Rate and Productivity in Manufacturing (Unit: % annually)				
period	Real wage rates			Productivity
	Total	Unskilled	Female	
1953–62	2.85	2.6	– 0.9	6.64
1963–72	6.55	3.3	6.6	9.87
1973–83	7.08	NA	NA	3.49
1953–83	5.54	NA	NA	6.67
Source: Wu (1985B).				
Note: NA: data are not available.				

increased from only 0.1 per cent in 1952–53, to 15.8 per cent in 1971–72 and further to 21.3 per cent in 1983–84. This shows a clear trend of decreasing importance of textile products in total exports and increasing weight of electrical machinery and apparatus between 1952–53 and 1984–85. The share of plastic products and metal manufactures also increased from zero in 1952–53 to 8.3 per cent and 5.8 per cent respectively in 1984–85. Thus, facing the persistent increase in wage rates, whether Taiwan can continuously maintain such a rapid shift of industrial structure from a labor-intensive to a technology-intensive one is crucial for her future development.

Table 9

Structure of Exports (Unit: %)				
	1952–53	1961–62	1971–72	1981–82	1984–85
Grude agricultural products	17.7	13.3	7.3	2.1	1.5
Rice	12.8	3.7	0.1	0.2	0.1
Bananas	3.8	4.0	1.5	0.1	0.1
Processed agricultural products	74.0	40.8	10.4	5.6	4.6
Sugar	63.2	24.7	2.9	0.5	0.1
Canned food	1.9	7.3	4.4	0.9	0.5
Tea	5.6	3.9	0.6	0.1	0.1
Industrial products	8.3	45.9	82.3	92.3	93.9
Textile products	0.8	17.8	30.6	21.9	19.8
Electrical machinery & apparatus	0.1	0.9	15.8	18.0	21.3
Plastic articles	0.0	0.0	2.3	7.0	8.3
Metal manufactures	0.0	0.6	1.9	4.6	5.8
Machinery	0.0	0.5	2.4	4.0	3.9
Wood products	0.0	0.8	3.4	3.5	3.5
Basic mentals	0.6	4.3	3.1	2.6	2.6
Chemicals	3.0	5.8	1.5	2.5	2.5
Total exports	100.0	100.0	100.0	100.0	100.0

Source: *Taiwan Statistical Data Book,* 1986.

Moreover, long-term policy of "export-as-first-priority" has resulted in rapid industrial growth. It also led to a continously huge trade surplus. In 1985, trade surplus amounted to US$10.6 billion, which was more than 33 per cent of total exports. In 1986, trade surplus enlarged further to a recorded hight of US$15.6 billion, which accounted for 39 per cent ot total exports. Thus foreign reserves accumulated to US$44 billion at the end of 1986, which is about 22 months of imports. The sustained trade surplus and the resulting accumulation of foreign reserves led to the continuing appreciation of the New Taiwan Dollar and the pressure of inflation. The appreciation of the NTDollar will hurt the international competitiveness of Taiwan's products. Otherwise, inflation pressure will strengthen. This is a dilemma of economic policy under the current situation in Taiwan. Therefore, a large scale trade liberalization such as reduction of tariff and other trade restrictions have been undertaken. The deregulation of capital movement is also for the first time considered seriously by the Central Bank. In addition United States are the largest market of Taiwan (about 50 percent of Taiwan's export went to U.S. market in 1984–86). The trade imbalance between Taiwan (Republic of China) and the United States is so serious that the trade surplus in favor of Taiwan amounted to US$13.6 billion in 1986, the third largest trade deficit country for the USA. Therefore, American pressure on opening the Taiwan market is very strong. How Taiwan can face these internal and external pressures and make a proper adjustment is another crucial factor for the future development. Fortunately, government has adopted liberalization and internationalization as the basic economic policies since 1985. It is almost consensus that it is decisive to the future development of Taiwan's economy how many policies of deregulation can be executed.

Notes

This paper is based on a research project financed by National Science Council, NSC 74-0301-H005-07. The author would like to thank professors Tein-Chen Chou, Gi-li Yen, T.F. Wang, C.F. Wang-Liang and W.T. Hsiao for their useful comments.

[1]   In fact, customs duties used to be the most important tax revenue in Taiwan. It was only replaced by income tax and became the second one since 1981. However, the difference between them was very limited. See Taiwan Statistical Data Book 1986.

[2]   Actually, the monthly minimum wage was set at NT$300 in 1956–63, NT$450 in 1964–67, NT$600 in 1969–77, NT$2.400 in 1978–79, NT$3.300 in 1980–82, NT$5.700 in 1983, and NT$6.150 in 1984. It was only 60 per cent of the average wage in manufacturing in 1950s, only 10 per cent in 1977 and 40 per cent in the 1980s. See Wu (1985).

[3]   Fields (1984) also argued that the wage in the four rapid-growth developing countries in East Asia – i.e. Hong Kong, Korea, Singapore and the Republic of China – has been determined by the supply of and demand for labor. However, government in Taiwan has taken several important institutional change on labor conditions recently. For example, Labor Standards Law had promulgated on July 30, 1984. Government announced to lift the 37-year-old Martial Law in 1987.

[4]   This rate changed several times. The current business income rate is 22 per cent for strategic products.

[5]   According to 1971 census data, see Wu (1975).

[6]   See Wu (1975, 1985B). For example, in the Taichung Export Processing Zone, female workers accounted for 79.5 per cent of the total production workers. Among female workers, 57.8 per cent were aged 16–19 and 29.7 per cent were aged 20–24. A similar situation prevailed at the Nantze Export Processing Zone. The 1971 Industrial & Commercial Censuses of Taiwan and Fukien Area also show that 50 per cent of the male workers and 78 per cent of the female workers in manufacturing are classified as unskilled labor. Taking into account the specific employment structure in the Taichung EPZ and Nantze EPZ, where female workers accounted for 80 per cent of total workers, we can estimate that the percentage of unskilled workers in the Taichung and Nantze was 72 per cent, assuming the same structure of skills.

References

Ballance, R. J. Austin & H. Singer (1982) *The International Economy and Industrial Development,* (Wheatsheaf, U.K.)

Brandt, Willy, (1980) *North-South: A Programme for Survival,* London; Pan Book.

Bruton H. J. (1970) "The Import-Substitution Strategy of Economic Development: A Survey," *Pakistan Development Review,* vol. 10, no. 2., pp.123–146.

Chou, Tein-chen (1985) "The Pattern and Strategy of Industrialization in Taiwan: Specialization and Offsetting Policy," *The Developing Economies* 23(2), pp.138–157.

Cline, William (1982) "Can the East Asian Model of Development be Generalized?" *World Development* 10(2), pp.81–90.

Fields, Gary S. (1984) "Employment, Income Distribution and Economic Growth in Seven Small Open Economies," *Economic Journal,* 94, pp.74–83.

Galenson, Walter, (ed.) (1979) *Economic Growth and Structural Change in Taiwan, The Postwar Experience of the Republic of China, Ithaca,* Cornell University Press.

Hsing, Mo-Huan (1971), *Taiwan: Industrialization and Trade Policies,* London, Oxford University Press.

Kirkpatrick, C.H., N. Lee and F.I. Nixson, (1984) *Industrial Structure and Policy in Less Developed Countries,* London, George Allen & Unwin.

Krueger, Anne O. (1981) "Export-Led Industrial Growth Reconsidered" in Wontack Hong and Lawrence B. Krause (eds), *Trade and Growth of the Advanced Developing Countries in the Pacific Basin,* Korea Development Institute, Seoul, Korea, pp. 3–27.

Kuo, Shirley W.Y. (1983) *The Taiwan Economy in Transition,* Boulder Westview.

Lall, Sanjaya (1984) "Transnationals and the Third World: Changing Perspectives," *National Westminster Bank Quarterly Review,* pp. 2–16.

Liang, K.S. (1974) "Agricultural Trade and Economic Development in Taiwan," *Economic Essay,* vol. 5, Graduate Institute of Economics, National Taiwan Univ., Taipei, pp.207–233.

Lin, Ching-yuan (1973) *Industrialization in Taiwan, 1946–72, Trade and Import-substitution policies for Developing Countries,* New York, Praeger.

Little, Ian, Tibor Scitovsky and Maurice Scott (1970) *Industry and Trade in Some Developing Countries: A Comparative Study,* Oxford University Press.

Myint, H. (1973) *The Economics of the Developing Countries,* 4th ed. Hutchinson University Library.

Ranis, Gustav (1981) "Prospects of Taiwan's Economic Development" *Conference on Experience and Lessons of Economic Development in Taiwan,* Dec. 18–20, 1981, Taipei, The Institute of Economics, Academia Sinica, pp. 681–705.

Robinson, Austin, (ed.) (1979) *Appropriate Technologies for Third World Development,* London, Macmillan.

Scott, Maurice (1979) "Foreign Trade," in: Walter Galenson (ed.) (1979), *Economic Growth and Structural Change in Taiwan,* ch.5.

Todaro, Michael (1981) *Economic Development in the Third World,* 2nd ed.

Tsiang, S. C. and Rong-I Wu (1985) "Foreign Trade and Investment as Boosters for Take-off: The Experiences of the Four Asian Newly Industrialized Countries," in: Walter Galenson (ed.) *Foreign*

Trade and Investment, Economic Development in the Newly Industrializing Asian Countries, Madison: The University of Wisconsin Press, pp.301–332.

Wu, Rong-I (1975) "Strategic Factors of Industrialization in Postwar Taiwan," *Proceedings of Chinese Economic Association Annual Meeting*, pp.155–178

—, (1975) "Taiwan's Export Boom: Causes and Prospects," *Mondes en Development* (Paris), no.10.

—, (1975) "Choice of Technology, Labor Absorption and Economic Development," *Taipei City Bank Monthly*, vol. 6, no. 1 and 2, (in Chinese).

—, (1976) "Urbanization and Industrialization in Taiwan: A Study on the Specific Pattern of Labor Utilization" *Proceedings of Conference on Population and Economic Development in Taiwan*, Dec. 29, 1975 – Jan. 3, 1976, Taipei.

—, et al (1980) *Impact of U.S. Investment on Taiwan Economy*, Taipei, Institute of American Culture, Academia Sinica, (in Chinese).

—, and Hsu Hwa-jen (1984) "Study on the Strategy of Industrialization in Taiwan," *Economic Studies* 25, pp. 1+22 (in Chinese).

—, (1985A) "The Distinctive Features of Taiwan's Development," paper prepared for the *Symposium of In Search of an East Asian Development Model*, June 28+30, 1985, New York, N.Y. mimeo.

—, (1985B) "Taiwan's Success in Industrialization," *Industry of Free China*, 64 (5).

Creating the Structures for an Efficient and Dynamic Economy: The Case of Ghana.

by James C. W. Ahiakpor

1. Introduction

Ghana is a typical less developed country (LDC) whose economy has retrogressed over time owing to the adoption of inconsistent development policies. Liberia, Mozambique, Niger, Tanzania, Uganda, Zambia, and Zaire, all in Africa, share this distinction. Between 1965 and 1986 real per capita income declined on an average annual basis in these countries, for several of them at almost – 2 per cent (World Bank, 1988, p. 222). However, this was hardly the intended outcome of policies adopted by various governments – civilian and military – that have ruled these countries. Thus, even now a vigorous search continues in Ghana to find policies that would promote economic development.

In this paper, I use recent economic history of Ghana to illustrate the argument that the perverse development performance in these countries has been due mainly to the types of institutions and policies adopted by their governments. I argue for a limited role of government, both direct and indirect, and the preservation of individual liberties and property rights. These conditions are required to promote efficient economic choices among individuals and harmonize the dynamics of these choices for development. I suggest that different though the institutions required to implement these policies may be from those that have been adopted by various past governments of Ghana and many other LDCs, they are more consistent with their avowed goals.

It is well known that making recommendations for creating the kinds of economic structures that would foster economic development is in the realm of art, not science. Thus, John Stuart Mill (1874, p. 124) argued, "Science is a collection of truths; art a body of rules, or directions for conduct. Political Economy does not of itself instruct how to make a nation rich." Yet, as Mill also pointed out, the study of economics provides us with the scientific basic for designing rules: "but whoever would be qualified to judge of the means of making a nation rich, must first be a political economist. Unless political economy be altogether a useless science, practical rules must be capable of being founded on it." Thus, from insights we gain from the scientific study of human motivation and the consequences of past policies in different economies, we may derive practical rules for the conduct of human affairs consistent with chosen goals. It is from the same perspective that Mill himself was an advocate of policies whose adoption he believed would be conducive to the efficient and dynamic economic development within politically free societies. To set the stage for developing my argument, I trace briefly the development experience of Ghana over the last 30 years or so.

2. Development Experience since Independence:

At independence in 1957, Ghana ranked among what would now be termed middle income countries by its per capita income level of about $500 (in 1980 U.S. dollars). But the country has since slipped into the ranks of poor LDCs, with a per capita income of $380 in 1985 (while the consumer price index had risen by a factor of 9 since 1980).

As *Table 1* shows, all basic indicators of economic performance show a general decline from the 1950s when the governance of the country started being passed into the hands of natives.[1] Thus between 1950 and 1960 gross national product (GNP) increased at an average annual rate of 4.2 per cent, but slowed to 2.0 per cent in the 1960s, and turned negative (– 0.2 per cent) in the 1970s. Similar worsening trends can be found in other categories of economic performance, including exports, imports, private consumption, and the consumer price index.

Table 1

Indicators of Economic Performance in Ghana: 1950–81 (Average annual per cent growth rates)			
	1950–60	1960–70	1970–81
Gross National Product	4.2	2.0	– 0.2
Imports of goods and non-factor services	8.9	– 2.0	– 5.4
Exports of goods and non-factor services	3.2	0.1	– 9.2
Private consumption	4.5	1.7	– 0.4
General Government consumption	12.9	7.2	7.4
Consumer Price Index	1.7	8.7	47.3

Source: World Bank, *World Tables*, 1983, p. 65.

Examination of these indicators over the decades may yield some usefull lessons, but they nevertheless mask some important epochs. The 1950s may usefully be considered together since they represent a period of fairly stable and open economic climate, most of it under the political supervision by the British. Though the country attained self-government status in 1951 and became politically independent from Britain from March 1957, no radical changes in economic policy were implemented until after the attainment of a republican status in July 1960. Thus, until 1961, the country relied mainly on the export of agricultural and forestry products and minerals, operated a relatively free foreign exchange system, while most of modern sector manufacturing activities were in private hands. State intervention took an indirect form. The government tried to assist the development of private local enterprise by granting financial assistance through a financing company, the Industrial Development Corporation (IDC).[2]

However, important changes in economic policy started to be made from 1961 when the government under Nkrumah declared its preference for state-led industrialization in pursuit of socialism as the appropriate path to economic development. That experiment ended in 1966 with the overthrow of the government. After about two years of attempting to arrest the downward direction of the economy under a stabilization programme, the new military government (National Liberation Council) in 1968 embarked on a policy of greater reliance on private enterprise and market forces as the instruments of development. These policies were continued under the Second Republic, beginning from October 1969, under Busia's Progress Party government. With the overthrow of the Second Republic in January 1972, the experiment with private enterprise-led development also ended. The years 1972 to 1979 were a period when soldiers bent on returning to state activism of the Nkrumah period ruled the country, initially under the National Redemption Council (NRC), later tranformed into the Supreme Military Council (SMC, 1 and 2).[3]

A new civilian government led by Limann took power in September 1979, but it too pursued the same state activist philosophy of the last military regime though with a greater tolerance of private foreign enterprise than the previous regime. Partly because of its openness to private foreign investment and partly for failing to pursue more overtly socialist economic policies, this government also was overthrown in December 1981. Thus, between 1982 and 1983, the Provisional National Defence Council (P.N.D.C.), a government composed of Marxist-Leninists who overthrew the Third Republic, tried policies aimed at establishing a Marxist-Leninist state. The significant failure of such policies to make any positive impact on the economy led the government, though with a substantially altered composition of personalities, to embark on more free-market and private-enterprise policies in its approach to economic development from the middle of 1983.[4]

Thus we learn more about development epochs in Ghana by dividing the period since the attainment of a republican status in 1960 into 1961–65 (Nkrumah's socialist experiment), 1966–1971 (National Liberation Council and Busia's private enterprise experiment), 1972–79 (National Redemption Council/Supreme Military Council nationalist and state-activist experiment), 1979–81 (state activism with external dependency). and 1982–85 (Rawlings's experiments). From these divisions we see significantly different trends within the decades (see Table 2). With the exception of the NLC/Busia period of liberalization (and the early 1980s, for which the relevant data are not available), real per capita national income declined on an average annual basis over the other periods. The deterioration gets worse in the 1970s, – 2 per cent during the military regime and – 5 per cent during the CPP revival period. On the other hand, the six years of economic stabilization and liberalization show a 1 per cent positive average annual growth in per capita income. The same contrasts can be found on other indicators, including the rate of inflation, growth of exports and imports, and growth in private consumption.

Though the numbers for the 1982–85 period appear to indicate a much better economic performance in terms of exports, imports and private consumption than for the 1966–71 period, these indications are more apparent than real. In the first place, they indicate growth rates from abysmal economic downturns, especially from 1983 when conditions got to their worst levels after more than ten years of continuing deterioration. Also note that the growth in the consumer price index (inflation) during 1982–85 is about nine times the rate in 1966–71 (48.8 per cent as against 5.7 per cent). Nevertheless, it is proper to regard the period after 1983 as indicating an economic upturn. An adequate explanation of the different economic performance is necessary for designing appropriate developmental policies and institutions. To this task we now turn.

3. Accounting for Development Experience:

The functioning of an economy is the end product of several factors, both internal and external to the country. The degree of external influence may be even more significant for a small open economy like Ghana's. However, because of being a major producer of the world's supply of cocoa, variations in Ghana's output affect the world price of this commodity. But the price of most other internationally traded goods are beyond the country's influence. Similarly, economic policy of the country has little impact on inter-

Table 2

Policy Regimes and Development Experience: 1961–1985					
	CCP Socialism 1961–66	NLC/Busia Liberalism 1966–71	NRC/SMC Nationalism 1972–79	Limann CPP Revival 1979–81	Rawlings's Experiments 1982–85
1. Growth of real per capita GNP	– 1.2	1.0	– 2.0	– 5.3	N.A.
2. Share of Gov. Expenditure in GNP	26.7	21.2	18.3	12.3	10.7
3. Ratio of Deficits to Gov. Expenditure	27.5	18.9	40.7	47.2	29.8
4. Growth of Private Consumption	9.7	10.1	1.2	– 5.6	49.7
5. Growth of Gov. Consumption	13.4	7.9	8.1	7.7	60.4
6. Growth of Exports	– 3.0	15.9	– 8.1	– 15.7	40.5
7. Growth of Imports	1.0	6.2	– 2.9	– 24.8	153.1
8. Growth of Consumer Price Index	11.9	5.7	47.0	73.7	48.8

Sources: Values calculated from *World Tables,* The World Bank, 1983, *International Financial Statistics,* The International Monetary Fund, 1987.

Note: Values are in percentages. Growth rates were calculated on an average annual basis.

national capital markets. Yet we get a sharper focus for our explanation by studying the role of government over the period. However vulnerable an economy may be to external factors, the exercise of the coercive powers of the state by government significantly affects the nature of resource utilization and new wealth creation. The focus on government also enables us to compare Ghana's experience with other open economies, but which have experienced impressive economic growth since the 1960s, including Japan, South Korea, and Singapore.

The role of government appears to have been the most important factor that influenced the direction of Ghana's economy since independence. In pursuit of its new policy of a socialist state intervention in the economy, the government in 1961 raised both the level and scope of taxation, and thus appropriated more resources under its direct control.

Tax revenues were also supplemented by a compulsory development levy as well as borrowing from the domestic banking system and foreign sources. To gain greater access to foreign exchange, the government also made private transactions in foreign exchange illegal. Only the Central Bank was authorized to exchange foreign currency. Foreign exchange receipts from official exports were to be deposited with the Bank and the local currency (Cedi) equivalent paid to exporters. All importers were to apply to the government, through the ministry of trade, for foreign exchange allocations for imports of both consumer and producers' goods. Private travellers faced even greater obstacles in trying to acquire foreign exchange. The government also established a number of state enterprises in such sectors as agriculture, banking, commerce, manufacturing, mining, and transportation.

These changes in policy resulted in an increase in the share of government spending in national income. From a level of 23 per cent in 1960, the share rose to 27 per cent in 1961, and to 36 per cent the year after. Though the level declined in subsequent years, the average share of government spending between 1961 and 1965 was 29 per cent. Within the same period, the annual share of deficits in government spending also averaged about 30 per cent. It rose from 20 per cent in 1960 to 27 per cent in 1961, and to 40 per cent in 1962. Such high rates of deficit spending partly reflect a lack of adequate financial discipline in government spending, and partly the haste with which government spending plans were carried out without much reference to the available financial resources.

The above indicators of change in economic policy since 1961 describe mainly the quantifiable aspects of government intervention in the economy. The government also significantly controlled the economy in other ways. For example, it determined the types of industries that were established. Thus investors in the modern sector (defined as firms employing 30 or more workers), were required to obtain prior approval from the government so that their selection of industries would be consistent with government preferences. Similarly, the composition of imports was significantly influenced by the government through a system of import licensing. Thus, besides the permit required to establish a firm, the government also controlled the composition of output through the regulation of raw materials imports.

The resulting centralization of economic power in the hands of the government raised the stakes of politics. It became more rewarding for people to be seen as being on the side of the ruling party in order for them to receive economic privileges dispensed by the government. On the other hand, the opportunity cost of being out of power increased for members of government and the ruling party. The interaction of these factors produced among the public, especially the business community, pressures to play sycophants to the party leadership or offer bribes to senior government officials.[5] On the side of the government, the pressure was to silence official opposition, culminating in the institution of a single party state in 1964 and the repression of all forms of political opposition, both from within and outside the party.

But as the evidence shows (table 2), the economy responded negatively to these policies. The association of increased economic control by government with overall economic decline may be explained thus: Where bureaucrats allocate the community's capital appropriated through taxation or government borrowing, the recipients often are not the most deserving of such allocation. They are not necessarily the most efficient investors, but mainly those whose political preferences are consistent with the government's or those who may have paid the highest bribes. If the capital is invested directly by the government in state enterprises, it is often not economic viability that dictates project selection but political preferences.[6] For a detailed documentation of such investments in Ghana during the 1960s, see Killick (1978), esp. chapter 9.

The high stakes of politics that the centralization of economic control often produces may cause political instability. This may arise from some individuals attempting to take over the government in order that they also might appropriate privileges to themselves. The political instability may discourage private investment both local and foreign. But where the government appears to have a firm, even dictatorial, grip on the country, private foreign investment may still be forthcoming, as has occurred in varying degrees in countries such as Ghana, South Africa, South Korea, and Taiwan. Thus, the political consequences of the centralization of economic power may not be as significant in retarding overall economic growth as the distortion of production incentives.

It is the above economic and political structures that subsequent governments in Ghana have tried to perpetuate, modify or completely change. The performance of the economy under these governments may be explained by the extent to which they failed or succeeded in changing them. Thus the significant reduction in the scope of government in the economy following the overthrow of Nkrumah's regime is associated with positive economic growth over the period, 1966 to 1971. The average share of government spending fell from 29 per cent over the 1961–1965 to an average of 21 per cent during the NLC and Busia's government era. The average share of deficits in government spending also fell from 27 per cent to 19 per cent over the same periods.

Both the NLC and Busia's governments also liberalized the process of foreign exchange allocation, culminating in only about 40 per cent of all imports requiring specific license in 1970, compared with 95 per cent in 1967. Some state enterprises were sold to the private sector while some workers in some public corporations were laid off. However, either from their sensitivity to public pressure not to divest the state completely from direct production, or their lack of total commitment to private enterprise, neither government was able to sell all state enterprises engaged in agriculture, manufacturing, and service industries such as hotels and transportation – air, road, rail, and sea.

Both the NLC and the Busia's governments were basically committed to the promotion of individual freedoms, although neither administration was devoid of acting arbitrarily on occasion (see, for example, Pinkney, 1972 and Killick, 1978, for details). We see the ultimate aspiration of the NLC towards the institution of a government respectful of civil liberties in the kinds of individual freedoms prescribed by some of its members. For example, Lt. General A. A. Afrifa, one of the leaders of the coup that overthrew Nkrumah's government, called for the establishment of a constitutional democracy under which the following freedoms would prevail:

Freedom of worship, of speech and of the press, the right of peaceable assembly, equality before the law, just trial for crime, freedom from unreasonable search, and security from being deprived of life, liberty or property, without due process of law. (Quoted in Pinkney, 1972, p. 142.)

He argued that it is from these freedoms that Ghanaians could find "the invisible sentinels which [would] guard the door of every home from invasion, coercion, intimidation and fear." Another important participator in the 1966 coup, Lt. General A. K. Ocran, also described his vision of a future political democracy in Ghana thus: "Democracy means respect for individuality, and other people's views, and tolerance. Consequently, there can be no democracy without certain well-known freedoms such as those of expression, of thought, of person, of assembly and of association."[7]

Busia's government tried to preserve many of these freedoms. Thus, during the term of that government (1969–71), opposition parties and press operated quite freely, guarantees of individual liberties under *habeas corpus* were protected by the courts, and there was considerable degree of market freedom. The years 1969–71 thus stand out as those in which Ghanaians enjoyed the most civil liberties since the country became a republic in 1960.

Thus, whatever may have been the external influences on the economy, leaving more resources in the private sector through reductions in the share of government spending and deficit financing, appears to have increased the overall level of efficiency in the economy between 1966 and 1971. The greater access importers had to foreign exchange without having to go through bureaucratic approvals also must have increased efficiency in the allocation of imports. Of course, this was not a period of complete laissez-faire in economic policy. The 21 per cent average share of government spending over the period also appears high compared with those of Japan, Singapore, and South Korea during the rapid development phase of these countries (see Table 3). Although the share of government spending in these countries has increased over time, it was less than 20 per cent during most of the 1960s and 1970s.

Table 3

Share of Government Spending and Growth of Per Capita Income in Japan, Singapore, and South Korea, 1960–1985 (per cent)								
Selected Years						*Average of Annual Values*		
1960	**1965**	**1970**	**1975**	**1980**	**1985**	**1960–69**	**1970–79**	**1980–85**
Japan:		*Share of Gov. spending*						
14.9	12.4	11.0	14.7	18.4	12.8	13.4	13.7	18.3
		Growth of per capita income						
12.4	16.0	8.2	1.4	3.4	4.0	11.0	4.0	3.3
Singapore:		*Share of Gov. spending*						
N.A.	N.A.	17.9	17.1	20.4	26.5	N.A.	17.7	21.7
		Growth of per capita income						
N.A.	N.A.	11.3	4.8	5.5	−1.8	N.A.	7.6	6.2
South Korea:		*Share of Gov. spending*						
13.8	11.1	16.2	15.9	17.9	19.1	15.0	15.9	19.1
		Growth of per capita income						
9.2	10.2	8.6	4.9	−6.1	4.3	5.3	7.7	5.4
Source:	Calculations based on data from International Monetary Fund, International Financial Statistics, 1987.							
Note:	N.A. = not available.							

On the other hand, subsequent governments have tried to reverse the free-market oriented policies. They have been characterized by attempts to control prices of both locally produced and imported goods, including food items, and the prosecution of people accused of buying or selling above control prices. Price controls were also extended to services such as private transportation, restaurants and hotels, as well as to wages (and conditions of employment) in the private sector. The governments also took over some private enterprises often as part of the penalty for their having violated some regulations, e.g. failure to pay taxes on time, or having been implicated in acts of bribery and corruption. As the military government pointed out in its Five-Year Development Plan (1977), the aim of these policies was to enable the state to take over the commanding heights of the economy, in the spirit of Nkrumah's vision. Thus it is declared in the plan that Nkrumah's "Seven-Year Plan (1963) set the pattern and in the post 1972 period, public and private Ghanaian participation in mining, plantations and industrial ventures has become an accepted fact. The Investment Policy Decree, 1975 (N.R.C.D. 229) has set the course which will accelerate this trend under the present plan" (p. viii). Until 1983 when the PNDC government changed policy, subsequent governments tried to follow this policy.

As the evidence shows, the economy responded negatively to these policies. Price control laws and other regulations stifled production. Unemployment immediately did not increase significantly because the government also prohibited lay-offs beyond five employees at a time without its approval. Meanwhile hopes of policy change kept firms from closing down as profits declined. Much of business enterprise also was turned into trying to get around regulations or influencing senior government officials to secure import licenses or higher regulated prices for their products. It is this economic climate that produced the breakdown in public morality, as evidence of corruption of public officials during the period later reveals.[8] The gap between revenue and costs was even wider in state organizations. They could not lay off workers, but were the most obedient of price control laws. However, their losses were passed on to the state treasury.

A significant consequence of the price controls and their negative effect on the profits of private businesses was that government revenues from taxes fell far short of its expenditures. This mainly explains the increased reliance of governments between 1972 and 1983 on deficit spending. The poor performance of the economy in turn also meant that most of the deficit could not be financed through borrowing from the private sector. Instead the governments relied on borrowing from the Central Bank, which also explains the significant increase in inflation over the period. Finally, the economic dislocation created by government policies caused large scale emigration of skilled workers and professionals, and financial capital from the country. For example, it is estimated that between 1975 and 1981 about 14,000 teachers left the Ghana Education Service to work outside the country, and about 3,000 of these were university graduates.[9] And by 1981 it was typical for departments in the country's universities to function with less than one half the staff required ten years earlier. The economic dislocation also generated considerable resentment among the population and led to several attempts to overthrow the governments between 1972 and 1983.

Government policy since 1983 has been characterized by a greater reliance on market forces, including floating the exchange rate, decontrol of prices and interest rates, and openness to foreign private investment. The government also has adopted a greater fiscal discipline by reducing the level of deficit spending and borrowing from the Central Bank. Economic growth since adoption of these policies has been positive, averaging about 6 per cent annual growth in real national income between 1984 and 1986.[10]

4. Lessons from Other Development Experiences:

The negative relation between increased government intervention and economic growth in Ghana has been observed in several other countries. For example, in a study of 65 LDCs, including 22 African and 11 Asian countries, Landau (1986) finds a statistically significant negative relation between government intervention, variously measured, and economic development over the period of 1960 to 1980. He also finds that democracy and incidence of coups – indicating a high degree of political instability – had negative effects on economic growth.[11] Similarly, Marsden (1983) also finds a negative relation between tax/GDP ratio and economic growth among 20 LDCs and more developed countries over the period of 1970 to 1979. These results are not surprising when we recall that increased government spending is always at the expense of private sector spending. Even if government borrows funds from abroad, future payments have to come from taxes levied mainly on the private sector. Thus, if the productivity of government spending is less than that of private spending, as theoretical analysis suggests, then the greater the share of government, the less growth would be generated in the economy. For some recent confirmation of the greater profitability of private enterprise over public ones in Brazil, Ghana, and Tanzania, see Tyler (1978), Ahiakpor (1986), and Perkins (1983), respectively.

However, some analysts do not accept the negative association between increased government intervention and economic growth in LDCs. They point to the emergence of the newly industrialized countries (NICs) of Asia, including South Korea, Singapore, and Taiwan as success stories of government intervention to promote economic development. In principle, there are grounds for skepticism over such claims. They, in effect, suggest that bureaucrats are better at directing other peoples' capitals into profitable investments than private entrepreneurs who stand directly to benefit or lose from the consequences of their investment choices. Recent studies also appear to confirm the skepticism, e.g. Crocker (1988) and Stoever (1986). The studies show that the interventions by governments of these Asian countries as well as in Japan to promote certain enterprises through subsidies, tax preferences, and other forms of industrial promotion, were not significantly responsible for their spectacular economic development since the 1960s.

Thus, writing on Japanese industrial policy, Crocker (1988) dismisses the myth that it was the Japanese government "through such agencies as the Ministry of International Trade and Industry (MITI) and the Ministry of Finance" that played "a powerful role ... turning a war-battered Japan into an economic juggernaut in 25 years" (p. 136). The limited positive impact of MITI on Japanese economic prosperity is illustrated by the fact that, although Japan is now noted for its exports of electronic products and cars, MITI "did not want Mitsubishi and Honda to build cars, and did not want Sony to purchase U.S. transistor technology" (p. 137). Thus, but for the entrepreneurial initiative of private investors, Japan's economic status might be significantly different now, most probably worse. As Charles Schultze (1983) also has observed, "In Japan as in any other democratic country, the public investment budget has been divided up in response to political pressures. It has not been a major instrument for concentrating investment resources in carefully selected growth industries."[12]

In the case of South Korea, Stoever (1986) explains that the country's success story of being transformed from one of "the world's poorer and less-industrialized nations" into a "newly industrializing [one]," was mostly the success story of private enterprise. The government relied "very heavily on private entrepreneurs," both foreign and local, to promote its goals including "the expansion of the industrial base, a rapid rise in exports, and improvement in technology" (p. 226). But the attempt to assist local firms through guaranteed foreign loans was mostly wasteful: "many domestic companies [took] out foreign loans and drain[ed] the money off into private individuals' hands shortly before the companies went bankrupt, leaving the government to pay off the debts" (p. 231). He also shows that whenever the Korean government tried to impose controls over private foreign investment, both the rate of investment and economic growth slowed down, especially in the mid to late 1970s. Thus the experience of these Asian countries appears consistent with those of Ghana's in suggesting that an extensive intervention of government in an economy is not necessarily conducive to growth.

5. Implications and Conclusion:

Governments of Ghana since independence have claimed improvement in the welfare of its people as the main motive behind policies they have adopted. But with the exception of the years 1966 to 1971, the record suggests they have been largely unsuccessful in achieving this goal.[13] Yet we have had prescriptions over the centuries on how to promote economic growth along with individual liberty. The age of empirical testing of scientific propositions, what some call "scienticism", may explain the reluctance among social scientists to accept propositions that derive from logical, introspective premises only. Were this not the case, the prescriptions of the classical economists, particularly Adam Smith and John Stuart Mill for promoting economic development would not need frequent restatement or attempts to verify statistically. Of course, resistance to the classical precepts is also partly due to misinterpretations of their ideas by later economists. For example, the failure of some to recognize that government spending is always a reallocation of capital from more efficient private uses to less efficient public sector may be explained by Keynes's misinterpretation of the classical fund concept of capital, which is only now becoming apparent.[14]

However, the lessons suggested by the above study of Ghana's recent economic history again give credence to the validity of the classical precepts on development policy. They include first, limiting the direct role of government in the economy. This may be reflected in a smaller share of government spending as well as the ratio of taxes to national income. Although it is difficult to designate a certain proportion of government spending as the only acceptable level, the evidence of Asia would suggest between 12 per cent and 18 per cent as tolerable margins for efficient development.[15] Indeed, the experience of the U.S. where growth and industrialization occurred while federal government spending remained well below 10 per cent until the Second World War, has led Milton Friedman to argue that "This remarkable fact should destroy once and for all the contention that economic growth and development require big government and especially centralized government."[16] But among some of the African countries experiencing difficulties in promoting economic growth, and whose governments have not lost control over revenue collection, the share of government spending in national income was significantly more than 20 per cent in 1980, e.g. Ethiopia (25 per cent), Kenya (26 per cent), Zaire (29 per cent), Cote D'Ivoire (30 per cent), Tanzania (33 per cent), and Zambia (35 per cent).[17]

There is always a need for government spending to protect national security, enforce law and order, and to protect property rights. In the absence of such public spending the feeling of security of life and property, which is a prerequite for widespread creation and accumulation of wealth among individuals, may be impaired. But beyond this requirement, allowing greater individual control over the employment of their wealth fosters greater efficient investment. It also prevents the conflicting preferences of individual wealth owners and bureaucrats from interacting to produce economic stagnation or decline.

Secondly, limitation of the role of government also means a curb on government deficit financing. The inability of government to raise funds through taxes is often an indicator of the resistance of income earners to cede large portions of their income to government. Deficit spending is thus an attempt to override the preferences of tax payers. Raising funds through borrowing may create the illusion of postponing the burden of government spending into the future, especially for private bond holders. The illusion may be even worse when deficits are financed from foreign borrowing. But all have to pay higher taxes for government debt to be retired. On the other hand, sale of bonds to the central bank extracts real resources through an inflationary tax. Furthermore, as in the case of direct taxation, there is always an opportunity cost to government spending in the form of the foregone output from the capital transferred from the private sector.

Thirdly, government also should limit its role in setting prices and interest rates. The difficulty of assigning clear property rights in some aspects of human activities may create externalities, which may require government intervention in the form of levying taxes and granting subsidies. But beyond such identifiable sources of externalities, government involvement in setting prices turns out mainly to be an attempt to impose the values of one group of market participants over another. The losers from such arbitrary designation of values tend to supply less while the potential gainers are never fully satisfied of their demands. The result is frustrated economic growth.

Limited involvement of government in the economy also means promotion of freedom of enterprise in production and sale of home and foreign goods. Like price controls, government attempts to direct the investment and consumption choices of individuals amounts to subjecting them to the tastes and preferences of a few politicians or bureaucrats. They may well be acting upon the preferences of some groups in the population. But it is the conflict of private and public preferences that produces smuggling, and bribery and corruption of public officials assigned the task of acting against private interests.

Finally, a limited role of government in the economy may create the conditions congenial for political democracy, including the freedom of speech and association. The failure of many LDCs to promote these elements of political democracy has tended to be dismissed with the excuse that "democracy is an expensive luxury for poor countries."[18] It is as though people in poor countries are less human, and thus require fewer human rights than those in the more developed countries where economic development has occurred along with extentions of human rights, e.g. Britain, Canada, and the U.S. But it is rather the attempt to keep individuals in line with the dictates of government that necessitates denial of such freedoms. Were respect for individuals as entities in their own right paramount rather than regarding people merely as of a community (whose preferences can be uniquely identified by the government), there would be no need to suppress individual freedoms, including those of speech and association.

At independence, the government of Ghana adopted the motto, "Freedom and Justice." If these ideals are to be realized by Ghanaians or citizens of other LDCs now living under forms of tyranny and economic deprivation, their governments need seriously to reconsider the interventionist roles they have assigned to themselves. They also need to recognize political freedom in terms of individual political rights rather than solely as freedom of a nation against the rest of the world. The latter view of freedom often leads to the suppression of individual liberties while representatives of governments pursue more rights for the nation at the international level. Discounting any genetic theories of underdevelopment, there is no good reason why Ghana and other African countries could not adopt the same path to economic development as has been taken by the more developed countries, including Japan and the newly industrialized countries of Asia.

Notes

[1]   Following political agitation for independence and riots during the late 1940s, internal self-government was granted by the British in 1951. The colonial administration still controlled key aspects of government, including finance, defense and external affairs. Full independence was granted in 1957 after two general elections in 1954 and 1956, both won by Nkrumah's Convention Peoples Party (C.P.P.). For a detailed political history of Ghana, see Austin (1970).

[2]   For a description of the activities of the IDC, see Killick (1972 and 1976).

[3]   Following agitation for a return to civilian rule and threats to law and order, General I. K. Acheampong, leader of the coup in 1972, was removed by his colleagues who then reconstituted the governing council as the second Supreme Military Council.

[4]   For an account of the policy failures of the PNDC and subsequent change of policy, see Ahiakpor (1985).

[5]   Accounts of the resulting bribery and corruption can be found in the reports of government committees of inquiry, e.g. the Abrahams, Akainyah, and Ollenu Reports. For a summary of these, see Killick (1978), chapter 10.

[6]   For example, in 1955, N. A. Welbeck then minister of Works and Housing and later General Secretary of the C.P.P. defended the government against the charge of using state corporations as the dumping ground for political supporters thus: "But that is proper: and the honourable [opposition] Member too would do it if he were there." Quoted in Killick (1976), p. 29. Also see the rest of the article for more discussion of government interference in the operations of state corporations, particularly the I.D.C.

[7]   Quoted in Pinkney (1972), p. 142.

[8]   Several of the officials implicated in these activities were later jailed, some including key members of the previous regime were executed by firing squad in 1979, while some others fled into exile.

[9]   See West Africa, 6 September, 1982, p. 2319.

[10]   See Chand and van Til (1988), p. 33.

[11]   But the negative association between democracy and growth, may have arisen from the pursuit of redistributive policies in several democratic LDCs, but which tend to dampen economic efficiency, rather than democracy per se undermining growth.

[12]   Quoted in Crocker (1988), p. 137.

[13] The change in economic policy since 1983 has not been accompanied by the restoration of individual liberties, including the freedom of speech and political association, and security from arbitrary arrest, all significantly repressed since 1982.

[14] See Ahiakpor (1988).

[15] For example, before the Second World War, the share of federal government spending in national income in Canada was less than 10 per cent, and until the mid-1970s, it averaged about 16 per cent (see Ahiakpor and Amirkhalkhali, 1987, table 1). A similar level of government spending obtained in the U.S. before 1940. However, the adoption of social welfare programmes in the 1960s, caused the share of federal government spending to reach 25 per cent of national income by 1970.

[16] Quoted in Fink and High (1987), p. 122.

[17] Calculations based on data from International Monetary Fund (1987).

[18] See Landau (1986), p. 64.

References

Ahiakpor, James C.W. (1988) "On Keynes's Misinterpretation of 'Capital' in the Classical Theory of Interest," Department of Economics, Saint Mary's University, Halifax, N.S., (mimeo).

—, (1986) "The Profits of Foreign Firms in a Less Developed Country: Ghana," *Journal of Development Economics,* 22, (July-August), pp. 321–35.

—, (1985) "The Success and Failure of Dependency Theory: The Experience of Ghana," *International Organization,* 39 (Summer), pp. 535–52.

—, and Amirkhalkhali, Saleh (1987) "On the Deficit Policy in Canada: Some Causality Tests," Department of Economics, Saint Mary's Univeristy, Halifax, N.S., (mimeo).

Austin, Dennis (1970) *Politics in Ghana: 1946–1960,* London: Oxford University Press.

Chand, Sheetal K. and van Til, Reinold (1988) "Ghana: Toward Successful Stabilization and Recovery," *Finance & Development,* 25 (March), pp. 32–35.

Crocker, C. Brandon (1988) "The Myth of Japanese Industrial Policy," *Freeman,* 38 (April), pp. 136–39.

Fink, Richard H. and High, Jack C. (1987) *A Nation in Debt: Economists Debate the Federal Budget Deficit,* Frederick, Md.: University Publications of America.

Ghana (1977) *Five-Year Development Plan: 1975/76–1979/80 – Part II,* Accra: Ministry of Economic Planning.

—, (1964) *Seven-Year Development Plan: 1963/64–1969/70,* Accra: The Planning Commission.

International Monetary Fund (1987) *International Financial Statistics,* Washington, D.C.

Killick, T. (1978) *Development Economics in Action: A Study of Economic Policies in Ghana,* London: Heinemann.

—, (1976) "The State Promotion of Industry: The Case of Ghana's Industrial Development Corporation - Part II," *Ghana Social Science Journal,* 3, no. 1, pp. 18–34.

—, (1972) "The State Promotion of Industry - The Case of the Ghana Industrial Development Corporation - Part I," *Ghana Social Science Journal,* 2, no. 1, pp. 27–49.

Landau, Daniel (1986) "Government and Economic Growth in the Less Developed Countries: An Empirical Study for 1960–1980," *Economic Development and Cultural Change.* 35 (October), pp. 35–75.

Marsden, Keith (1983) "Links between Taxes and Economic Growth," *Staff Working Paper* No. 605, The World Bank, Washington, D.C.

Mill, John S. (1874) *Essays on some Unsettled Questions of Political Economy* (2nd ed.), London: Longmans.

Perkins, F.C. (1983) "Technology Choice, Industrialization and Development Experiences in Tanzania," *Journal of Development Studies,* 19 (January), pp. 213–43.

Pinkney, Robert (1972) *Ghana Under Military Rule: 1966–1969,* London: Methuen.

Stoever, William A. (1986) "Foreign Investment as an Aid in Moving from Least Developed to Newly Industrializing: A Study in Korea," *Journal of Developing Areas,* 20 (January), pp. 223–48.

Tyler, William G. (1978) "Technical Efficiency and Ownership Characteristics of Manufacturing Firms in a Developing Country: A Brazilian Case Study," *Weltwirtschaftliches Archiv* 114, no. 2, pp. 360–78.

World Bank (1988) *World Development Report 1988,* New York: Oxford University Press.

–, (1983) *World Tables,* (3d ed.), Baltimore, Md.: Johns Hopkins University Press.

Index of Names

Subject Index